Agrarian Structure and Productivity in Developing Countries

A Study Prepared for the International Labour Office within the Framework of the World Employment Programme

R. Albert Berry and William R. Cline

The Johns Hopkins University Press
Baltimore and London

1000339622

Manufactured in the United States of America

The World Employment Programme (WEP) was launched by the International Labour Organisation in 1969, as the ILO's main contribution to the International Development Strategy for the Second United Nations Development Decade.

The means of action adopted by the WEP have included the following:

—short-term high-level advisory missions;
—longer-term national or regional employment teams; and
—a wide-ranging research programme.

Through these activities the ILO has been able to help national decision-makers to re-shape their policies and plans with the aim of eradicating mass poverty and unemployment.

A landmark in the development of the WEP was the World Employment Conference of 1976, which proclaimed inter alia that "strategies and national development plans should include as a priority objective the promotion of employment and the satisfaction of the basic needs of each country's population." The Declaration of Principles and Programming of Action adopted by the Conference have become the cornerstone of WEP technical assistance and research activities during the closing years of the Second Development Decade.

This publication is the outcome of a WEP project.

The Johns Hopkins University Press, Baltimore, Maryland 21218
The Johns Hopkins Press Ltd., London

Library of Congress Catalog Number 78-20524
ISBN 0-8018-2190-8

Library of Congress Cataloguing in Publication data will be found on the last printed page of this book.

Agrarian Structure and Productivity
in Developing Countries

Contents

Foreword

The World Employment Conference held in Geneva in June 1976 unanimously recommended that the alleviation of poverty and the satisfaction of the population's basic needs be included as an explicit priority objective of national development plans of the developing countries.* In order to make a major stride in the fulfillment of the basic needs of the masses, national policies and strategies will have to focus on the rural sector. The reasons for this emphasis on rural development are obvious. A large proportion of the world's poor work and reside in rural areas. And food production, an important component of the basic needs basket, will have to be substantially increased.

However, the acceleration of economic growth in the developing nations, measures aimed at improving employment and earning opportunities, and more productive use of resources by the lowest income groups are recognized as essential prerequisites to the provision and satisfaction of basic needs. A basic needs approach to development requires consideration of major policy measures aimed at both higher levels of productivity and improving the prevailing agrarian structures in developing countries. The World Employment Conference in its program of action specifically recommended reorganization of the agrarian structure, including land redistribution measures.

This study by Albert Berry and William Cline (with a contribution from Surjit Bhalla) deals with a question of fundamental importance to any agrarian reform measures—the relationship between farm size and factor productivity. Although some scattered empirical evidence on this relationship already existed, the authors, perhaps for the first time, have brought

*Meeting Basic Needs: Strategies for Eradicating Mass Poverty and Unemployment: Conclusions of the World Employment Conference (Geneva: International Labour Office, 1977), p. 24. Basic needs are defined to contain two elements. First, they include certain minimum requirements of a family for private consumption: adequate food, shelter, clothing, certain household equipment, and furniture. Second, they include essential services provided by and for the community at large, such as safe drinking water, sanitation, public transport, and health, educational, and cultural facilities.

together evidence from a number of developing countries extending over three continents and provided a systematic treatment. Evidence from extensive international cross-sectional data is considered along with an intensive analysis of data obtained from six major developing countries, namely, Brazil, Colombia, the Philippines, Pakistan, India, and Malaysia.

The general conclusion of this study is that the small farm sector makes better use of its available land (higher production per unit of land) than does the large farm sector, largely through applying higher levels of labor inputs (family labor) per unit of land. Small farms are, furthermore, almost universally characterized by higher land utilization either in the form of high multiple cropping ratios or in higher shares of total land cultivated. As a result, small farms tend to achieve higher production relative to the (social) value of their total factor inputs (land, labor, and capital) than do large farms.

The central policy implication of the analysis is that agricultural development strategies focusing on small farms—whether they involve land redistribution or improved access of smallholders to credit, new technology, etc.—are likely not only to have beneficial distribution and employment effects but also to be efficient means of reaching higher output levels. Land reform, for its part, represents a potentially important instrument for rural development, not only in land-abundant Latin American countries but also in land-scarce Asian countries. Concern that land redistribution or emphasis on small farm production might entail loss of potential efficiency, or dynamic growth influences, appears to be unwarranted. There is widespread evidence of constant rather than increasing returns to scale in agriculture. Cross-country data do not show a positive influence of farm size on agricultural growth rates and there is growing evidence, particularly in the Asian Green Revolution, that small farmers achieve adoption rates of new grain varieties as high as those on larger farms.

The present study represents a joint research effort between the Technology and Employment Branch of the ILO's World Employment Programme and the Employment and Rural Development Division of the Development Economics Department of the World Bank.

Mark W. Leiserson, Chief,
Employment and Rural
   Development Division,
The World Bank,
Washington, D.C.

Ajit S. Bhalla, Chief,
Technology and Employment
   Branch,
International Labour Office,
Geneva

Preface

The influence of agrarian structure upon agricultural productivity, technical change, and employment in developing countries remains an issue of considerable controversy. Despite the recurrent calls in the United Nations and other official bodies for land reform as a means of spurring development, the concentration of land ownership remains severe and land reform movements remain moribund in most developing countries. Aside from the underlying political forces opposing land reform, an important reason for its slow progress is the apparent perception of many economic planners that dynamic agricultural development must depend upon the large, modern farm and that the small-farm sector is backward and inefficient. This perception appears to have been strengthened by the advent of the Green Revolution, in light of the widespread view that it has been the large farms that have adopted newly available technologies.

Students of agrarian structure have long been aware, however, of empirical evidence pointing in the opposite direction. The studies on Latin American countries by the Comite Inter-Americano para Desarrollo Agricola more than a decade ago, and the literature on farm size and productivity in India dating from the 1950s, found a systematically negative relationship between farm size and the ratio of production to land available. Thus, there has long been evidence that a small, family farm structure could be more favorable for agricultural production than a structure based upon the concentration of land ownership into the hands of a small rural elite. The authors have participated in the literature on agrarian structure in their earlier detailed studies of Colombia (Berry) and Brazil (Cline).

More recently, a heightened concern (both among analysts and international development agencies) about unemployment and the maldistribution of income in developing countries has set the stage for what should be a renewed interest in programs of small farm development and land reform. The purpose of this study is to consider the issues of agrarian structure and productivity at the theoretical level and to bring together recent empirical evidence on these issues from a wide range of countries. This evidence should permit a more global extension of the analyses conducted earlier in the context of individual countries or regions, taking into account the possibility of changing relationships caused by the Green Revolution. The analysis here also permits an examination of the differences among countries in the scope for increasing agricultural production and employment through land reform and through programs focused upon small farm development. At the level of policy, the study seeks to contribute to a more accurate assessment of the role of land reform and small farm development in addressing today's critical developmental problems, which include the need to address basic human needs through the expansion of employment and the reduction of the incidence of severe poverty (and, by implication, the degree of concentration in income distribution) as well as to achieve rapid growth in the agricultural sector.

The authors are, respectively, Professor of Political Economy, University of Toronto, and Senior Fellow, The Brookings Institution. Views expressed in this study carry no implication of endorsement by the institutions with which the authors are associated nor by the International Labour Office and the World Bank. The authors are indebted to Surjit Bhalla of the World Bank for his invaluable participation as author of the special Appendix A on India, and to Carl J. Dahlman and Kathy Terrell for research assistance. They wish to thank the World Bank for making available detailed data from farm sample surveys for Muda River, Malaysia, and northeastern Brazil (for which the cooperation of the Superintendencia para o Desenvolvimento do Nordeste is gratefully acknowledged), and for computational assistance. For helpful comments and encouragement the authors thank Ajit S. Bhalla of the I.L.O., Mark W. Leiserson of the World Bank, and Bruce F. Johnston of the Stanford University Food Research Institute.

R. Albert Berry
William R. Cline

Abbreviations

AID	Agency for International Development (United States)
ARIS	Additional Rural Income Survey (India)
BAECON	Bureau of Agricultural Economics (Philippines)
CES	Constant elasticity of substitution
CIDA	Comite Inter-Americano para Desarollo Agricola
DANE	Departamento Administrativo Nacional de Estadistica (Colombia)
FAFBS	Farm Accounts and Family Budget Surveys (Pakistan)
FAO	Food and Agriculture Organization
FMS	Farm Management Studies
HYVs	high-yielding varieties
IBRD	International Bank for Reconstruction and Development
ILO	International Labour Office
INCORA	Instituto Nacional de Colonizacion y Reforma Agraria (Colombia)
INCRA	Instituto de Colonizacao e Reforma Agraria (Brazil)
IPEA	Instituto de Planejamento Economico e Social (Brazil)
MPL	marginal product of labor
MPS	marginal propensity to save
NCAER	National Council of Applied Economic Research (India)
OECD	Organization for Economic Cooperation and Development
SUDENE	Superintendencia para Desenvolvimento do Nordeste (Brazil)

Agrarian Structure and Productivity
in Developing Countries

ONE

Introduction

Rural poverty of severe proportions afflicts most developing countries. A priority policy question in these countries is how to increase productive employment and incomes for the rural poor, often the bulk of the population. Agricultural development policies typically have focused on "modernization," often using subsidized inputs (including imported farm machinery) and frequently through a strategy favoring the expansion of large capitalized farms, while leaving behind the majority of the farm population on small farms and the landless labor force. This "bimodal" strategy[1] appears to have been both inequitable and inefficient: inequitable, for obvious reasons; inefficient, because the developing countries possess abundant labor but lack capital and land, and it is precisely the small-farm sector that is most successful in achieving high levels of production relative to modest inputs of capital and land—through the ample use of labor. Moreover, the new technology of high-yielding varieties (HYVs) can be applied on small farms, since it requires no threshold scale.

It is time that policy-makers turn in earnest to the present and potential small-farm sector in the search for a feasible means of achieving the joint objectives of agricultural production growth and rural equity. Two policies in particular warrant consideration: land reform, redistributing land from existing large farms into new small-scale family farms; and the channeling of improved inputs and credit to the existing small-farm sector in countries where land redistribution is not a feasible option in political terms. It is the objective of this study to contribute to the analytical and empirical basis for answering the policy question of whether and to what

1

extent these two measures could successfully increase agricultural production and improve rural employment and income distribution in developing countries. Note that the "farm" under discussion is the "operating" unit, not the owned unit. Although the distribution of operated units may be reasonably similar to that of owned units in many countries, they are by no means the same thing. Our analysis relates directly to the social efficiency of different distributions of land among operators, with this analysis relating in turn to the social efficiency of different ownership distributions.

The specific questions addressed in this study include the following. (1) Do large farms tend to be more or less efficient than small farms, given the overall resource endowments of developing countries? (2) Are there systematic distortions in the utilization of existing resources, caused by the structure of land ownership and by imperfections in the factor markets? (3) How much do countries and continents differ in their potential for increased output and employment from land reform or from policies channeling improved inputs to existing small farms? Specifically, is land reform a potentially important instrument for rural development only in land-abundant Latin American countries, or does it have comparable potential in other developing regions, including land-scarce Asian countries? (4) Has the Green Revolution changed the relationship between farm size and factor productivity? Has it transformed large owners from traditional landlords into a vanguard of agricultural modernization, whose replacement by a small-farm structure would spell agricultural stagnation? (5) Do other aspects of land tenure, especially sharecropping, affect the social efficiency of agricultural production?

The authors have previously explored several of these issues in detail for Colombia[2] and Brazil.[3] This study examines a wider spectrum of developing countries in the hope of reaching more general conclusions on the possible production and equity effects of land reform and of agricultural development strategies emphasizing small farms. Theoretical arguments relating farm size to productive potential and, more specifically, to factor productivity are reviewed in Chapter 2. Hypotheses relating efficiency to sharecropping and farm size to dynamic influences of technical change and savings rates are also discussed. Then two empirical examinations are presented, the first an extensive analysis of many countries, using the sparse available data common to them all (Chapter 3), and the second an intensive analysis of six countries for which relatively rich data sources are available: Brazil, Colombia, the Philippines, Pakistan, India and Malaysia (Chapter 4). A more detailed analysis for India, separately authored by Surjit S. Bhalla, is presented as Appendix A, and a brief review of the literature bearing on these issues in other countries appears as Appendix B. Chapter 5 synthesizes the policy implications derived from the extensive and intensive empirical analysis.

The main focus of this study is on differences in the productivity of existing farms by size, and some of the factors—including technological change—that determine these differences. We do not attempt to consider in detail the institutional factors that affect the likelihood of land-reform policies supportive of small farms, or the probable success of such policies when these institutional factors are taken into account. It is obvious that they are usually controversial policies and will generate political opposition that may sidetrack, dilute, or otherwise prevent their achieving the technically feasible results. In not discussing such matters, our analysis is technical; it suggests the potential of certain strategies without considering in detail how they might best be carried out from the political and administrative points of view.

Related to the above omission is our failure to consider the various dynamic phenomena that may surround a process like land redistribution or increased services to small farmers. Thus, while the factors that appear to underly the high land productivity on small farms should eventually come into play whenever a large farm is split into small ones, such productivity also depends on the operators. If they have had little previous managerial experience, there may be a learning period before they achieve the productivity levels of existing small farms. Again, land redistribution may often involve considerable conflict and loss of capital (as in cases like Mexico and Bolivia). Consideration of such matters is obviously important to the policy-maker, but we have elected here to focus on what appear to be the more basic, general, and long-run factors in the relationship between farm size and productivity. Accordingly, we would not presume to suggest that the same policy would be appropriate in all countries. The technical potential of both land reform and better support for small farms varies among countries, according to existing land productivity and total factor productivity differentials by farm size, to the availability of the entrepreneurial talent needed to expand the small-farm sector, and so forth. The pay-off to expanding the land under small farms and increasing its productivity also depends on how long the country will have a surplus of labor at low opportunity cost. The administrative capacity to support small farms must be developed in countries that have a history of neglecting them. And there are, of course, the political problems.

The evidence presented in the remaining chapters points to

systematically higher land productivity on small farms than on large ones, and to total factor productivities that are at least comparable. What these findings suggest is that the expansion of the small-farm subsector of agriculture may be a more effective way of increasing both employment and output than pro-large-farm strategies and thus warrants serious consideration in almost all developing countries.

TWO

Theories on the Relationship of Farm Size to Productivity and Technical Change

2.1   RETURNS TO SCALE

The first question to be answered in an assessment of productivity as related to farm size is whether there exist increasing (or decreasing) returns to scale in agriculture. It is essential to distinguish this issue of "technical input-output efficiency" from the broader question of efficiency of resource utilization.[1] The first refers strictly to the engineering relationship of production per inputs actually used in the production process. The second, examined below, considers as well the selection of those inputs, and especially the degree of utilization of the available land resource and the related use of labor. Thus, for crop production only the land actually cultivated enters the "technical production function" in an evaluation of returns to scale. But, for overall assessment of social efficiency, the share of available land actually put into cultivation and the share double- or multiple-cropped must also be considered.

Solely with regard to inputs actually used, there are strong reasons to expect returns to scale to be approximately constant in developing country agriculture and, therefore, neutral with respect to the more general issue of farm size as related to productivity. In terms of actual practices, it is common to observe even large plantations repeating many-fold the operations carried out by the single farmer on a small family establishment, so that changes in efficiency with scale would not be anticipated. One basis on which increasing returns to scale might be expected would be that crops requiring farm machinery would need some minimum scale in order to utilize the machinery fully. However, this consideration is generally of limited relevance to most developing countries, where the scarcity of capital and abundance of labor recommend against the use of costly machines, at least in terms of social (if not private) costs and benefits.[2] Even in cases where fairly large farm machinery is appropriate it can be made available to small farms on a rental basis; and, as the Japanese case clearly showed, small machines can be developed. Either approach helps to remove the minimum-scale requirement for machinery use.

Another argument sometimes made in support of increasing returns to scale is that cattle production, in particular, requires large land areas for extensive grazing. Yet livestock operations can be carried out either on an extensive or an intensive basis (such as feedlot activities), and there appears to be no rigid minimum scale required for cattle raising.

Other considerations suggest decreasing returns to scale in agriculture. Thorough knowledge of the peculiarities of the farm's land and the corresponding basis for making appropriate decisions in choice of inputs, techniques, and products will be maximized on farms with a limited area directly managed by one operator.[3] Furthermore, the small farm, on which the principal workers are the owner himself and his family, will have a much more highly motivated labor force than the larger farm using hired labor.

The empirical studies on returns to scale in developing-country agriculture generally have found approximately constant returns. In an early survey of agricultural production functions in many developing and industrial countries, Heady and Dillon[4] consistently encountered results of constant returns to scale, even in many of the developed countries. Cline's estimates of Cobb–Douglas type production functions for eighteen state-product sectors in Brazil systematically found returns to scale not significantly different from constant returns.[5] For India, several recent production function studies have shown constant or decreasing returns to scale.[6]

In summary, on *a priori* grounds, one would expect approximately constant returns to scale in agriculture in developing countries (the alternative arguments for increasing or decreasing returns are either largely irrelevant for developing countries or tend to cancel each other out); and by far the majority of the studies in the quite substantial body of literature containing empirical production-function estimates reach the conclusion that observed returns are, in fact, nearly constant.[7] Such studies create no presumption that planners should fear losses of production efficiency (aside from temporary disruption effects) from the division of existing large farms into small family parcels, nor the sacrifice of potential future efficiency through the establishment of such parcels rather than large state farms. If returns to scale for inputs actually utilized are constant, then the crucial determinant of the farm-size-efficiency relationship becomes the behavioral pattern of resource utilization by farm size.

2.2   FARM SIZE AND FACTOR UTILIZATION

Overview.   In an agricultural structure composed of very large estates holding most of the land on the one hand, and a large number of small farms on the other, agricultural production tends to be below its maximum potential level because land is underused on the large farms, while excess labor without opportunity for fully productive work is crowded onto the small farm sector (or in the landless labor force). Agrarian reform redistributing land from the large estates into new family farms of a moderate size can combine the underused land with the underused labor and raise production (as well as total capital and seeds-fertilizer requirements). The potential increase in production will often be sufficient to allow a substantial rise in the incomes of the rural poor, even if they are expected to compensate former landowners for the land transferred, paying the market price of land.[8]

There is a substantial body of literature that investigates the theoretical relationship between farm size and the utilization of land and labor.[9] The central theme of this literature is that the incentives facing large farms systematically differ from those facing small farms: the effective prices of land and capital are low for the former and high for the latter, while the situation is the reverse for the effective price of labor. The specific arguments behind this theme are discussed below, but the general prediction is relatively low utilization of land on large farms. As will be discussed, there are various influences beside differing factor prices that lead to poor utilization of land on large estates, and all of them—except for the possibility that land quality or access to markets is below average on large farms—point to the same policy conclusion—that redistribution of land would raise potential output.

Another aspect of the effect of agrarian structure on production concerns the impact of sharecropping. In this area, there has recently been an intense flurry of theoretical work, as discussed in section 2.4 below. However, in light of the ambiguity of both the theoretical conclusions and the empirical evidence on this issue it probably deserves far less attention than does the influence of the size distribution of land on the social efficiency of agriculture.

Labor Market Dualism.   It is well known that in the economies of most developing countries a substantially "modern" sector coexists with a more "traditional" sector, and that whereas relatively highly capitalized activity takes place in the former, using labor only to the point where its marginal product[10] equals the modern sector wage rate, in the latter sector there may exist a large supply of labor with a very low marginal product, possibly below the income received.[11] This same dualism typically pervades agriculture and causes distortions in the sector's utilization of available land and labor resources. Several factors typically conspire to produce a different marginal productivity of labor across farm sizes.

One such factor is the tendency to income-sharing on smaller farms, where family labor is the sole or dominant labor force. Each family member receives a share of total family output. In the family context, even if the marginal product of labor is quite low, this means that when the individual makes the decision whether to hire out his labor services or to migrate, his supply price may be closer to the "average product" of labor on the small farm. When labor's marginal product on such farms is quite low, this supply price will exceed it. Since marginal product in the large-farm sector will not be below the wage rate, which in turn equals the supply price of labor, it then follows that the marginal product of labor will be lower on small farms than on large. Now the effective price, or opportunity cost, of a worker who does not have to be hired is his marginal product on the farm. Under the circumstances just cited, therefore, the effective price of family labor to the small farm—its marginal product there—is lower than the effective price (wage of hired labor) on large farms.

Under family decision-making this result would be less likely; the family would hire out labor until its marginal product on the family farm rose to equal the wage obtainable outside, after allowing for costs of transportation to the alternative site and any preferences to have or not have family members working on the farm. These latter factors would generally contribute to a marginal product of labor on the farm below the wage rate for work elsewhere. Further, some wage-labor opportunities carry the risk of not obtaining a job, so that the marginal product of the family worker at home would be compared not to the outside wage but to that wage multiplied by the probability of obtaining full-time work outside. If that wage rate were low enough, it would be necessary for those remaining on the family farm to supplement the wage income of the family worker sent to work elsewhere; if this requirement were infeasible, because of physical distance or unwillingness on the part of the remaining family workers to share the farm output with the absent family member, market pressures pushing the marginal product of labor on small and large farms toward equality would again be weakened.

Still other factors could be at work to keep wage rates above marginal product of labor (MPL) on small farms. In conditions of severe excess labor, a complete clearing of the market could drive the wage close to zero. In this situation, the collective behavior of the labor force in trying to "hire out" would reduce total labor earnings, even though any individual family might still raise its income by hiring out family labor. In such a situation social traditions could develop, preventing the acceptance of such low, market-clearing wages—since social custom would tend to "internalize" for the laboring community as a whole, the effect of driving down wages, an "externality" from the standpoint of the individual family. The very calculus of caloric expenditure on physical labor compared with food buying power from outside earnings would set some absolute minimum below which the wage could not fall. Thus, whether off-farm work by family members is at the discretion of the individual or the family, or a combination of the two, it is to be expected that the marginal product of labor on the small, family farm will be below the market wage rate.

The gap between the marginal product of labor on family farms and that on large estates is often further widened by the fact that the landowners may consider labor to have a higher real cost than its wage alone, because of the risk of strikes or of the establishment of workers' claims to property rights in the event of land reforms, and by monopsony power they may have in the labor market. When large landlords in a given region possess monopsony power over the local labor market (that is, expansion of their own hiring pushes up the wage), they will hire fewer workers and produce less than would a group of smaller competitive farmers operating the same total area.

In sum, the family-farm sector faces incentives that lead it to apply its own labor to the point where the marginal product is likely to be below the rural wage,[12] whereas the large-farm sector uses relatively less labor, only to the point where its marginal product equals or even exceeds the wage. The effective price of labor is lower on the small farm which, as a result, can exploit more marginal land, bring a larger share of its given land under cultivation, and achieve a larger output per unit of available land resource. In short, labor-market dualism leads to the phenomenon of higher utilization of the available land resource on small farms than on large.

Land and Capital-Market Imperfections. Not only is the effective price of labor frequently lower for small family farms but, in addition, the effective prices of land and capital are likely to be higher. The land price may be higher for two reasons. First, purchases of small plots probably carry a higher price per hectare than do purchases of large tracts of land, for land of constant quality. Many more individuals are potential buyers for small plots, because of the low total cost. The inconvenience of selling off odd fragments of land also makes the large owner insist on a higher unit price for such sales than for a sale involving a large block, or all, of his land.[13] Second, land purchase sometimes involves medium- or long-term borrowing, and because large operators have better credit ratings than small farmers, the interest and maturity terms will be more favorable for large farmers, making the real price of land lower for them than for small farmers. Land price differences[14] thus reinforce the difference in effective labor costs in leading to higher labor/land ratios on small farms than on large and, as a result, higher output per hectare available on the small farms.

Imperfections in the capital market tend to reinforce still further the tendency to low labor use on large farms, but to offset somewhat the tendency to low output per unit of land. Typically, special government credit programs or machinery import subsidy programs channel capital disproportionately to the large farms, artificially lowering the price of capital to them. The price of capital on the small farms, by contrast, tends to be set by the high interest rate charged by traditional moneylenders, or by the opportunity cost to the family of reducing its own consumption. This gap between the price of capital to large and small farmers frequently encourages the substitution of capital equipment for labor on the large farm.

In other situations, capital and labor may be complementary, as where more capital permits a farmer to hire more labor; this relationship is observed on large farms in some Asian and African countries, where capital is very scarce and advanced mechanical technologies not in common use. As capital becomes more readily available, along with capital-intensive techniques, the dominant relationship between labor and capital becomes one of substitution.

Whether the relatively cheap capital available to large farms goes far toward encouraging high output per land area (offsetting the influence of labor-market imperfections) depends on two related considerations. First, there is the question of whether or not the *ratio* of capital price to land price is in fact lower on large farms than on small; the drop in the price of capital as farm size rises would have to be proportionately larger than that of land in order for the phenomenon of cheaper capital to lead to the prediction of higher capital/land ratios on larger farms. Second, the impact of this cheaper capital will depend on the substitute/complement relationships between capital and both land and labor. If capital and land are substitutes, then cheaper machinery will lead to the combination of more machinery with each unit of land; this type of substitutability could exist if mechanized production achieved higher yields, for example. However, most available evidence shows little influence of mechanization *per se* on yields,[15] and it appears that generally the degree of substitutability between land and machinery is very low.

Where capital and labor are complements, a low price of capital helps to offset the influence of labor-market dualism on relative land productivity; where they are substitutes, that influence is accentuated. The substitutability between certain machines and labor may be substantial.[16] In economies that have reached the stage of incipient labor-saving mechanization, a lower capital price to large farmers tends to do little in raising their land productivity, and its main influence is to replace labor by machinery in existing production—thereby exacerbating the problem of underemployment without ameliorating the problem of underutilization of land on larger estates. In other economies, the effects may be less pernicious as far as labor demand is concerned; capital sometimes permits the hiring of more labor and some types of physical capital can raise the demand for labor (e.g., irrigation works, tubewells, etc.). But the evidence from most empirical studies (see Chapter 4 and Appendixes A and B) shows markedly lower labor/land ratios on large farms than on small ones; this implies either that the capital and land market imperfections work in this direction, i.e., complement the effects of labor-market imperfections, or that if they work in the opposite direction, they are not strong, *and* the effects of labor-market imperfections are quite strong.

Landholding for Asset or Prestige Purposes.   Another influence leading to low production activity levels relative to land available on large farms is the holding of land for purposes of asset placement rather than for production. In countries with poorly developed capital markets, especially those with chronic inflation, landowners may find it attractive to hold land for speculative gain—or merely to accomplish the "store of value" objective. In this situation, they may be unprepared to incur the expense and risk of using the land in highly productive ways, and they may also be unwilling to lease out or sharecrop the land to tenants for fear of jeopardizing their ownership rights in the event of land reform.

Still another possible influence is that large landlords hold land primarily for purposes of prestige or political power rather than for production. This phenomenon has frequently been asserted to be important in Latin America, although in view of the other rational economic influences leading to low land utilization, it is difficult to ascertain just how important its effects have been. In any case, the more objectives, other than production for profit, which figure in the decisions of landowners, the lower land productivity is likely to be.

Monopoly. Monopoly in the product market is less likely to exist than monopsony in the labor market, because many product markets are national or even international in scope, and even very large owners are too numerous to collude in control of the national product market. Nevertheless, in some food items the market may be a local one, in which case a large producer may be constrained from producing too much for fear of driving the price down, whereas, a group of small farmers would not. The impact of this difference is to reduce the relative productivity of larger farms, when measured at fixed prices—though not if each farm sale was valued at the actual price received.[17]

Own-Consumption and Risk. An advantage of many small farms over larger ones is that the family has the option of consuming a significant part of production in the event that prices are unfavorable. This lowers the degree of risk involved in production and encourages higher output per unit of land on the small family farm relative to larger establishments. The net impact of risk considerations on relative productivity by size is not clear, however. Small farmers, having lower incomes, are often constrained to produce the items they need to consume for fear of relative price changes; if they specialize in a nonstaple crop and its price falls sharply, their subsistence is threatened. If that nonstaple crop is a high-value one, this affects negatively their average land productivity over several years.

Land Quality and Market Access. A final influence on land

utilization and productivity by farm size is land quality and localization. If large farms tended to have below average productive potential, either in the physical sense or because of inaccessibility to markets, then it would be neither surprising nor socially inefficient that they cultivate smaller shares of their land and achieve lower levels of output per land area than do small farms.

It has been argued in some Asian countries that larger farms tend to have poorer quality land (Appendix A). In the Latin American context, it is undeniable that on a nation-wide basis some of the largest holdings are located in inaccessible regions where economic potential, if not soil fertility, is low. But in the established agricultural areas it is just as often the case that the very large estates have land of better quality than that of the small farms (see the discussion of Brazilian data below; that of Muda River, Malaysia, tells a similar story). With respect to the inverse relationship between size and nearness to market, it seems probable that it exists in many countries, for one or more of the reasons cited above, although in some countries the preference of the urban rich to have their (usually medium or large) farms nearby may work in the other direction.[18] In short, *a priori* generalization is not possible on the question of potential economic productivity; it is necessary in each case to allow for such differences as exist in physical quality and location of land in large and small farms before drawing policy conclusions on land reform or the relative focus of public policy on small farms. In so doing, it must be borne in mind that the principal indicator of land quality, the land's price (which reflects both its inherent quality and its location) will tend to be a downward biased measure of the relative land quality of large farms, if the land market imperfections are as described in section 2.2.[19] The ratio of output to the value of land is, in any case, a more interesting indicator than the ratio of output to land area.[20]

Yields, Cultivation Rates, and Product-Mix.   All of the factors discussed above except for the land quality, possibly the risk considerations, and sometimes the capital market imperfections, point to the prediction that larger farms will use their land less fully than smaller farms, combining lower levels of other inputs with each unit of land and achieving lower output per total farm area. It is important to clarify the exact forms that this divergence may take. Decreasing output per land area may manifest itself in one or more of three alternative ways as farm size rises: (a) a falling "yield" per hectare cultivated in a given crop; (b) a falling share of total farm area placed under cultivation or, a falling share of cultivated land double-cropped; and (c) a product-mix shifting away from items with high values of output and input per hectare toward items with low value per hectare.

Perhaps the most deceptive of these dimensions is that of yield per hectare cultivated. It is often maintained that yields are higher on large farms, with the implication that larger farms are therefore more efficient. Yet it is perfectly consistent for yields per cropped area to be higher on large farms than on small ones, while at the same time the underlying degree of land utilization on the large farms is lower because a smaller portion of land available is cropped. Indeed, with equal quality land, and with an internal "Ricardian margin" of decreasing land quality within each farm, this phenomenon is precisely what one would expect. Since large farms cultivate smaller portions of their total area they enjoy the luxury of limiting cultivation to a higher quality subportion of their land (or, equivalently, to areas maintained at higher levels of fertility through more leisurely fallowing sequences), so that on the area actually planted yields would be expected to be higher for larger farms.[21]

Yields that are constant or even rising as farm size rises, therefore, do not imply size neutrality for social efficiency of land use, because of the strong tendency for the cultivation rate to fall with increasing farm size. Almost without exception census and survey data show a declining proportion of land placed in cultivation as farm size rises (see, for example, the cross-country data presented in Chapter 3). Moreover, where double-cropping is practiced, the cropping intensity almost invariably declines as farm size rises, even if the percent of land cultivated does not.

However, a valid interpretation of the systematic relationship between cultivation rates and farm size raises the question of the third dimension of land use: product-mix. Especially in the Latin American context, a decline in the percent of land cultivated means a rise in the percent of land placed in natural pasture. The question is, then, whether any diagnosis of underutilization of land on large estates is justified on the basis of their lower cultivation rates, since their livestock production may replace the crop production typical on smaller farms. In reality, the income generated per hectare placed under extensive grazing is much lower than that from crop production, so that the product shift toward livestock only partially moderates the decline in land productivity implied by declining portions of land under cultivation as farm size rises.

Two alternative approaches may be followed in analyzing the issue of product-mix. The evaluation of the size-productivity relationship may be confined to individual "product sectors" composed of farms producing only, or primarily, a specified product. If analysis of output per farm area demonstrates a decline as farm size rises, even in this narrow approach holding product-mix constant, then the evidence is unambiguous that small farms make fuller use of their land resources than do larger farms. However, this approach is overly lenient to the large farms in its assessment of their relative performance, because it fails to capture falling output per area attributable to the shifting of product-mix.

The alternative approach is to consider output achieved relative to available land area, regardless of product sector. So long as land quality is taken account of, this second approach is more meaningful for an accurate evaluation of the social efficiency of land-use patterns. It might be objected to in that it fails to allow for the possibility of "fixed coefficient" production characteristics, whereby some products inevitably require more land input per value of production (and lower inputs of labor and capital) than do other products. There are several flaws with this objection. First, agricultural production is not generally characterized by fixed coefficients. For individual crops, yields may be varied by changing the applications of fertilizers and other inputs. For livestock, production may be conducted anywhere along a spectrum from extensive grazing to an intensive-fodder basis. Second, even if there were strictly different fixed coefficients for alternative products, there would be no reason to expect the systematic result that those products requiring much land per unit of output value would be produced on large farms—unless the agricultural sector were indeed affected by the systematic distortions in factor markets that have been outlined above. Finally, and most basic, if fixed coefficients did exist and large farms specialized in land intensive products with relatively low land productivity, the implication would not be that because they had no technological alternatives they should be defined as efficient, but rather that the socially optimal product-mix would include less of these land-intensive items. Where, as in Latin America, large farms tend to specialize in extensive cattle raising, there is no doubt that social benefits could be achieved by changing the product-mix somewhat in the direction of the more labor-intensive crops produced on smaller farms and forming the major portion of the consumption basket of the poor. In sum, even if agricultural products had different fixed coefficients of production, the "product-mix" consideration would not remove the policy conclusion that the agrarian structure distorts productive efficiency in situations where larger farms consistently select products using relatively more land and less labor than those chosen by small farms.

To recapitulate, the declining degree of land utilization as farm size rises is likely to take one or more of the following forms: falling proportions of total area placed under cultivation, or double-cropped; less focus on products using little land and much labor per value of output and more on products using the reverse combinations; and, less commonly, falling yields per hectare cultivated (sometimes the opposite happens). The diagnosis of an inefficient agrarian structure remains valid, even if yields per area cultivated actually rise rather than falling as farm size rises, because of the more than offsetting decline in the share of land cultivated.

Social Efficiency. To this point the discussion of farm size and efficiency has focused on land utilization, or land productivity—the ratio of output to the available land resource. Because the salient result of maldistribution of land is declining land utilization as farm size rises, land productivity serves as a shorthand indicator of the influence of farm size on the social efficiency of production. However, a more precise formulation must consider total factor productivity—the ratio of output to the social cost (i.e., opportunity cost) of all factors used in production. With labor abundant but land and capital scarce to the economy, the systematic shifts toward lower output per area and the heavy use of land and capital, rather than labor, as farm size rises will frequently imply a general decline in total factor productivity (with factors evaluated at social prices) as farm size increases. That is, when "social efficiency" is defined as total factor productivity, its relation to farm size is likely to be in the same direction though quantitatively less strong than that of the simpler measure—land productivity. The main qualification to this proposition is that where the social cost of labor is substantial, its abundant use on the smallest farms, combined with small inputs of capital, and especially land, will generally imply a lower total factor productivity (with factors socially priced) than at a somewhat larger family-farm size. This result would hold in cases where productive employment is available in other sectors, but where excess workers remain on these small farms as a result of income sharing (the labor surplus model). If such alternative employment is not available, the social cost of labor must be very low (possibly zero) and the farms in question will not tend to be inefficient, indeed, they may be the most efficient of all.

Total factor productivity is, of course, not the only interesting measure of overall performance. It is the appropriate measure when the goal sought is maximization of the economy's total output. If the society places weight on an equitable income distribution and/or on the number of employment opportunities, different farm sizes could be compared using a more complex indicator of performance, one giving weight to these goals as well as to output. With such an indicator, small farms would come out still better than under the total factor productivity criterion, given their high labor absorption and the low incomes of most of the persons who live on them.

Predicted Static Effects of Land Redistribution on Output. Where the total factor productivity of large farms is below that of small farms, a redistribution of land would be expected to raise total output, if the new small farms created are as efficient as the existing ones. To predict the impact of land reform in practice, this last assumption must be held up to scrutiny and the dynamic effects of redistribution on capital formation, technological change, etc. must be considered. As a first step, however, it is useful to estimate the static output effects, assuming that new small farms will indeed be as efficient as existing ones. Chapter 5 presents estimates of the potential impact of land redistribution using this assumption (and taking land quality into account whenever possible).

Because our analysis relates to size of operated units, not the size of owned units, the "reform" under consideration involves literally a redistribution of land from large to smaller operators. This redistribution could involve the transfer of land ownership from large operators to smaller units, or simply the rental of land by currently large operators to small operators. For large owners who rent out their land, there are essentially three cases. In the first case, where owners already rent out all of their land to small tenants of the size that would be established more generally after a land reform, there is no reason from our central analysis to expect land redistribution to increase output.[22] In the second case, where large owners rent out all of their land, but to medium or large-sized renter operators, one would expect land redistribution into smaller, owner-operated units to raise production, following the general analysis of farm size and productivity. In the third case where owners rent out only a portion of their land, whether to small or large renters, one would also expect positive output effects of land redistribution with respect to that portion of the land operated by the owner. It is a matter for more theoretical inquiry (perhaps following the analytical lines established in the sharecropping debate) whether large owners who rent may be expected generally to do so on an exhaustive and small-tenant basis, thereby attaining production characteristics similar to those of an aggregate of small operations; or whether, instead, they may be expected to rent only part of their land, and to rent to medium or large renters, thereby tending to replicate the production characteristics of large owner-operated farms. At the level of actual land-reform implementation, it is important to recognize that the reforms in Eastern Asia typically involved transfer of ownership to existing small tenants rather than the fragmentation of large operations into new small operations, whereas, reform in Latin America more typically would involve redistribution from large operating units to small units. For this reason one might expect the impact of reform on production to be greater in the Latin American case than in the East Asian case.

Finally, although the reform to which we refer is not technically identical to redistribution of land ownership (the usual definition), in practice a redistribution of land by operator is likely to require a redistribution by owner. Large operated units are normally based on large owned units, and the chances of encouraging large owners to rent their land out in small parcels, if they are not already doing so, is extremely limited. The current trend is in quite the opposite direction, as land-reform fears encourage large owners to displace tenants and operate the land on their own.

The optimal postreform farm size, in the absence of technical returns to scale, will necessarily be merely the total agricultural area divided by the total number of families in the agricultural labor force (after adjusting for land quality). That is, since total factor productivity falls as farm size rises in the relevant range, the most productive agrarian structure will be that composed of the smallest farms possible, consistent with full allocation of the available land and labor force, i.e., total area divided by the total number of farm families.[23] Although such considerations as varying family size and economies of scale in a few products tend to imply that the optimal distribution would have some variance, this might be achieved satisfactorily through rental (i.e., the distribution of land by operator could have some variance, even though that by owner did not). Alternatively, a moderate degree of inequality in the distribution of land by owner would be expected to emerge through land sales, where the economic logic of some larger farms was compelling. If the equal distribution of all available land among all families implies a labor/land ratio equal to that of the same sized farms in the existing agrarian structure, the land productivity of these latter farms can provide a rough prediction of average land productivity after redistribution, subject to a few caveats. Most obvious, perhaps, is the fact that output composition tends to shift toward items produced on small farms and, unless demand patterns shift in an offsetting way, there will be some changes in relative prices. These complicate predictions of output increases from the redistribution. Where the labor intensity of the postreform farms is different from that of the current farms of the same size, predicting the new level of output is further complicated (Chapter 5).

It is important to clarify that the approach of this chapter does not permit an evaluation of the social efficiency of prospective large state or cooperative farms as the units of postreform agrarian structure. The general absence of increasing returns to scale noted in section 2.2 does suggest that large state farms are not required for technical efficiency, and there are a number of issues concerning incentives suggesting that, unless correctly organized, state or cooperative farms may fall below private family farms in productive potential.[24] However, both the *a priori* analysis of this chapter and the empirical analysis of the following chapters are confined to the likely effects of land redistribution from large to small private holdings. Neither our knowledge of existing private market imperfections nor the data on existing relationships between farm size and productivity under private ownership provide any basis for predicting the output or employment effects of a land reform creating large state or cooperative farms.

2.3   LAND-UTILIZATION PATTERNS ACROSS COUNTRIES

Following the above discussion, agrarian structures with unequal land distribution would be expected to lead to underutilization of land and therefore low land productivity (output per total farm area) on larger farms. However, it is important to know whether the severity of this phenomenon varies across countries, and, if so, what determines the variation. This question has received virtually no theoretical attention. Yet the policy issue that it raises is important: Can the production gains from land reform be expected to be relatively similar across many countries in varying situations? More specifically, it is frequently thought that land reform has substantial potential for output gains only in certain Latin American countries with abundant land and very large estates. It is argued that land-scarce countries, such as India, could expect little production gain from land redistribution, because the division of current "large" farms, already of a modest size by international standards (due to land scarcity), into the very small parcels that would be necessary to absorb the rural population might cause agricultural stagnation rather than raise output.[25]

Three main forces suggest themselves as primary determinants of the variation across countries in the potential for increasing output and employment through land reform: (1) the degree of concentration in land operation; (2) the relative abundance of the land endowment of the country; and (3) the country's state of development, as represented by its per capita income.

The concentration of land determines the share of total land operated by the minority of large farms. The higher this share the more severe will be the overall productive impact of given productivity differentials by farm size.

The per capita income level of the country should be an important factor for several reasons. More developed countries have less labor-market dualism, because of the greater wage-labor opportunities in their relatively more important modern sectors. On the basis of the discussion in section 2.2, a decline in the influence of labor-market dualism should lead to a narrowing of the divergence in intensity of land utilization across farm sizes. Similarly, more developed countries have more perfect markets for credit, capital, and land, and more viable alternatives to land for the objective of asset-holding, so that the land-use distortions associated with these factors should diminish as per capita income rises.

A third plausible determinant of relative large-farm land utilization across countries is the abundance or scarcity of land. At the intuitive level, one might expect the "luxury" of holding land idle or using it poorly in large estates to be limited to countries with abundant endowments of land per capita. A more rigorous analysis, however, suggests that, while the "most likely" result appears to be that the land-scarce country will have less serious underutilization of land in its large-farm sector than the land-abundant country, it is not at all improbable that the two types of countries will have similar degrees of underutilization of land on large farms relative to small farms (given identical proportionate distributions of land), and it is even possible (but not likely) that the land-scarce country will have more serious underutilization of land in the large-farm sector.

Appendix C presents a mathematical model that demonstrates these points in the case where the agrarian structure is identical in two countries—in the sense that a large-farm sector holds the same (high) share of total land and employs the same (low) share of total labor in each. A measure, Z, of "relative large-farm land utilization" is defined as the ratio of output per farm area in the large-farm sector to that in the small-farm sector. Then, if the "elasticity of substitution" between land and labor is

(1) less than unity (probably the "normal" case), the land-scarce country will have a higher relative large-farm land utilization, Z (and therefore less potential for increased output through land reform) than the land-abundant country; (2) equal to unity, the two countries will have identical levels of relative large-farm land utilization; (3) greater than unity, the land-scarce country will have *lower* relative large-farm land utilization (Z) than the land-abundant country and *greater* potential for output gains through land redistribution.

The "elasticity of substitution" represents the degree of ease with which land and labor can replace each other in the production of agricultural goods. When this elasticity is unity, the two can be substituted relatively easily, and, more specifically, a one percent change in the ratio of the price of land to that of labor will cause a one percent change in the ratio of land to labor used in production by a profit-maximizing farmer. When the elasticity is lower, technical conditions are more rigid and it will require more than a one percent change in the ratio of land's price to that of labor to make it profitable to change the factor ratio by one percent; if the elasticity is above unity, technical substitutability is easier and the factor ratio will be more sensitive to relative factor prices. (These statements refer to the absolute value of the elasticity, since it carries a negative sign.)

Before proceeding to an elaboration of the economic logic of the result on relative large-farm land utilization in relation to the country's land endowment, it is important to state the major policy implication. Because the degree of substitutability between land and labor is usually relatively high (that is, close to unity, but probably somewhat below it), the model in Appendix C suggests that the potential for increased output from land reform normally will be almost as great in land-scarce countries as in land-abundant countries, for a given degree of concentration in land ownership and assuming no differences in available technology with size. It is generally agreed that there is a greater ease of factor substitution in agricultural production than in the industrial sector. Labor may be applied more heavily on a given plot of land through more careful weeding and the more thorough application of other cultivation practices to achieve a higher yield, which in turn calls forth more harvesting labor per hectare. There is much potential for factor substitution in varying product-mixes. At the empirical level, agricultural production functions of the Cobb-Douglas type—which have a unitary elasticity of substitution between all factors, including land and labor—do quite well in explaining output achieved (see the references in section 2.2). However, the few existing production function analyses using estimating forms that do not constrain the elasticity of substitution to unity (particularly the constant elasticity of substitution or CES function) are inconclusive, some finding the elasticity to be well below unity and others finding it close to unity.[26] Thus, the scant available evidence suggests that the elasticity of substitution between land and labor is somewhat below unity, but probably not far below—meaning that land redistribution could be expected to increase output almost as much (in proportionate terms) in land-scarce as in land-abundant countries, if the degree of land concentration is the same.

The intuitive logic behind the proof presented in Appendix C is as follows. In the land-scarce country, the large farmer already has relatively much land combined with relatively little labor. In the land-abundant country, the large farmer (who has more land than his counterpart in the land-scarce country) combines still more land with the same relatively low amount of labor (by assumption). If technical options in production are very limited, so that it is difficult to combine the extra land with the given labor (that is, substitutability between the two factors is low), then the large farm in the land-abundant country will produce little more than its counterpart in the land-scarce country, despite its greater land availability. Its output per area will therefore be much lower than that on large farms in the land-scarce country. On the other hand, the small farms have relatively little land and much labor in both countries. Comparing them, the additional land (the factor in short supply) available to the small farmers in the land-abundant country will mean a greater output advantage vis à vis the land-scarce country counterparts than holds for the large farms in the land-abundant country vis à vis their counterparts in the land-scarce country. These two comparisons taken together mean that (1) not only would the average degree of "land utilization" (output per hectare, or fraction of area cultivated, for example) be lower in the land-abundant country than in the land-scarce country for *all* farms taken together but also (2) this differential would be more pronounced as between the large farms in the two countries than as between the small farms. The implication of these considerations is that the measure of the large-farm/small-farm land-use distortion would be more severe—that is, output per total area on large farms, relative to that on small farms, would be lower—in the land-abundant country than in the land-scarce country.

Now, suppose instead that land is fairly easily substitutable for labor in the production process. Then, considering the large farms only, the extra land of those in the land-abundant country can be used productively (since it can be smoothly substituted for labor) rather than becoming more and more redundant (as in the limited substitutability case), so that output of large farms in the land-abundant country will be significantly higher than output of their counterparts in the land-scarce country. The difference in output between small farms in the land-scarce and the land-abundant countries will be less dramatic because, since it is relatively easy to substitute labor for the land in short supply, the small farm in the land-scarce country is not at too great a disadvantage and will generate an output not too much less than for the small farm in the land-abundant country. The overall result will be that the relative output per farm area between large farms and small farms will be about as great in the land-abundant country (although the overall country average of output per land area will be lower in that country).

Figures 2-1 through 2-3 present a graphical exposition of these points. Each graph shows isoquant curves that specify the alternative combinations of land and labor that will produce a given level of output. The isoquants of Figure 2-1 have unitary elasticity of substitution; those of Figure 2-2, elasticity of substitution below unity; and those of Figure 2-3, infinitely high elasticity of substitution. Country 2 is assumed to have twice as much land as country 1, both in large farms (L) and in small ones (S). In all three cases, large farms in country 1 are assumed to have the same output as small farms (at L_1 and S_1; both points lie on the isoquant for 100 output units); the large-farm sector uses more land and the small-farm sector more labor. The land ordinate is twice as high for both large and small farms in country 2, while the labor quantity (on the abscissa) remains unchanged for each. In Figure 2-1, the new isoquant (at 150 output units) passes through both points L_2 and S_2—that is, output rises by the same proportion for both large and small farms. But in Figure 2-2, with low substitutability between factors, output rises very little for large farms, going from country 1 to country 2 (L_2 is only on isoquant 125), whereas it rises a great deal more for small farms (S_2 is on the higher isoquant 175). Finally, with infinitely elastic substitution in Figure 2-3, output rises much more for large farms than for small farms, going from country 1 to country 2 (L_2 is on a higher isoquant, 180, than is S_2, which lies on 140).[27]

In summary, the extent to which the underutilization of land in large farms reduces output below its potential may be expected to vary across countries with the degree of land concentration, per capita income, and the abundance of land endowment. On the basis of the analysis in Appendix C, an important policy conclusion is that, other things being equal (including the concentration of land), this relative large-farm underutilization of land will probably be only a little less important in land-scarce than

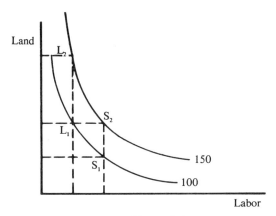

Figure 2-1

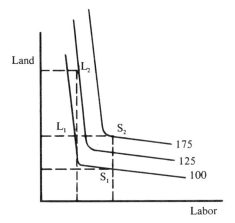

Figure 2-2

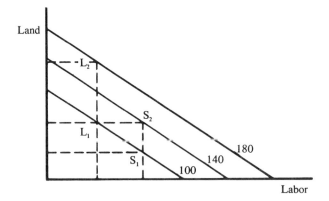

Figure 2-3

in land-abundant countries, if land and labor have close to unitary elasticity of substitution in production—which we have reason to expect to be the case. Operationally, the implication is that comparable production gains might be expected from land reform in land-scarce Asian countries and land-abundant Latin American countries, for a given degree of concentration in the distribution of land ownership.

2.4   SHARECROPPING

Whereas there has been limited theoretical discussion of the farm-size-productivity relationship, and virtually none on its cross-country patterns, there exists a large theoretical literature on the influence of sharecropping on the efficiency of the agricultural sector.[28] The traditional viewpoint is that sharecropping causes inefficient allocation of resources because, unless landowner and sharecropper share all input costs in the same proportion as output (unlikely by definition for the labor input, which is fully the sharecropper's), the sharecropper will apply below-optimal levels of variable inputs, since he will equate the full marginal cost of such inputs with *his share* of their marginal product, not with the total marginal product.

A recent debate centers on the failure of this viewpoint to recognize that the shares (of inputs and outputs) are themselves endogenous to the contractual process, rather than being exogenously given. Cheung[29] proposed a maximization model in which the share that emerges is just that level at which net income accruing to the sharecropping worker equals the wage and the share going to the landlord equals the rent per unit of land in the cash rental market; thus, although the medium of sharecropping is used, the result is the same combination of factors and level of output as in the neoclassical land-rental market solution.

As Bardhan and Srinivasan[30] have pointed out, Cheung's conclusion requires the extreme assumption that the landlord precisely stipulates all input levels (including labor) that the sharecropper must apply, removing the possibility that the wedge between the share of output results and the full cost of inputs can affect the sharecropper's production decisions. This one-sided relationship is not likely to exist. Bardhan and Srinivasan offer an alternative model, involving maximization from the standpoint of the sharecropper, which returns to the marginalist conclusion of inefficiency in sharecropping production. Their model involves a general equilibrium analysis in which the demand and supply of leases is a function of the rental share, while the landowner's alternative to sharecropping is cultivation of the land himself, and the sharecropper's alternative is wage labor elsewhere. However, the model requires the unrealistic assumption that the sharecropper can obtain land to the point where its marginal product falls to zero.[31]

A more recent analysis by Bell and Zusman[32] takes a game-theoretic approach to address the problem that a realistic solution involves neither complete domination by the landlord (Cheung), nor maximization only from the standpoint of the sharecropper (Bardhan–Srinivasan), but the outcome of bargaining between the two. The Bell–Zusman analysis indicates that bargaining is not likely to generate a share precisely consistent with the market solution under direct rental (as proposed by Cheung) and, thus, that the problem of incentive distortion under sharecropping remains.

For policy purposes, the relevant question is how severely the existence of sharecropping lessens the productive potential of agriculture (if at all), and, accordingly, how large the output gains might be of a shift from sharecropping to small-farm ownership or cash-rental operations. When the implementation of a policy forcing the conversion of sharecropping into cash rental is considered, it becomes obvious that another major factor must be taken into account, risk. Namely, although under complete certainty such a conversion might increase efficiency, when risk is considered, it is evident that the landless class might be unwilling to lease as much land under cash rental as under sharecropping for fear of bad crops or low product prices and the resulting risk of being unable to cover both cash rents and subsistence costs. In other words, for any given expected income from cash rental the worker would insist on a risk premium leading to a lower expected rental rate than that which he would be prepared to accept under sharecropping. A recent theoretical study by Stiglitz[33] emphasizes the importance of risk in the evaluation of sharecropping and concludes that in the absence of alternative arrangements for risk-sharing the system is not inefficient. Empirical studies that would indicate which sets of assumptions are most likely to be valid have only begun to be undertaken, so it is not clear which theoretical analyses will turn out to be relevant. What has become increasingly clear, however, is the lack of any general evidence of lower productivity on sharecropped farms.

Most empirical attempts to find important inefficiencies associated with sharecropping have been unsuccessful[34] (and tests reported in Chapter 4 fail to find significant effects of tenancy on land use or productivity). Land productivity is as often found to be lower on owner-operator farms as higher. In view of this, and the fact that our understanding of the microeconomics of peasant agriculture in general and land rental markets in particular is inadequate to choose one theoretical specification over another, it would seem that, although the issue has evoked a stimulating body of theoretical work, the efficiency impact of sharecropping remains, to put it mildly, ambiguous. Further, it is clearly of much less importance as a determinant of agricultural output and employment than is the relationship emphasized in this study—the influence of farm size on the utilization of available resources.[35]

2.5   DYNAMIC EFFECTS: TECHNICAL CHANGE, SAVINGS, AND FARM SIZE

An argument frequently invoked against land redistribution, or other strategies relying on small farms, is that large farmers are more dynamic in the adoption of technological innovations. The premises are that their superior education makes them more aware of technical advances, and that their greater margin for risk-taking and access to capital enables them to shift to new techniques sooner. The observation in some countries of higher yields per hectare from the land put into cultivation on large farms is often cited as empirical evidence in support of this notion, although the tendency mentioned above on these farms to confine cultivation to a more fertile (smaller) proportion of total area, must contribute to such differentials. So is the common assertion that it is the larger farmers who have adopted the new techniques of the Green Revolution in Asia, while small farmers have lagged behind.

Whether a greater receptivity to new techniques gives large farms an advantage in terms of dynamic efficiency is a matter for empirical examination,[36] and the data and tests presented below address this question (particularly for Colombia, Pakistan, and India). However, certain general considerations should be borne in mind from the outset. (1) The same capital market imperfections that lead to the economizing of capital inputs on small farms confer an advantage to larger farms in access to credit for modern inputs. The main policy implication is that the channels for credit and modern inputs to small farms should be improved—not that a large-farm structure is essential for the adoption of new techniques. Indeed, precisely because of their disadvantage in access, the small farms will frequently have a high production return on the supply of additional units of credit-financed modern inputs.[37] (2) The popular association of mechanization with more dynamic adoption of new techniques is generally erroneous. Large-farm adoption of mechanized techniques may just as well reflect the distortions of the factor price incentives facing them (cheaper capital, dearer labor) away from the social scarcity values of factors, as any technical superiority over small farms in the appropriate choice of modern techniques. (3) There exists a well-known S curve relating the percentage of farmers adopting an innovation to time.[38] Even though the larger farms are likely to be the first to adopt innovations, small farms are likely to follow—and sometimes to do so very soon. The phenomenon of the S curve is important to keep in mind when addressing the policy assertion that, even if large farms in the past had relatively poor land productivity, their current performance is much improved because of their participation or leadership in the Green Revolution. This viewpoint fails to recognize that once adoption of new techniques and varieties takes place along the full extent of the S curve, the earlier size-productivity relationship is likely to be reestablished in relative terms, with a higher output per farm area at all sizes.

Another dynamic superiority sometimes claimed for larger farms is their greater contribution to capital formation than small farms, because of higher savings rates. Such assertions typically fail to distinguish between average and marginal savings rates; the latter determine the savings effect of an income (or, in this case, land) redistribution. Household surveys find them usually much more similar for families at different income levels than are average savings rates. Moreover, under various of the more fully specified theories of savings (i.e., ones including variables other than income as determinants of savings), income redistribution leaves savings unchanged.[39] Simulation experiments with rural savings data for Brazil indicate that rural income redistribution would have only limited impact on the rural savings rate.[40] A recent analysis of Indian NCAER household survey data finds rural savings behavior of a nature that also would indicate little if any loss in total savings resulting from rural income redistribution.[41]

The issue of savings rates in relation to farm size is addressed only peripherally in this study, although relevant data are reported for Pakistan and Malaysia. In the absence of compelling evidence to the contrary, it would appear that the issue of rural savings does not constitute a basis for reversing the policy implications of the farm-size–productivity relationship. This conclusion is reinforced by two other considerations. First, it must be remembered that the increase in total production likely to be associated with land redistribution tends to offset any negative effects on savings rates from the associated rural income redistribution, so that the absolute level of total savings may be unchanged, or higher, than before redistribution. Second, a dollar's worth of savings on a small farm will generally lead to a greater output increase than on a larger farm, due to the greater amount of complementary labor. Indeed, since after reform agriculture would be less capital-intensive than before (with a lower capital/output ratio), a lower savings rate could support the same growth rate as before reform.[42] This consideration, in fact, implies that if savings rates did not decline substantially after land reform, the dynamic effects would be positive rather than negative; the long-run growth rate would rise, as well as the static output level.

2.6   CONCLUSION

Several theoretical considerations lead to the expectation that in developing countries large farms will tend toward lower production than small farms, per unit of constant quality land available. An especially important influence is labor-market dualism, or the dichotomy between the use of family labor on small farms and hired labor on large farms. This phenomenon leads to a lower effective price of labor and, therefore, a higher rate of land cultivation on small farms than on large. A broad result is that land goes relatively underused on large farms, while excessive labor is crowded onto small farms. Land redistribution should therefore be expected to raise total output by combining underused labor from small farms and the landless work force with underused land on large farms. Nor is there likely to be a sacrifice of potential efficiency from land redistribution, because it is unlikely that there will be significant economies of scale for actual farming operations, especially in developing countries where highly mechanized techniques are inappropriate because of the relative scarcity of capital.

Imperfect capital markets aggravate the distortions of factor use, generally causing large farms with preferential access to cheap credit to substitute machinery for labor and to choose even lower labor/land ratios than would result from labor-market dualism alone. The result is an aggravation of the problem of rural underemployment.

Because the social opportunity costs of land and capital are likely to be high, while that of labor is likely to be low in the developing economy, total social factor productivity (the ratio of value-added to factor cost at social prices) is likely to decline as farm size rises, although perhaps by somewhat less than the ratio of output to land alone.

The differing degree of potential output increases from land redistribution, among different developing countries, is an unexplored subject. Analysis in this chapter and in Appendix C concludes that if the elasticity of substitution between labor and land is close to unity (a reasonable case for agriculture), the relative underutilization of land by large farms will be almost as severe in land-scarce (Asian) countries as in land-abundant (Latin American) countries. Therefore, the potential output gains from land reform may be more comparable between the two categories of countries than is generally thought to be the case.

The possible distortions of sharecropping have received a great deal of theoretical attention. However, both the ambiguous theoretical conclusions and the inconclusive empirical evidence on the subject suggest that it is of considerably less importance for policy purposes than the issue of productivity in relation to farm size.

Finally, the consideration of dynamic factors, such as technological change and savings behavior, need not reverse the policy implications that arise from the static output gains to be achieved from land redistribution and other programs favoring the small-farm sector. Indeed, to the extent that large farms enjoy temporary advantages in the greater use of improved techniques because of preferential access to credit, a major policy implication is the need for expanded programs making credit and improved inputs available to small farms (where the return may be higher because of more limited current use).

Chapters 3 and 4 present empirical examinations of these issues relating the agrarian structure to productivity of the agricultural sector. Chapter 3 investigates the limited data available internationally, in order to explore these questions on a comparative basis across countries. Chapter 4 examines the rich sample survey data bases available for six countries in order to carry out rigorous empirical tests of the hypotheses posed in this chapter.

THREE

Cross-Country Tests: Extensive Data

3.1   RELATIVE LAND UTILIZATION BY FARM SIZE

The sets of agricultural data available on a common basis for a wide range of countries, and thus usable for the "extensive" testing of hypotheses raised in Chapter 2, are quite limited in detail. The most satisfactory data for this purpose come from the agricultural censuses for the censal year 1960, which have been compiled into cross-country analytical tables by the Food and Agriculture Organization (FAO).[1] Unfortunately, agricultural censuses generally do not contain data for total value of production by farm size, reporting instead data relating to land use and, in some cases, physical magnitudes of output of selected crops or numbers of animals existing on farms. Nevertheless, these data do provide an indication of the pattern of land use by farm size, on the basis of the percent of total farm area placed under cultivation by each size group. They may be used to examine the hypothesis raised above, relating "relative large-farm land utilization" to the degree of concentration in land operation, the abundance of the land endowment, and the per capita income. Recall that, in this data, as in almost all that is available, a farm is defined by the size of the operated unit, not the size of the owned unit.

Table 3-1 presents cross-country data on the land utilization of large farms relative to that of small farms for twenty developing countries. For each country, the large-farm sector is defined as all farm-size classes making up the top 40 percent of total land area, and the small-farm sector as those constituting the bottom 20 percent. (Identification of the floor and ceiling sizes, respectively, requires interpolation from the data presented by size-classes.) The table indicates the percentage of farm area dedicated to cultivation in each of the two sectors—small- and large-farm—as well as the farm-size ceiling for the small class and floor for the large class. The final column reports the ratio of the large farm-size floor to the small farm-size ceiling. This ratio provides an indication of the degree of concentration in the distribution of land in farm establishments (that is, the ratio would be unity for a completely equal distribution; the higher the ratio, the more unequal the land distribution).

Column E of Table 3-1 presents an indicator of relative large-farm land utilization: the ratio of the percent of land under cultivation in the large-farm sector to that in the small-farm sector. Two features are readily apparent from this indicator. First, it is almost always below unity, regardless of country, meaning that the percent of land cultivated is lower on large than on small farms within each country. Second, the indicator tends to be higher for the land-scarce Asian countries and lower for the land-abundant Latin American countries, tending to confirm the hypothesis for the cross-country pattern of relative large-farm land utilization under the "normal" case of somewhat less than unitary elasticity of substitution between land and labor.

Figure 3-1 presents a scatter diagram that permits visual confirmation of the declining "relative large-farm land utilization" indicator Z, as land endowment rises. The land endowment variable is "agricultural" land per capita of agricultural population (column F of Appendix Table D-2).

The data of Table 3-1 may be used to conduct a statistical test of the three hypotheses proposed in section 2.3 above, concerning relative large-farm land utilization across countries. A regression[2] of the following form is fitted to the data:

$Z = a + b \log A + c \log y + dC,$

where Z is the index of relative large-farm land utilization (percent of farm area cultivated on large farms divided by that on small); $\log A$ is the natural logarithm of the per capita land endowment; $\log y$ is the natural logarithm of per capita income; and C is the indicator of land concentration (column F of Table 3-1).

The logarithm is chosen as the form for inclusion of the land endowment and per capita income variables, because of the extreme range of variation of each, compared with a more limited range of variation in

Table 3-1. Relative Land-Use Intensity: Large Farms Compared to Small Farms (Selected Countries)

| | Weighted average % of farm area cultivated: | | | | "Z": relative intensity large-farm land use | Ratio, size group limits |
| | Small-farm sector (bottom 20% of total area) | | Large-farm sector (top 40% of total area) | | | |
Country	A %	B ceiling (ha)	C %	D floor (ha)	E= C/A	F= D/B
Brazil	33.0	91	2	1,000[a]	0.06	11.00
Chile	41.4	467	6	1,000[a]	0.15	2.14
Colombia	48.8	38	4.5	525	0.09	13.82
Peru	46.4	263	5	1,000[a]	0.11	3.80
Uruguay	31.0	320	7	1,000[a]	0.23	3.12
Venezuela	51.8	452	10	1,000[a]	0.19	2.21
Costa Rica	43.8	42	17	413	0.39	9.72
Nicaragua	43.6	48	9.8	419	0.22	8.64
Panama	67.5	18	11.1	120	0.16	6.70
Ceylon (Sri Lanka)	86.9	1.28	80.6	9.25	0.93	7.23
Taiwan	71	0.60	80.2	1.86	1.13	3.10
India	93.9	2.12	87.8	7.95	0.93	3.75
Japan	91	0.65	75.4	1.87	0.83	2.88
Korea (Rep.)	33	0.38	46.3	1.21	1.40	3.18
Pakistan	87.5	2.03	67.5	8.0	0.77	3.94
Philippines	96.5	2.78	75.3	8.45	0.78	3.04
Thailand	90.4	2.78	85.6	7.20	0.95	2.59
Turkey	97.1	4.34	76.3	15.6	0.79	3.59
Kenya	49.5	7.45	13	1,000[a]	0.26	134.2
U.A.R.	99.8	1.21	90.1	5.7	0.90	4.71

[a]Area over 40% of total. Brazil 44.1; Chile 72.6; Peru 69.7; Uruguay 56.9; Venezuela 71.8; Kenya 44.3.
Source: Appendix Table D-1, this volume.

the relative large-farm land-use indicator Z. The choice of the logarithmic specification is supported by the nonlinear relationship evident in Figure 3-1.

Table 3-2 presents the results of these regression estimates. They provide good levels of explanation, especially considering the cross-country nature of the data. The land endowment variable is consistently significant (statistically) and has the predicted sign; the same goes for the variable for land concentration. By contrast, per capita income does not prove to be statistically significant, and it even has the opposite sign to that expected. (To determine whether the extreme values of per capita income for Uruguay and Japan, or the extreme value of the land concentration variable for Kenya, affect the results, variants 4 and 5 in the table are included; their results do not differ meaningfully from those for the full set of data.)

In sum, these cross-country regression results are consistent with two of the three hypotheses raised earlier: that the degree of relative large-farm underutilization of land is more severe in countries with more unequal land distribution and in land-abundant countries (in the normal case of less than unitary elasticity of substitution). The tests may be somewhat misleading, however. They, as well as the scatter diagram, indicate a rather sharp decline in relative large-farm land utilization as land endowment rises. The evidence, referred to earlier, suggesting a substitution elasticity lower than, but close to, unity would imply instead only a gentle decline in relative large-farm land utilization as land endowment rises. This apparent inconsistency may be because the variable Z used in the test, the share of land cultivated on large farms relative to that on small, almost certainly introduces an upward bias in the measure of relative large-farm land use for land-scarce countries and a downward bias for land-abundant countries (and, as a result, a bias toward an overly steep decline in the relationship of Z to the land endowment variable). The reasons are: first, in land-scarce countries, double-cropping is the main manifestation of fuller utilization of land on small farms; yet the measure of Z here takes no account of double-cropping and counts all cultivated land equally, whether double-cropped or not. Second, in land-abundant countries (at least in Latin America) there is a systematic shift in product-mix toward the extensive raising of livestock as farm size rises, and, therefore, a shift in land use away from cultivation toward natural pasture. In light of these considerations, the relative degree of large-farm land utilization based on output per total farm area is probably substantially lower than that measured here

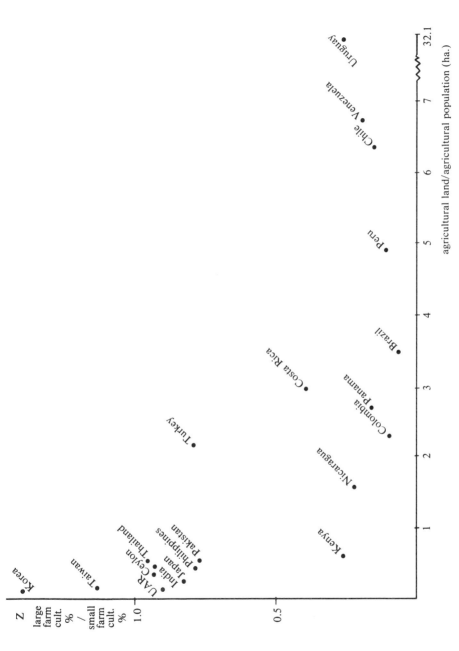

Figure 3-1. Relative Large-Farm Land Utilization and Land Endowment

Table 3–2. Cross-Country Regression Results: Relative Large-Farm Land Utilization Based on Percent of Area under Cultivation (Top 40 percent Total Area Farms Relative to Bottom 20 percent)

	Regression coefficient (standard error in parentheses)				
Form	Constant	Land endow- ment[a]	Per capita income (1970 $)	Concentra- tion index[b]	$\overline{R}^2$
1	0.60 (.05)	−0.23 (.04)	—	—	.6721
2	0.6936 (.490)	−0.2265 (.045)	−0.0159 (.084)	—	.6728
3	1.458 (.402)	−0.2087 (.033)	−0.0936 (.064)	−0.1885 (.047)	.8383
4[c]	0.7956 (.704)	−0.2226 (.060)	−0.0325 (.124)	—	.6604
5[d]	1.421 (.362)	−0.2471 (.034)	−0.0861 (.055)	−0.2090 (.07)	.8861

[a] Agricultural land (hectares) per agricultural population.
[b] Ratio of the floor of farm size for farms holding top 40 percent of total area, to the ceiling of farm size for farms holding the bottom 20 percent of total area.
[c] Excluding Japan.
[d] Excluding Kenya and Uruguay.
Source: Calculated from data presented in Tables 3-1, D-2, and *World Bank Atlas.*

on the basis of cultivation rates for land-scarce countries and higher for land-abundant countries. The policy implication of this qualification is that the scope for increased output from land reform is probably much closer for the land-scarce and land-abundant countries than suggested by Figure 3-1 and by the coefficients on land endowment in the regression estimates. This question can only be examined more accurately by the use of data on output per farm area rather than cultivation rates. Such data are not available on an extensive cross-country basis, but are discussed in detail in the "intensive" analyses for six countries, in Chapters 4 and 5.

3.2   EVIDENCE ON DYNAMIC EFFECTS OF AGRARIAN STRUCTURE

If large farms are more conducive to dynamic growth than small ones, then one would expect, other things being equal, to observe higher agricultural growth rates in (1) countries with a larger average farm size and (2) countries with more unequal distributions of land and, therefore, a larger share of total land in large farms.

Table 3-3 presents data for thirty developing countries on agricultural growth during the 1960s: average farm size; population growth rate; the concentration of farm land distribution (Gini coefficient)[3]; and land endowment (in this case, total land per capita of agricultural population). The output growth rates are from FAO indexes of the volume of total agricultural production. The table is arranged in ascending order of average farm size, and there is no immediately apparent association between average farm size (column 1) and the agricultural growth rate (column 2).

Table 3-4 reports the results of alternative regression estimates, attempting to relate agricultural growth rate to the other variables included in Table 3-3. The population growth rate is included as an independent variable, because of its influence on the supply of, and demand for, agricultural output. That is, more rapid population growth provides both more agricultural labor and a wider market for foodstuffs. The land endowment variable is included to remove the influence of resource base (countries with higher land endowments would be expected to achieve higher agricultural output growth).

Neither of the two hypotheses cited above receives serious statistical support. The agricultural growth rate is neither related in a statistically significant way to average farm size (whose coefficients are usually negative, but not significant), nor to the concentration of land distribution—Gini coefficient (whose coefficient is positive, but not significant). The only explanatory variable that is significant is the population growth rate, a result that is reasonable but that tells nothing about the influence of agrarian structure on the dynamism of agricultural growth.

3.3   LAND PRODUCTIVITY, EMPLOYMENT,
       AND AGRARIAN STRUCTURE

The World Bank has compiled an additional set of cross-country evidence on the relationship of agrarian structure to productivity. These data, presented in Table 3-5, indicate that both production and employment per hectare are higher in those countries that have (a) smaller average farm size and (b) more equal distribution of land ownership.[4] Thus, in the table it is evident that production per hectare is much higher and average farm size much smaller in Asia and Africa than in South America. Within Asia, output per hectare is much higher in China (Taiwan), Korea, and Japan, where land concentration is

Table 3-3. Comparison of Agricultural Growth Rates to Average Farm Size, Population Growth Rates, Land Concentration, and Land Endowment (30 selected Developing Countries)

Country	Average farm size (ha) (rank in parentheses) 1	Agricultural output growth rate,[a] 1961–71 (percent) 2	Population growth rate, 1960–70 (percent) 3	Gini coefficient for farm land distribution[b] 4	Total land area per agricultural population, 1970 (ha) 5
Japan	1.18 (1)	1.6	1.0	.411	1.73
Indonesia	1.20 (2)	2.7	2.0	.553	2.18
Taiwan	1.27 (3)	3.8[c]	2.9	.401	0.57
United Arab Republic	1.59 (4)	0.7	2.5	.598	0.19[d]
Sri Lanka	1.61 (5)	1.9	2.4	.665	1.00
Korea	2.06 (6)	3.9	2.7	.195	0.57
Pakistan	2.35 (7)	4.7	2.7	.631	1.84
India	2.70 (8)	1.9	2.3	.584	0.90
Uganda	3.29 (9)	1.0	2.7	.485	2.63
Philippines	3.59 (10)	2.9	3.0	.507	1.13
Thailand	3.47 (11)	3.7	3.1	.455	1.86
Senegal	3.63 (12)	−2.2	2.1	.399	6.48
Turkey	5.03 (13)	3.4	2.5	.629	3.18
Dominican Republc	5.05 (14)	3.2	3.0	.798	1.85
Guatemala	8.34 (15)	4.8	3.1	.828	3.40
Morocco	9.82 (16)	2.4	2.9	.640	4.73
Kenya	11.74 (17)	2.8	3.1	.822	3.40
Tunisia	15.40 (18)	2.0	3.0	.645	6.65
Panama	18.81 (19)	5.1	3.3	.737	11.97

Nicaragua	37.41 (22)	3.5	5.5	.801	11.51
Costa Rica	41.05 (23)	3.3	6.3	.782	6.32
Brazil	74.86 (24)	2.9	3.6	.831	20.95
Venezuela	81.21 (25)	3.5	4.4	.927	32.31
Paraguay	108.53 (26)	3.1	3.1	.938	32.03
Chile	118.32 (27)	2.3	1.4	.933	30.47
Mexico	123.87 (28)	3.5	3.4	.747[e]	8.56
Uruguay	195.26 (29)	1.3	-0.6	.820	36.83
Argentina	371.06 (30)	1.5	1.0	.836	75.11

[a] Average for 1971–72 compared with 1961–62 average, FAO indexes for total agricultural production.

[b] Calculated as: $G = 1 - 2\{\Sigma_i n_i z_{i-1}\} - \Sigma_i n_i a_i$, where n_i is the fraction of holdings in size class i, a_i is the fraction of total area in size class i, and z_i is the cumulative fraction of total area up through size class i.

[c] Calculated from United Nations, Yearbook of National Accounts Statistics: 1972. Figure refers to growth of real value of agricultural output, 1964–70.

[d] Inhabited and cultivated area only.

[e] Calculated from CIDA, Estructura Agraria y Desarrollo Agricola en Mexico, Tomo I (Mexico: Comite Interamericano para Desarrollo Agricola, 1970), pp. 95–97, 117. Treats ejido land as equally distributed among all ejidatarios. Unadjusted figure computed from FAO Report on the 1960 Census is 0.950.

Sources

Col. 1: FAO, Report on the 1960 Census of Agriculture, Vol. 5: Analysis and International Comparison of Census Results (Rome: Food and Agriculture Organization, 1971), Table 2.10.

Col. 2: FAO, Production Yearbook: 1972, Vol. 26 (Rome: F.A.O., 1973), Table 8.

Col. 3: International Bank for Reconstruction and Development, World Bank Atlas: Population, Per Capita Product, and Growth Rates (Washington, D.C.: International Bank for Reconstruction and Development, 1972).

Col. 4: Calculated from FAO, Report on the 1960 Census, Tables 1.5, 2.4, and 2.10.

Col. 5: Calculated from FAO, Production Yearbook: 1972, Tables 1, 5.

Table 3–4. Regression Results: Agricultural Growth Rates in Relation to Agrarian Structure for 30 Developing Countries

	Estimation form:		
	1	2	3
Regression coefficient (standard error in parentheses) for:			
X_1	−.0075 (.01)	—	—
$(X_1)^2$	.000021 (.000032)	—	—
$\log X_1$	—	−.0637 (.38)	−.125 (.234)
X_2	1.962 (.51)	1.899 (.45)	1.925 (.43)
X_3	.773 (1.93)	1.109 (2.26)	1.007 (2.16)
$\log X_4$	—	−.0895 (.44)	—
Constant	−2.859 (1.42)	−2.785 (1.38)	−2.775 (1.36)
$\overline{R}^2$	.398	.395	.417

Notes: X_1 is average farm size, hectares; X_2 is percentage annual population growth rate, 1960–70; X_3 is Gini coefficient for land distribution; X_4 is land endowment—total land area per agricultural population (ha.).
Source: Calculated from data presented in Table 3–3.

relatively low, than in India, Iran, Pakistan, the Philippines, and Turkey, where land concentration is much higher.

These cross-country data suggest that countries with a relatively even distribution of land on a small-farm basis will achieve higher agricultural production and more agricultural employment, relative to their available land resources, than will countries with more concentrated distributions of land.[5]

3.4   CONCLUSION

It is possible to examine several hypotheses about the effect of agrarian structure on productivity by making comparisons among countries. The first broad question examined on this basis is whether land-use intensity is higher on small farms than on large (as hypothesized in Chapter 2). Using agricultural census data for thirty developing countries, this chapter finds that in practically all of these countries

Table 3-5. Productivity, Employment and the Distribution of Land, in Selected Countries

Country	Data year	Farm GDP per hectare (US $)	Farm GDP per worker (US $)	Employment per hectare	Size of average holding (hectares)	Gini's Index of Land Concentration
Europe						
Greece	1961	424	848	0.50	3.18	0.597
Spain	1962	90	980	0.09	14.85	0.832
Central America						
Costa Rica	1963	83	951	0.09	40.70	—
Dominican Republic	1971	129	463	0.28	8.64	—
El Salvador	1961	186	489	0.38	6.95	—
Guatemala	1964	144	492	0.29	8.17	—
Mexico	1960	22	569	0.04	123.90	—
Nicaragua	1963	55	580	0.09	37.34	—
South America						
Argentina	1970	18	1,903	0.01	270.10	0.873
Brazil	1960	14	285	0.05	79.25	0.845
Chile	1965	18	692	0.03	118.50	—
Colombia	1960	67	663	0.10	22.60	0.865
Paraguay	1961	11	479	0.02	108.70	—
Peru	1961	50	477	0.10	20.37	0.947
Uruguay	1966	14	1,333	0.01	208.80	0.833
Venezuela	1961	31	925	0.03	81.24	0.936
Asia						
China, Republic of	1960–61	841	410	2.05	1.27	0.474
India	1960	172	141	1.22	6.52	0.607
Indonesia	1963	323	149	2.17	1.05	—
Iran	1960	187	581	0.32	6.05	0.624
Korea, Republic of	1970	1,085	377	2.88	0.85	—
Japan	1960	1,720	1,188	1.45	1.18	0.473

Table 3-5. (Continued)

Country	Data year	Farm GDP per hectare (US $)	Farm GDP per worker (US $)	Employment per hectare	Size of average holding (hectares)	Gini's Index of Land Concentration
Nepal	1961–62	352	138	2.54	1.23	—
Pakistan	1960	240	249	0.96	2.35	0.607
Philippines	1960	250	200	1.25	3.59	0.580
Sri Lanka	1962	376	337	1.12	1.61	—
Thailand	1963	166	137	1.21	3.47	—
Turkey	1963	155	243	0.64	5.03	0.611
Viet-Nam, Republic of	1960	355	127	2.79	1.33	—
Africa						
Botswana	1969–70	168	142	1.18	4.75	—
Egypt, Arab Republic of	1960–61	681	360	1.89	1.59	—
Kenya	1969	183	140	1.31	4.20	—
Malagasy Republic	1961–62	293	88	3.32	1.04	—
Mali	1960	98	48	2.06	4.35	—
Morocco	1961	144	295	0.49	4.62	—
Senegal	1960	209	174	1.20	3.62	—
Togo	1961–62	189	180	1.05	2.62	—
Tunisia	1961–62	42	341	0.12	15.41	—
Uganda	1963–64	167	198	0.84	3.29	—
Zambia	1960	68	101	0.67	—	—

Source: World Bank, *Land Reform: Sector Policy Paper* (Washington, D.C.: International Bank for Reconstruction and Development, 1975), p. 26.

the large-farm sector (with the top 40 percent of land area) uses its land less intensively than the small-farm sector (with the bottom 20 percent of area), based on the percent of farm area under cultivation.

In the previous chapter it was also hypothesized that while large farms could be expected to have a low level of land use generally, the degree of this underutilization would tend to be more extreme in land-abundant countries (under the normal assumptions about substitutability between land and labor). A formal model of this proposition is presented in Appendix C. The statistical tests conducted in this chapter support this hypothesis. Relative land-use intensity on large farms, measured by the percent of land under cultivation on large farms compared to that on small farms, does decline as the land endowment per population rises across countries. Because the measure omits double-cropping (important in Asia) and extensive grazing (important in Latin America), the true decline of relative large-farm land utilization as land becomes more abundant is probably considerably less than that suggested by the measurements here, however. The tests also confirm the hypothesis that larger farms make relatively poorer use of their land in countries where the distribution of land is more unequal.

A second set of statistical tests using cross-country data finds no evidence of faster growth of agricultural output in countries with larger average farm size (casting doubt on the proposition that an agrarian structure based on large farms will be more dynamic, because of greater responsiveness to technical change). Nor is the agricultural growth rate related, positively or negatively, to the degree of concentration in the distribution of land. Finally, further cross-country data from the World Bank suggest that farm output and employment per area of available land are higher in countries with smaller average farm size and more equal distribution of land. These various cross-country results are broadly consistent with the analysis of the economic effects of agrarian structure presented in Chapter 2.

FOUR

Intensive Hypothesis Tests for Selected Countries

The cross-country tests, employing a large number of countries with limited data for each, suggest the following results: (a) the relative underutilization of land on large farms is more severe as the distribution of land is more unequal and is somewhat less severe in land-scarce countries than in land-abundant countries; and (b) the evidence does not support the notion that a large-farm structure or unequal land distribution are conducive to agricultural growth for dynamic reasons. Problems of comparability among countries (e.g., in land quality) mean that these results are suggestive rather than definitive.

The availability of a limited number of highly detailed data sets for selected countries makes it possible to explore much more fully and rigorously the various hypotheses raised in Chapter 2 on the influence of the agrarian structure on agricultural production and employment. These analyses are conducted for six countries or regions, each important in its own right; two represent the land-abundant Latin American case and the other four the land-scarce Asian case.

4.1   BRAZIL

Land Productivity by Farm-Size Group.   The question of what impact land reform would have on agricultural output and employment in Brazil has been examined at length elsewhere by one of the authors.[1] The principal results of that study were the following. (1) Production function estimates showed constant returns to scale for inputs actually used, sug-

44

gesting no sacrifice of efficiency from current levels through dividing existing large farms, nor from potential future levels through establishing family parcels instead of large state farms.[2] (2) Alternative tests verified the hypothesis that land utilization declines as farm size rises. This result held at the level of individual product sectors, and it held even when the influence of land quality was removed by the inclusion of land price as an explanatory variable. (3) Factor ratios were found to vary systematically away from labor and toward land and capital as farm size rose. In addition, the study calculated the likely increase in total output and inputs to be expected from alternative types of land reform (Chapter 5).

The data for this prior study were from a 1962–63 sample survey in seven major agricultural states throughout Brazil conducted by the Getulio Vargas Foundation, and from a second survey by the same institution concerning sugar farms. Recently, comparable data have become available from a sample survey in Brazil's Northeast, conducted jointly by the International Bank for Reconstruction and Development (IBRD) and the Superintendencia para o Desenvolvimento do Nordeste (SUDENE). This survey, carried out on approximately 8,000 farms, refers to production in 1973 and provides an exceptionally rich empirical base for analysis. The discussion of this section is based on analysis of these data, from which calculations requested by the authors have most generously been provided by the IBRD.

The first hypothesis that may be examined, using these data, is whether production relative to the available land resource declines as farm size rises. Since the answer to this question was affirmative in the earlier study, using 1962–63 data, the persistence of a similar declining pattern would indicate that little has happened in the subsequent decade to alter the influence of the agrarian structure on efficiency. Such a finding would be anticipated, especially considering the fact that there has been no dramatic revision in seed varieties and techniques applied comparable to the Green Revolution in Asia and thus little room for the argument that a sweeping technical change would have raised the relative performance of large landowners.

Table 4–1 presents the basic data relating land productivity to farm size. The data are reported for seven separate physiographic regions in the Northeast, thereby minimizing the introduction of spurious patterns by the mixture of areas with different agricultural potential. In each of the zones (except zone F, the rich cocoa plantation area), output per land area systematically declines as farm size rises. The drop is particularly dramatic in the zone containing some of the most fertile land of the entire

Table 4–1. Northeastern Brazil, 1973: Production per Unit of Available Land Resource, by Farm-Size Group

Zone	Size group	A Avg. farm size (ha.)	B Avg. land value ($US)	C Avg. gross receipts ($US)	D Avg. gross receipts/ area (C/A)	E Avg. gross receipts/ land value (C/B)
A	1	3.7	189	318	85.92	1.68
	2	25.5	763	782	30.73	1.03
	3	71.9	2,452	1,165	16.19	0.48
	4	138.9	4,247	1,223	8.80	0.29
	5	313.2	11,112	1,565	5.00	0.14
	6	1,178.0	17,119	2,589	2.20	0.15
B	1	3.7	293	289	78.25	0.99
	2	26.6	785	880	33.14	1.12
	3	68.8	1,553	1,034	15.03	0.67
	4	138.9	2,448	1,174	8.45	0.48
	5	317.2	5,458	1,900	5.99	0.35
	6	1,396.9	16,773	6,141	4.40	0.37
C	1	4.9	549	295	60.41	0.54
	2	27.5	1,558	978	35.54	0.63
	3	72.4	3,600	2,040	28.19	0.57
	4	143.3	16,593	2,626	18.33	0.16
	5	288.1	9,244	4,571	15.87	0.49
	6	1,059.2	37,049	11,799	11.14	0.32
D	1	4.8	[a]	100	21.00	[a]
	2	24.2	5,796	1,262	52.16	0.22
	3	71.8	10,715	3,381	47.06	0.32
	4	138.4	20,065	1,926	13.91	0.10
	5	282.5	34,669	4,003	14.17	0.12
	6	1,210.6	179,671	11,859	9.80	0.07
E	1	3.7	1,238	1,310	353.03	1.06
	2	26.1	5,231	1,668	63.88	0.32
	3	72.8	8,916	3,396	46.64	0.38
	4	143.6	19,182	5,061	35.24	0.26
	5	283.5	45,923	12,989	45.81	0.28
	6	2,303.6	834,200	17,870	7.76	0.02
F	1	5.6	2,618	970	173.13	0.37
	2	27.1	25,339	6,601	243.65	0.26
	3	70.6	104,048	18,979	268.71	0.18
	4	142.3	179,126	44,736	314.40	0.25
	5	294.6	372,763	74,671	253.46	0.20
	6	620.0	[a]	141,046	227.49	[a]
G	1	4.0	828	790	197.11	0.95
	2	26.5	3,957	1,445	54.49	0.37
	3	73.3	11,135	3,766	51.34	0.34
	4	143.4	19,642	4,372	30.49	0.22
	5	299.1	43,077	8,640	28.88	0.20
	6	1,135.3	83,794	17,817	10.17	0.21

region—the coastal "Zona de Mata" dominated by sugar-cane plantations (zone E).

To permit an examination of whether the decline in land productivity may be attributed to a falling quality of land as farm size rises, the table includes the ratio of output value to total land value for each size group, under the premise that the value of land incorporates the relevant locational and physical aspects of the land into a single measure of land quality. It is clear that the pattern of declining output per land resource available remains, even when land quality is taken into account in this way (and even the exception, zone F, shows declining land productivity on this basis).

Regression analysis may be used to obtain a more rigorous test of the hypothesis of declining land utilization, as represented by output per unit of land resource. The size-class grouped data (for the zones and classes shown in Table 4-1) are pooled for purposes of estimating a single regression, with dummy variables to account for the differences among zones. The following regressions are estimated with these pooled data:

(a) $Q/X = a + b \log X$
(b) $Q/V = a + b \log V$
(c) $Q/X = a + b \log X + c P + d_1 D_1 + d_2 D_2 \cdots + d_6 D_6$
(d) $Q/X = a + b \log X + c P + d_1 D_1 + d_2 D_2 \cdots d_6 D_6$
$\qquad + e_1 D_1 \log X \cdots + e_6 D_6 \log X,$

where Q is gross output value, X is farm size in hectares, V is total land value, P is the average land price per hectare, and

Footnotes to Table 4-1.

---

[a]Land-value data not available. Sample estimate negative (land-value data obtained by residual: total value of land, structures, equipment, livestock minus nonland items).

Source: International Bank for Reconstruction and Development/Superintendencia para Desenvolvimento do Nordeste farm survey.

Zones: A—low demographic density (west of Maranhao, Piaui, Bahia); B—middle north (east of Maranhao, north of Piaui); C—semiarid sertao (portions of Ceara, Rio Grande do Norte, Paraiba, Pernambuco, Bahia); D—semihumid southeast (portion of Bahia); E—humid east (coastal zone of Rio Grande do Norte, Paraiba, Pernambuco, Alagoas, Sergipe, northern Bahia); F—humid southeast (cocoa zone of Bahia); G—Agreste (transitional zone of Rio Grande do Norte, Paraiba, Pernambuco, Alagoas, Sergipe, Bahia).

Size groups: 1   0- 9.9 ha.   4   100-199.9
  2   10-49.9   5   200-499.9
  3   50-99.9   6   500 and over

D_1 through D_6 are dummy variables with the value 1, if data are from the zone in question, and 0 otherwise. (The final zone has no separate dummy variable, but acts as the base for the regression.)

Form (c) shifts only the constant term for each zone, whereas form (d) not only shifts the constant but alters the slope coefficient on the log X variable for differing zones.

All four forms use the logarithm of the land resource as the specification for the farm-size variable. Some of the theoretical propositions, especially that concerning labor-market dualism, would suggest that land productivity would decline more rapidly at first and then more slowly, as farm size rose. Moreover, good results were obtained with this form in past analyses.

As shown in Table 4–2, reporting the results of these tests, even in the first form, using the natural logarithm of farm size as the sole explanatory variable and making no adjustment for zone, the negative relationship of output per farm area to farm size is statistically significant. The second form, relating output per land value to the logarithm of land value (as a quality-adjusted measure of the land resource), also shows a significantly negative relationship and increases the degree of explanation. The third and fourth forms, accounting for land quality with the land-price term and introducing the zonal dummy variables, not only raise the explanatory power to quite high levels but also find highly significant and correctly signed coefficients on farm size and land price.

Tests at the Farm Level, by Product Group. To test the hypothesis of declining land utilization (land productivity) under the more stringent condition of holding product-mix constant, it is necessary to resort to farm-level data sorted into alternative categories by principal product.[3] Once the farm is classified into a product category, its total output value (regardless of product composition) is included in the dependent variable of output per farm area.

The farm level regressions by product sector are conducted in the following form:

$$VA/X = a + b \log X + cP + dS + e_1D_1 + e_2D_2 \cdots + e_6D_6,$$

where VA is value-added; X is total farm area in hectares; P is the average land price per hectare on the farm; and S is the percent of land on the farm under operation by sharecroppers.

Table 4-2. Northeast Brazil: Regression Results, Land Productivity by Farm Size, Grouped Farm Data,[a] 1973

Form	Dependent variable[b]	Regional dummy variables:[c] intercept	Regional dummy variables:[c] slope	Constant	Log. of farm area[d] (ha.)	Log. of land value[d]	Land price per ha.	$\overline{R}^2$
				(standard error in parentheses)				
1	Q/X	no	no	153.3 (34.8)	−44.93 (16.9)	—	—	0.1323
2	Q/V	no	no	1.431 (.164)	—	−0.2634 (.041)	—	0.5061
3	Q/X	yes	no	110.7 (22.7)	−39.91 (7.9)	—	0.1963 (.046)	0.8137
4	Q/X	yes	yes	141.5 (36.7)	−56.44 (16.3)	—	0.2033 (.062)	0.8856

[a]Each observation is the average for all farms in a given farm size group, by physiographic region. See Table 4-1.

[b]Q: total output value. X: farm area, ha. V: total land value.

[c]Dummy variables for each of the first six physiographic zones listed in Table 4-1; the seventh zone is the base. "Intercept": dummy variables shift constant term only. "Slope": dummy variables shift the coefficient on logarithm of farm size as well as constant. Note: coefficients estimated for dummy variables are not reported here.

[d]Logarithms are to the base ten.

The form chosen for the test is the same as form (c) above, except that the somewhat preferable concept of value-added per hectare is used as the dependent variable, and an additional explanatory variable is included to account for the influence of sharecropping.

The results for these farm-level, product-specific tests are reported in Table 4-3. The most important finding is that in all six product sectors the coefficient on farm size is negative and statistically significant. That is, even holding the product-mix constant (as well as removing the influences of regional zone, land quality as represented by land price, and the extent of sharecropping on the farm) the result remains confirmed that output per available land resource declines as farm size rises. On a

Table 4-3. Northeast Brazil: Regression Results,[a] Land Productivity by Farm Size, Farm-Area Basis (Farm Level Data, by Major Product,[b] 1973)

Product sector	Constant	Coefficient on:[c] Log. of farm area (ha.)[d]	Land price per ha.	Fraction of area administered by share-croppers[e]	$\bar{R}^2$
		(standard error in parentheses)			
Livestock	84.45 (21.1)	−19.33 (3.7)	0.3619 (0.24)	26.58 (81.0)	0.217
Rice	63.91 (12.2)	−12.23 (1.01)	0.0447 (.026)	58.97 (15.7)	0.304
Cocoa	214.1 (50.3)	−9.87 (9.8)	0.0853 (.019)	−78.9 (182.7)	0.474
Sugar	155.6 (18.9)	−20.16 (3.6)	0.0207 (.0196)	264.1 (291.3)	0.277
Subsistence: manioc, corn, beans	75.5 (4.5)	−11.91 (.93)	0.0108 (.0061)	31.45 (14.3)	0.151
Other crops	253.6 (18.8)	−29.41 (3.4)	0.00395 (.0052)	58.86 (36.1)	0.114

[a]Dependent variable: value-added per hectare of farm area, in 1973 U.S. dollars.

[b]A farm observation is included in the livestock category if it obtains more than 50 percent of total output from livestock. For nonlivestock farms, an observation is included in a particular crop sector if the crop provides more than 50 percent of the value of crop output or more than 30 percent of the value of total output.

[c]The regressions include dummy variables that shift the constant, for each of the regions 1 through 6 listed in Table 4-1. Results here do not report the coefficients estimated for these dummy variables.

[d]Logarithms: Naperian base.

[e]Fraction of total area classified in this product sector that is administered or operated by sharecroppers.

basis of comparison between the constant and slope terms, the rate of decline is the most dramatic for the livestock sector (as might be expected for a shift from fodder operations to extensive grazing). It is the most gradual for the cocoa sector, suggesting a relatively high land utilization on large capitalized cocoa plantations.

The land-price variable remains significant for only half of the sectors; nevertheless, its inclusion in the estimation form means that the coefficient on farm size should represent the size-productivity relationship after removal of the influence of land quality.

The sharecropping variable is significant in only two of the six sectors: rice and subsistence crops. Moreover, it has the wrong sign for consistency with the conventional argument that sharecropping distorts incentives for resource allocation. If sharecropping leads to the inadequate application of labor and other variable inputs (because tenants equate only their share of, rather than full, marginal value product with marginal costs), then output per area should be lower, not higher, on farms under sharecropping.

The earlier study of Brazilian agrarian structure by Cline, using 1962-63 farm sample survey data, also found no statistical significance of a land tenure variable (for owners versus tenants) in regressions explaining output per unit of area (with farm size and land price entering as the other independent variables).[4] In addition, in a recent analysis Scandizzo and Barbosa have found statistical evidence that total factor productivity is higher for sharecroppers than for owners (rather than lower) in Northeastern Brazil.[5] These various results all suggest that the conventional microeconomic view on the inefficiency caused by sharecropping is not of practical significance, at least in the Brazilian case. Moreover, this evidence supports the view set forth in Chapter 2 that farm-size considerations are more important than the issue of sharecropping in assessing the productive impact of the agrarian structure.

The explanatory power of the regressions reported in Table 4-3 is somewhat reduced, but this result is to be expected when extremely large data sets are used.[6]

Results for the alternative regression formulation, using output per land value regressed against the logarithm of land value, are reported in Table 4-4. Once again the inverse relationship between land productivity and farm size is confirmed at the level of the individual product sector by highly significant estimates. The explanatory power of the estimates is quite modest, both because of the large number of observations at the farm level and because zonal dummy variables are excluded (although

Table 4-4. Northeast Brazil: Regression Results,[a] Land Productivity by Farm Size, Land-Value Basis (Farm-Level Data, by Major Product)[b]

| Product sector | Coefficient on:[c] | | $\bar{R}^2$ |
	Constant	Logarithm[d] of land value	
	(standard error in parentheses)		
Livestock	5.755	−0.5593	.043
	(.696)	(.081)	
Rice	9.555	−1.0733	.118
	(1.13)	(.145)	
Cocoa	2.026	−0.1585	.148
	(.413)	(.039)	
Sugar	4.548	−0.4113	.093
	(.91)	(.098)	
Subsistence: manioc, corn, beans	7.960	−0.8991	.087
	(.705)	(.092)	
Other crops	12.996	−1.4067	.081
	(1.29)	(.155)	

[a]Dependent variable: value-added divided by land value.
[b]See note b, Table 4-3.
[c]The regression estimates do not utilize dummy variables for physiographic zones; results reported are for the full model estimated.
[d]Naperian base logarithms.

specification of the variables on a land-value basis should reduce the need for dummies).

Factor Combinations. The final statistical tests conducted with the SUDENE–IBRD data, in Table 4-5, are for the hypotheses that factor combinations systematically shift away from labor toward land, capital, and seeds-fertilizer inputs as farm size rises. These hypotheses are tested by regressing the logarithm of each nonland input against the logarithm of farm area (that is, of the total land input available). In this type of equation, the coefficient on the explanatory variable is the "elasticity" of the dependent variable with respect to the independent variable. That is, the coefficient indicates how large a percentage rise in the use of the factor will occur as farm size rises by one percentage point.

The results in Table 4-5 confirm the hypotheses stated in Chapter 2. Factor combinations shift away from labor to land and capital as farm size rises. The elasticity of the use of labor with respect to farm size is only 0.38, so that the labor/land ratio declines rapidly as farm size rises. The elasticity of capital use with respect to farm size is 0.63, meaning that the

Table 4–5. Northeast Brazil: Regression Results, Factor Use in Relation to Farm Size (Grouped Farm Data,[a] 1973)

Regression	Dependent variable	Coefficient on: (standard error in parentheses)		$\overline{R}^2$
		Constant	Logarithm of farm area (ha.)	
1	logarithm of labor[b]	−0.2183 (.098)	0.3845 (.047)	.6199
2	logarithm of capital[c]	2.722 (.126)	0.6263 (.061)	.7239
3	logarithm of purchased inputs	0.898 (.240)	0.6944 (.116)	.4635

[a]Each observation corresponds to the average for all farms in a given farm-size group and physiographic region. See Table 4-6.
[b]Man-years of labor utilized.
[c]Value of structures, equipment, livestock, and capitalized value of equipment rental.
Note: All logarithms to base ten.

ratio of capital to land available falls as farm size rises, but by much less than the labor/land ratio—confirming the expected shift from labor to capital as size rises. The use of purchased inputs shows an elasticity of 0.69 with respect to farm size. The closeness of this elasticity to that for capital suggests that, as proposed in section 2.5, it is more the imperfections in the capital market than any inherent inferiority in capacity for modernization that leads small farmers to use less intermediate inputs (such as fertilizers) than larger farmers, relative to labor used.

The same phenomenon of shifting factor combinations as farm size rises is documented in Table 4-6, which presents average factor ratios by farm-size group. For each of the seven physiographic zones the table reports labor per hectare of total farm area, capital per farm area, and the corresponding capital/labor ratio, by farm-size group. In practically every zone, as farm size rises labor per hectare declines very rapidly, capital per hectare also declines, but less dramatically, and, accordingly, the ratio of capital to labor rises substantially.

The existence of similar analyses of land utilization and factor combinations by farm size, using data from a decade earlier, provides an unusual opportunity to examine whether the performance of large farms relative to small in Northeastern Brazil improved during the 1960s and early 1970s. Estimates for directly comparable product sectors from Cline's earlier study and from the results here are available for only two sectors—livestock and sugar cane. In both cases the negative relationship between farm size and output per farm area appears to have remained practically unchanged over the decade.[7] An alternative means of examining the same issue is to compare the factor-use elasticities with respect to farm size for the 1962–63 data with those found here. These elasticities also remained practically unchanged over the decade; although precise comparison is difficult, it would appear that if there were any change it was toward a slight decline over the period in the elasticity of labor use and a slight rise in the elasticities of capital and seeds-fertilizer use with respect to farm size—in other words, an accentuation of the factor-use distortions already present with regard to labor on the one hand and capital and intermediate inputs on the other.[8]

Social Factor Productivity. As a final test of the relative economic performance of large and small farms, it is useful to consider a measure of "total social factor productivity" relating total output to the value of factor inputs as evaluated at "social" prices. An exercise of this nature necessarily involves arbitrary judgments about the correct social factor prices to apply. It does provide, however, an assessment of the relationship of farm size to social efficiency, taking into account all factor inputs, not just the land factor.

On the basis of the data contained in Tables 4–1 and 4–6, it is possible to calculate a measure of total social factor productivity for each farm-size group in each of the seven regions examined in Northeast Brazil, as follows. Total social factor productivity is measured as the ratio of gross output to the sum of land, capital, and labor input costs, with each evaluated at its respective social price. For the social price of land and capital, an opportunity cost of 15 percent per annum is applied to the asset value reported for each of these two factors.[9] In the case of labor, the regional minimum wage is used as a benchmark.[10] It is assumed that the social cost of labor ranges from zero up to one-half of the minimum wage. For purposes of comparison only, the measure of total factor productivity is also included when labor is evaluated at the minimum wage. This wage is almost certainly too high for the social cost of labor (in the presence of high underemployment), and it even overstates the private cost of labor, because hired labor frequently is paid below the minimum wage in the Northeast.

The measure used here is probably biased in favor of large farms, because it includes gross output instead of merely value-added in the numerator, while the value of intermediate inputs does not appear in the denominator for factor costs. Considering that larger farms tend to use

Table 4–6. Northeast Brazil: Factor Ratios by Farm-Size Group, 1973

Zone	Size group	Average farm size (ha.)	Labor input/ farm area (man-years/ hectare)	Capital[a] /farm area ($US/ha.)	Capital /labor ($US/ man-year)
A	1	3.7	.257	453.9	1767.9
	2	25.5	.068	143.9	2116.9
	3	71.9	.031	57.8	1863.8
	4	138.9	.016	44.2	2789.0
	5	313.2	.008	30.0	3555.3
	6	1178.0	.003	9.9	3056.2
B	1	3.7	.203	336.7	1656.6
	2	26.6	.061	97.3	1586.0
	3	68.8	.030	46.7	1559.6
	4	138.9	.013	30.1	2258.2
	5	317.2	.009	21.3	2462.7
	6	1395.9	.004	12.1	3033.6
C	1	4.9	.190	193.8	1019.0
	2	27.5	.065	97.8	1494.8
	3	72.3	.038	76.6	1998.0
	4	143.2	.023	61.7	2636.9
	5	288.1	.017	49.8	2932.8
	6	1059.2	.009	41.0	4403.8
D	1	4.8	.187	458.4	2446.8
	2	24.2	.070	178.0	2534.7
	3	71.8	.040	124.7	3143.8
	4	138.4	.019	98.3	5235.5
	5	282.5	.015	125.1	8455.4
	6	1210.6	.007	105.7	16054.1
E	1	3.7	.356	914.2	2569.4
	2	26.1	.091	154.1	1697.7
	3	72.8	.045	113.7	2501.7
	4	143.6	.033	87.3	2656.0
	5	283.5	.044	88.7	2032.3
	6	2303.6	.004	29.6	6889.0
F	1	5.6	.270	76.4	283.4
	2	27.1	.145	215.6	1482.4
	3	70.6	.090	322.4	3574.5
	4	142.3	.101	243.8	2412.8
	5	294.6	.072	228.3	3178.1
	6	620.0	.097	125.3	1292.8
G	1	4.0	.297	312.3	1052.3
	2	26.5	.085	164.7	1941.1
	3	73.4	.049	131.9	2687.1
	4	143.4	.036	120.6	3319.7
	5	299.1	.029	132.1	4545.7
	6	1135.3	.030	119.6	4043.2

[a]Value of buildings, equipment, and livestock, plus capitalized value of equipment rentals discounted at 10 percent per annum.

Note: See Table 4–1 for details on zones and size groups.

higher levels of intermediate inputs (seeds, fertilizers) relative to gross output, the result is a bias in measured efficiency in favor of large farms.

Table 4–7 reports the measures of total social factor productivity in columns A (at zero labor cost) and B (with labor evaluated at one-half the minimum wage). The table shows the following patterns. (1) In general, total social factor productivity declines as farm size rises, reinforcing the conclusions above, based on declining output per land area and per land value as farm size rises. (2) The decline is more rapid (and the total factor productivity of small farms considerably higher) when a zero social price is applied to labor. This pattern reflects the relatively heavy use of labor as a production input on small farms. (3) When a social price of labor of one-half the minimum wage is used, there is a tendency for total factor productivity to be higher in the second and third size groups than in the first, or smallest, size group. This finding indicates that when some social cost is applied to labor, the very smallest farms are found to be using too much labor (just as the larger farms, size groups 4 to 6, are using relatively too little). (4) When the full minimum wage is used as the price of labor, total factor productivity still declines as farm size rises in four of the seven regions (A, D, E, and G). This result suggests that, in addition to a higher effective cost of labor in comparison with small farms, large farms

Table 4–7. Total Social Factor Productivity[a] by Farm-Size Group, Northeastern Brazil

Zone	Size group	A At zero labor cost	B At labor cost one- half minimum wage	C With labor cost at minimum wage
A	1	1.134	0.717	0.525
	2	1.177	0.814	0.622
	3	1.173	0.848	0.664
	4	0.786	0.632	0.528
	4	0.509	0.446	0.398
	6	0.601	0.527	0.469
B	1	1.254	0.806	0.594
	2	1.744	1.125	0.831
	3	1.445	0.967	0.726
	4	1.180	0.900	0.728
	5	1.036	0.676	0.676
	6	1.215	1.022	0.882
C	1	1.316	0.771	0.545
	2	1.532	1.036	0.783
	3	1.492	1.110	0.884
	4	0.689	0.600	0.532
	5	1.290	1.044	0.876
	6	0.977	0.861	0.769

Table 4-7. (Continued)

Zone	Size group	A At zero labor cost	B At labor cost one- half minimum wage	C With labor cost at minimum wage
D	1	n.a.	n.a.	n.a.
	2	0.833	0.603	0.603
	3	1.145	0.981	0.859
	4	0.381	0.350	0.323
	5	0.381	0.356	0.335
	6	0.257	0.249	0.242
E	1	1.885	1.422	1.142
	2	1.201	0.924	0.758
	3	1.318	1.082	0.918
	4	1.065	0.909	0.794
	5	1.218	1.016	0.871
	6	0.132	0.130	0.129
F	1	2.122	1.355	0.996
	2	1.412	1.234	1.097
	3	0.997	0.944	0.895
	4	1.395	1.306	1.210
	5	1.132	1.073	1.020
	6	n.a.	n.a.	n.a.
G	1	2.530	1.532	1.098
	2	1.157	0.884	0.715
	3	1.205	1.007	0.864
	4	0.790	0.681	0.599
	5	0.698	0.623	0.563
	6	0.351	0.298	0.259

[a]Equals: $q/[0.15 (V + k) + w^*N]$ where q = gross receipts per area, V = land value per area, k = capital value per area, N = man-years per area, and w^* = social price of labor (zero or ½ minimum wage for columns A and B, respectively).

Source: Calculated from Tables 4-1 and 4-6.

perceive a lower opportunity cost of land and capital (such that only with a correspondingly lower imputation of capital cost for these size groups would their total factor productivity rise to levels found on smaller farms, even using the full minimum wage as the cost of labor).

As noted in Chapter 2, it would be misleading to identify a single farm size as "optimal," even in the light of these measures of total social factor productivity. The logic of declining land use as farm size rises leads to the conclusion (in the face of constant returns to scale) that the optimal size is that compatible with equal distribution of land among rural families (taking into account land quality). Nevertheless, the results found here, using measures of total social factor productivity, do confirm the thrust of the earlier analysis of land productivity: that the large-farm sector uses its available land inefficiently (from the standpoint of the economy as a whole) and, in particular, that employment and output could be expected to rise as the result of measures that redistributed land from the large-farm sector into smaller family farms.

Conclusion.   Statistical tests, using farm survey data for Brazil in 1962-63 and for Northeastern Brazil in 1973, systematically confirm the hypotheses concerning the distortions imposed on agricultural production by the agrarian structure. These tests show that output per farm area declines as farm size rises, even after taking account of land quality; that labor is replaced by land and capital as farm size rises; and that sharecropping tenancy has little evident effect on the efficiency of land use. Moreover, these patterns appear not to have changed over the decade in question, at least for Brazil's Northeast.

Finally, although total social factor productivity was not measured in the earlier study for lack of firm estimates of factoral shadow prices,[11] the measurements, using the 1973 data under alternative assumptions about the shadow price of labor, confirm the conclusions about socially inefficient land use on larger farms as evaluated in the analysis of the relationship of production to available land (or land value) by farm size.

4.2   COLOMBIA

Evidence on land productivity and utilization by farm size for Colombia relates to the period 1960 and later. Although there are suggestions of minor modifications since 1960, the basic pattern is one of substantially lower land productivity on larger farms, related to much lower labor inputs per hectare, a lower share of land cropped, and a lower cropping intensity on the land cropped. One factor working in the opposite direction is the higher yields of some crops on larger farms than on small ones.

Table 4-8 presents Berry's estimates of the above relationships, based mainly on the 1960 agricultural census.[12] Value-added per hectare was approximately 15 percent as high on farms of over 500 hectares as on those of 3 to 5 hectares; value-added per effective hectare (that is, constant quality hectares after normalization based on land value) was 45 percent as high. The single proximate factor determining these differentials was the rapidly decreasing share of land cropped as farm size rose; this share declined from 77 percent for farms between 2 and 5 hectares to only 6 per-

Table 4–8. Land Productivity and Farm Size in Colombia, 1960–61 (Values in Thousands of 1960 Pesos)

Farm size (hectares)	Number of farms (1,000)	Value-added per:		Value of crop output per hectare of cultivated land (including fallow)	Man-years of labor per:	
		hectare	effective hectare[a]		hectare	effective hectare[a]
0–3	606.4	1.37	0.75	1.05	0.82	0.45
3–5	150.2	0.86	0.79	1.02	0.41	0.38
5–10	169.2	0.73	0.73	1.04	0.19	0.19
10–50	201.0	0.44	0.57	0.96	0.12	0.16
50–500	76.0	0.23	0.38	0.88	0.036	0.06
over 500	6.9	0.13	0.35	0.89	0.008	0.023
All farms	1,209.7	0.285	0.46	0.95	0.08	0.128

[a] Number of effective hectares equals physical hectares divided by ratio of land price on farms in group relative to overall average land price.

cent for those larger than 500 hectares (Table 4-9). Whether value of crop output per cultivated hectare rises or falls with farm size depends on whether fallow land is included as part of cultivated area; if it is, the ratio falls by about 15 percent between the cited farm sizes; if it is excluded, the ratio rises by over 60 percent, primarily because of the fact that yields for many crops increase with farm size. A yield index, weighted according to the relative importance of crops in the sector as a whole, is 50 to 60 percent higher in the larger-size category (Table 4-9, column 1).

To explain the higher output per hectare on the small farms is thus essentially to explain the higher share of their land used in crops. In lesser degree, it reflects the fact that within the livestock category small farms focus on high-value animals (hogs, poultry) and large farms on cattle. The obvious hypotheses are those discussed in Chapter 2. The land, labor, and capital markets all are imperfect, with the ultimate result that the opportunity costs of land and capital are higher on small farms, while that of labor is lower. As Table 4-8 reveals, the input of man-years per hectare is approximately one-fiftieth as high on farms over 500 hectares as on those of 3 to 5 hectares; the input of man-years per effective hectare is approximately one-fifteenth as high.

Most of the differences in factor proportions are probably explained by factor price differentials. In addition, different levels of efficiency of resource utilization could play a role; if these differentials exist, they could be attributable to different degrees of incentive, differing risk aversion, or any of a number of other factors. Table 4-10 presents estimates of total factor productivity that suggest that farms in the size range of 5 to 10 hectares are the most efficient. The coefficient of efficiency is defined as the value of output divided by the opportunity cost of inputs, under various assumptions about the relationship of market prices to marginal social productivity. The calculations assume that the social opportunity cost of labor is only one-half the market wage rate. For the various sets of assumptions considered in Berry's study, the efficiency of the largest size category compared to that of farms of 5 to 10 hectares ranged from a low of 0.55 to a high of 0.88. Farms smaller than 5 hectares emerged as less efficient than those of 5 to 10 hectares, except when the social opportunity cost of labor was assumed to be close to zero.

With respect to the relationship of technology to farm size, data available for 1960, indicating utilization of fertilizer and machinery by size group (Table 4-11), show that a somewhat larger proportion of small farms than large ones used fertilizer, but a larger share of the large farms used mechanical power. The former pattern is noteworthy in view of the

Table 4–9. Differences in Yield by Farm Size, Colombia, First Semester of 1966

Farm size (ha.)	Index No. 1[a]: value of product per hectare cropped (1)	Index No. 2[b]: value of product per hectare cropped and fallowed (2)	Value of crop output		Cropped land as percent of	
			per ha. cropped (1,000 pesos) (3)	per ha. cropped & fallowed (1,000 pesos) (4)	arable and pasture land (5)	cropped and fallowed land (6)
0–2	94.2	80.5	1.23	1.05	.87	.85
2–5	96.8	81.6	1.22	1.03	.77	.84
5–10	96.7	79.4	1.27	1.04	.66	.82
10–20	100.0	78.5	1.34	1.05	.56	.78
20–50	96.8	68.1	1.25	.88	.44	.70
50–200	117.8	68.8	1.50	.87	.28	.58
200–500	140.3	70.7	1.79	.90	.18	.50
over 500	147.4	67.3	1.99	.89	.06	.46

[a] Average for farms of all sizes equals 100. For each crop, yields in kilograms per hectare and expressed as relatives to their average for all sizes of farms. These relatives for individual crops are combined, weighting them by the share of all cropped land devoted to the specific crop. This assumes that the percentage distribution of crops in each farm-size category is the same as that for all sizes of farms.

[b] Same as Index 1 except that shares of all cropped land plus fallowed land are used as weights.

Source: A. Berry, "Land Distribution, Income Distribution, and the Productive Efficiency of Colombian Agriculture," Food Research Institute Studies 12 (3) (1973):224. Column 1 is based on 1966 area and yield data by size of farm from U.S. Dept. Agr., Agricultural Productivity in Colombia (For. Agr. Rept. 66, 1970), and on unpublished data from Banco de la Republica (prices used in constructing the national accounts), Cuentas Nacionales, 1950–1967 (Bogota, 1968). Columns 2 and 6 use fallow to cultivated land ratios based on Colombia, Departamento Administrativo Nacional de Estadística, Directorio Nacional de Explotaciones Agropecuarios (Censo Agropecuario), 1960: Resumen General (segunda parte) (Bogota, 1964). Columns 3 and 4 are as for column 1 and Table 11, A. Berry, "Land Distribution . . . ," and column 5 is based on the 1966 census cited above.

Table 4-10. Indicators of Relative Social Efficiency of Farms by Size: Product Prices Unadjusted and Adjusted, 1960–61

Farm size (hectares)	Product prices unadjusted		Product prices adjusted			
	Coefficient of efficiency	Implied social rate of return to capital	Coefficient of efficiency		Implied social rate of return to capital	
			Est. R	Est. S	Est. R	Est. S
0–3	1.16	20.5%	1.09	1.07	15.9%	16.2%
3–5	1.30	24.1	1.17	1.15	17.7	18.2
5–10	1.36	24.5	1.18	1.16	17.3	17.8
10–50	1.16	19.0	1.06	1.05	14.5	15.1
50–500	0.87	13.3	0.92	0.93	12.1	13.0
over 500	0.81	12.5	0.98	1.00	12.9	14.2
All farms	1.01	15.8	1.00	1.00	13.3	14.2

Source: A. Berry, "Land Distribution, Income Distribution, and the Productive Efficiency of Colombian Agriculture," *Food Research Institute Studies* 12 (3) (1973):222. The first two columns are Case 2 from Table 11, ibid. Product prices are adjusted in Estimate R on the assumption that social value/market price ratios are as follows: coffee, 0.6; bananas, rice, sugar, and cotton, 1.5; and all other products 1.0. Estimate S adjusts on the same assumptions as R, except that the ratio for cattle is 1.2.

Table 4-11. Percent of Farms Using Fertilizer and Mechanical Power, 1960-61[a]

Farm size (hectares)	Fertilizer (organic or inorganic)	Inorganic fertilizer	Mechanical power	Human power only
0-3	10.44	6.09	3.62	73.71
3-5	13.57	7.54	6.62	60.56
5-10	14.09	8.00	7.87	55.90
10-50	10.11	6.12	9.21	43.74
50-500	6.38	4.49	12.50	52.39
over 500	6.46	5.11	28.83	31.59

[a]Farms not listed under either mechanical or human power use animal power only.

Source: Directorio Nacional de Explotaciones Agropecuarios (Censo Agropecuario), 1960: Resumen General (segunda parte) (Bogota, 1964), pp. 56, 58.

common assumption that larger farms utilize more modern technology. However, the data for fertilizer do not include details on rates of application. Moreover, they clearly reflect the relative importance of the crops traditionally receiving fertilizer in the different size categories. The data concerning the use of mechanical versus human power represent the expected pattern of increasing mechanization as farm size rises, due to increasing effective cost of labor relative to that of capital and, perhaps, because of indivisibilities in the use of farm machinery (that is, a minimum size requirement) as well.

Data from the 1970-71 agricultural census permit comparison with the 1960 census and the identification of certain trends. In Colombia, unlike most or all of the other countries reviewed in this chapter, the total agricultural labor force appears to have begun to decline during the decade 1960-70/71, in the face of rapid expansion of the economy. While the land area used for agriculture rose by 13.4 percent (according to the two agricultural censuses), the number of farm units fell by 2.7 percent (Table 4-12). Overall concentration of land did not change measurably during the decade; both the larger and smaller farms tended to increase in size (Table 4-13).

Substantial changes in the structure of land tenure occurred between the two census years, with operation by owners or their administrators increasing in relative importance and rental arrangements diminishing.[13] The increase in the share of land owned by the operator was noticeable for farms under 10 hectares, but not for larger ones. The decrease in importance of rental and sharecropping was much more pronounced on the smaller farms, below say 20 hectares. One obvious question about these

Table 4-12. Some Key Trends in the Agricultural Sector, 1960-70 (Values in Millions of 1958 pesos)

	1960	1970	Growth rate 1960-70
Agricultural output[a]	7,447.8	10,661.0	3.65% annually
Index of crop output[b]	104.2	148.9	3.63% annually
Index of livestock output[b]	107.7	160.1	4.05% annually
Agricultural labor force (thousands)	≈2,400	≈2,400[c]	0 % annually
Agricultural labor force/total labor force	0.495	0.384	—
Land reported in agricultural censuses (1,000 ha.)	27,338	30,993	13.4% period total
Crops	5,047	7,659	31.9% period total
Livestock[d]	14,606	17,465	19.6% period total
Other	7,685	5,870	−23.6% period total

[a]Value-added at factor costs: National Accounts Statistics.
[b]Physical volume: National Accounts Statistics, Index, 1958 = 100
[c]Very rough estimate. Departamento Nacional de Estadistica 1970 *Encuesta de Hogares* implied about this level, whereas preliminary estimates from the 1973 population census indicate a much lower figure. The latter, however, is suspect in several respects.
[d]Meadows.
Sources: 1960-61 and 1970-71 agricultural censuses, National Accounts Statistics.

trends is whether they are, in part, the results of the land reform legislation. In 1968, INCORA (Instituto Nacional de Colonizacion y Reforma Agraria) issued a decree indicating its intention to make rented or sharecropped land available to its operator; clearly, this policy could have led to decreased willingness on the part of owners to rent land. Earlier discussion had revolved around the proposition that rental was evidence of underutilization of land.

As of 1960, a considerable amount of modernization had already occurred in Colombia's agricultural sector. Many large farms were using tractors and machinery pulled by tractors. Although a minority of farms used fertilizers, their use was widespread for certain crops, such as potatoes. Over the 1960s, modern practices were expanded, and improved varieties became available for a number of crops. Between the agricultural censuses of 1960-61 and 1970-71 real value-added per hectare is calculated to have risen by 26.2 percent, or approximately 2.4 percent per year.[14] This period seems to have been characterized by an increase in the intensity of land use on larger farms (Table 4-14), although it remained far below that on small farms.

At first glance, Table 4-14 suggests that farms up to five hectares experienced a slight decline in the intensity of land use; their area under

Table 4–13. Colombia: Land Concentration, 1960–61 and 1970–71

Percentage of land operated by:	1960–61	1970–71
Smallest 20% of farms	0.31	0.33
Second 20%	1.12	1.00
Third 20%	2.58	2.47
Fourth 20%	6.50	6.61
Fifth 20%	89.49	89.59
Top 10%	81.16	80.40
Top 5%	70.71	69.44

Source: 1960 and 1970–71 agricultural censuses.

temporary and permanent crops fell (the former showing a considerable decline, not fully offset by a rise in the latter), while their land in pasture increased. At the same time, the table indicates that the intensity of land use rose for farms of 50 hectares and above, whose share of land dedicated to crops rose substantially in proportional terms (although from a low base). However, the precision of these intercensal comparisons is limited because of the different seasons in which the two censuses were taken as well as the apparently differing definitions of the categories "pasture," "fallow," and "other uses." Taking these changes into account, it seems probable that intensity of land use rose on all farm sizes, but did so more markedly on farms larger than 5 hectares, for which the share under both crops and pasture is reported to have risen.[15]

Both the apparent trend toward more intensive land use on larger farms during the 1960s and the general evidence of increasing yields add interest to the question of whether small farms' land productivity is as far above that of large farms now as it was in 1960. Unfortunately, the census of 1970–71 is insufficiently detailed to permit the type of analysis of relative land productivity that has been conducted with the 1960 census data. The only recent evidence on the relationship between farm size and productivity is that from a 1969 sample of approximately 3,000 farms for which INCORA collected information in connection with its lending activities. The U.S. Agency for International Development (AID) has conducted extensive analysis of the results of this sample. The most relevant evidence for our purposes is summarized in Table 4–15.

In the INCORA sample value of production per hectare falls sharply as farm size rises, by almost tenfold between the category 5–10 hectares and that of 50–100 hectares. In Berry's 1960 estimate, the corresponding differential was only slightly over 2.5 to 1.

Table 4-14. Colombia: Land Use in 1960-61 and 1970-71 (Percentages)

Farm size (hectares)	Temporary crops			Permanent crops	All crops (in use)[a]	Pasture	Other[b]
	In use	Fallow	total				
			A. 1960-61				
All farms	7.14	5.78	12.92	5.54	12.68	53.43	28.11
Less than 5	35.91	10.78	46.69	23.91	59.82	17.65	11.75
5-50	15.96	9.49	25.45	14.91	30.87	36.13	23.51
Over 50	3.14	4.51	7.65	2.01	5.15	60.06	30.28
			B. 1970-71				
All farms	6.81	10.32	17.13	7.58	14.39	56.40	18.89
Less than 5	29.08	7.99	37.07	29.53	58.61	24.85	9.05
5-50	13.45	14.59	28.04	18.53	31.98	39.15	14.58
Over 50	4.17	9.42	13.59	3.92	8.09	61.97	20.52

[a]Excludes fallow land.
[b]Land not used for crops or pasture.
Sources: 1960 and 1970-71 agricultural censuses.

Table 4-15. Farm Size and Land Productivity in Colombia, based on 1969 Sample of INCORA Borrowers

Farm size (hectares)	Gross farm income/hectare (pesos)	Net farm income/hectare (pesos)	Net farm income/ total family income (percent)
0- 0.99	37,970	6,645	29.2
1- 4.99	7,589	3,649	82.4
5- 9.99	3,896	1,950	88.9
10-14.99	2,742	1,171	89.0
15-19.99	2,008	1,022	89.4
20-49.99	895	475	87.9
50-99.99	377	220	89.1
100 and over	198	115	90.7
All farms	775	396	87.4

Source: Table D-3, Appendix D.

It would appear that in the INCORA sample the smallest farms are atypically productive and the large farms are atypically unproductive. The small farms serviced by INCORA tend to be selected from among the best small farms and presumably enjoy still further stimulus as a result of credit received. The large farms in the INCORA survey, on the other hand, are mostly located in zones of colonization. As a result, the decline in land productivity as size rises is presumably greater—probably substantially greater—than that characterizing agriculture as a whole in 1969.[16]

Table 4-16 suggests the extent to which the declining value of production per hectare as farm size rises is related to the allocation of land between crops and livestock. Figures on the breakdown of output by crops and livestock are available for a 474-farm subset of the total sample (Table D-4, Appendix D). For crops alone and for livestock alone the land productivity has no clear trend over the 5 to 100 hectare range (there were only two farms above 100 hectares). In this subsample, as in the full sample, many high-income farms are small and many low-income farms are large, although average value of production does increase almost monotonically with size, as does cash farm income (Table D-4, Appendix D). Off-farm income is highest on the smallest and the largest farms, averaging almost 20 percent of income for this set of farms.

Table 4-17 compares the relationship between labor per hectare and farm size on the basis of the INCORA sample with that calculated by Berry on the basis of the 1960 agricultural census. The two sets of data show generally similar patterns. For example, the 1960 census data indicated that labor per hectare was approximately 20 percent as high on

Table 4-16. Colombia: Land Use by Farm Size, 1969 (INCORA Sample)

Farm size (hectares)	Number of farms	Percentage share of land in:			
		Annual crops	Permanent crops	Pasture	Other
0- 0.99	36	34.93	29.59	47.13	−11.64[a]
1- 4.99	516	49.61	22.73	52.06	−24.40[a]
5- 9.99	538	35.74	18.66	30.82	14.77
10-14.99	336	25.29	16.30	47.83	10.58
15-19.99	212	17.57	13.56	46.38	22.50
20-49.99	528	11.00	8.41	51.20	29.09
50-99.99	439	9.89	2.99	44.92	42.20
100 and over	281	6.39	1.10	30.98	61.53
All farms	2,886	11.00	4.78	39.56	44.66

[a]Negative figures for "other" may be due to some form of double counting.

Source: Agency for International Development, Sector Analysis Division, Bureau for Latin America, *General Working Document #17L, Small Farm Analysis: Preliminary Results: Land Use and Land Tenure*, by James R. Horst and Thomas Walker, December 1972, p. 5.

farms of 20 to 50 hectares as on farms of 1 to 5 hectares; the INCORA data showed a corresponding ratio of about 15 percent. The absolute values were lower for the INCORA farms, presumably because these data reflect the situation nearly a decade after the 1960 census, and also because of a likely bias in the 1969 sample estimates toward low labor intensity.[17]

Because of the fact that the INCORA sample was not representative, with typical large farms not included at all (those included were principally in the colonization zones) and with the smallest farms apparently being unusually productive, the sample cannot be of much assistance in an attempt to judge whether size/productivity differentials changed significantly during the 1960s. Nevertheless, the results do tend to reconfirm the high potential and, in many cases, actual land productivity of small farms, and they constitute some circumstantial evidence that, if the land productivity differential between small farms and large farms did narrow over the 1960s, the change was not dramatic.

4.3   THE PHILIPPINES

Farm Size and Productivity.   With its low land to labor ratio in agriculture, the Philippines is naturally characterized by small farms. In

Table 4-17. Colombia: Comparison of Man-Years per Hectare, Berry 1960 Estimates Based on Agricultural Census, and INCORA Borrowers' Survey of 1969

Farm size (hectares)	Berry: 1960		INCORA survey: 1969	
	Est. A	Est. B	Est. A[a]	Est. B[b]
0- 0.99	1.510	2.470	1.290	1.026
1- 4.99	.533	.463	.257	.293
5- 9.99	.270	.201	.167	.173
10- 14.99	} .170	} .164	.112 } .098	.144 } .117
15- 19.99			.083	.087
20- 49.99	.103	.101	.041	.039
50- 99.99	.059	.053	.018	.015
100-199.99	.037 } .023	.037 } .027	} .009	} .008
200 and over				
All farms	—	—	.033	.033

[a]Assumes 280 days as one working year.
[b]Assumes a man-year involves the same number of days per hired worker as per family worker; this estimate thus reflects differences in days worked per year for family workers.

Sources: A. Berry, "Land Distribution, Income Distribution, and the Productive Efficiency of Colombian Agriculture," *Food Research Institute Studies* 12 (3) (1973); A.I.D., Sector Analysis Division, Bureau for Latin America, *General Working Document #17L, Small Farm Analysis: Preliminary Results: Land Use and Land Tenure,* by James R. Horst and Thomas Walker, December 1972, p. 5.

1960, only 38 percent of farms were larger than 3 hectares and only 19 percent larger than 5 hectares.

The agricultural census of 1960 provides the basis for our aggregate estimates of the relationship between farm size and land productivity (Table 4-18). The sharp decline in land productivity with increasing size can be seen to result from both (1) a considerably lower crop output per cultivated hectare on large farms—that on farms above 50 hectares was 32 to 45 percent below that on farms of 1 to 3 hectares; and (2) a much lower livestock output per hectare or per noncropped hectare on larger farms. Total value-added per hectare was 22 to 39 percent as high on farms above 50 hectares as on those of 1 to 3 hectares, depending on which of the output estimates is chosen. Estimate 1 is designed to be the central, unbiased estimate, whereas an upper limit to the relative productivity of the larger farms is represented by the alternative Estimate 2.

The share of land used for temporary crops falls from about three-fourths for the smaller size classes to approximately 30 percent for farms over 200 hectares; the shares in both fallow and forest cover are quite low for the smaller farms and high in the range of 5 to 100 hectares (Table 4-19).

As of 1960, yield differentials by farm size were not very striking in the Philippines, especially when distinctions are made between upland and

Table 4-18. Philippines: Relationship of Value-Added per Farm Area to Farm Size (Pesos per Hectare), 1960

Farm size (hectares)	Number of farms (1,000)	Total area (thousands of hectares)	Value-added /area		Cultivated area (thousands of hectares)		Value-added in crops[a] /cultiv. area	
			Est. 1	Est. 2	(Excluding fallow)	(Including fallow)	Est. 1	Est. 2
	(1)	(2)	(3)	(4)	(5)	(6)	(7)	(8)
0 - 0.2	20.0	2.0	9,559	6,994	1.1	1.2	953	918
0.2- 0.5	69.1	21.0	1,388	1,258	19.4	19.9	478	466
0.5- 1	160.7	101.5	811	777	94.6	98.1	380	366
1 - 2	642.1	795.6	556	557	736.6	774.1	344	327
2 - 3	458.9	1,000.5	443	478	906.3	971.2	321	300
3 - 4	252.5	797.0	397	431	699.4	766.3	321	293
4 - 5	152.4	629.5	359	397	522.6	596.3	323	283
5 - 10	289.7	1,845.3	292	316	1,296.6	1,642.0	329	260
10 - 15	86.2	964.8	229	251	542.2	785.4	338	233
15 - 20	13.7	224.7	249	260	129.9	182.8	374	266
20 - 25	9.3	206.6	215	226	107.4	160.3	358	240
25 - 50	7.1	232.7	215	242	131.7	182.3	330	239
50 -100	2.5	162.9	196	277	95.0	123.8	298	228
100-200	1.2	154.7	143	300	92.1	112.6	207	170
Over 200	1.0	633.9	82	157	205.4	280.0	196	144
All farms	2,166.2	7,772.5	331	362	5,580.2	6,696.2	325	271

[a]Includes permanent and temporary crops only.

Source: Census of the Philippines: 1960, Agriculture Vol. II, Summary Report Table 10b, Table 3, and tables giving output of specific products by farm size. Outputs were multiplied by average national farm-gate prices to estimate value of output for most crops. For some relatively unimportant crops, no output figures were available by size, so total output was divided among the size categories by area dedicated to the crop. For livestock, figures on stock were available from the census, rather than figures on current output. These were used as the basis for output estimates. The differences between Est. 1 and Est. 2 come mainly from the imprecision of our estimates of value-added in livestock. Est. 1 is designed as a "best estimate," Est. 2 to give an upper limit of the relative productivity of large farms compared to small ones.

Table 4–19. Use of Farmland by Crop Categories, by Size of Farm, Philippines, 1960

Size of farm	Area planted to temporary crops/ Total area %	Area planted to permanent crops/ Total area %	Area planted to temporary or permanent crops/ Total area %	Arable land lying idle/ Total area %	Permanent pasture/ Total area %	Areas covered with forest growth/ Total area %	All other lands/ Total area %
	(1)	(2)	(3)	(4)	(5)	(6)	(7)
Total	48.69	23.10	71.79	14.35	4.88	7.50	1.47
Under 0.2	35.71	20.92	56.63	2.19	a	1.15	40.03
0.2 and under 0.5	71.62	21.00	92.62	2.30	a	.89	2.41
0.5 and under 1	73.64	19.54	93.18	3.51	a	.56	1.40
1 and under 2	72.28	20.30	92.58	4.73	a	1.16	1.52
2 and under 3	69.02	21.56	90.58	6.48	a	1.63	1.29
3 and under 4	64.43	23.32	87.75	8.40	.003	2.59	1.25
4 and under 5	57.65	25.37	83.02	7.90	.01	4.09	1.22
5 and under 10	44.33	25.93	70.26	18.71	.35	9.22	1.43
10 and under 15	31.66	24.53	56.19	25.20	1.39	15.68	1.52
15 and under 20	27.92	29.88	57.80	23.56	2.58	14.76	1.30
20 and under 25	24.74	27.23	51.97	25.63	3.87	17.15	1.38
25 and under 50	28.40	28.21	56.61	21.74	6.36	13.96	1.34
50 and under 100	34.77	23.51	58.28	17.67	11.38	11.23	1.44
100 and under 200	41.67	17.90	59.57	13.26	17.12	7.84	1.52
200 and over	20.12	12.28	32.40	11.77	45.17	8.78	1.89

a Negligible.
Source: *Census of the Phillippines Agriculture, 1960.*

lowland, irrigated and nonirrigated areas. Even without allowance for these distinctions, the differentials in rice yield by size were moderate. Sugar cane and corn yields were higher on large farms, coconut yields on small farms (Table 4-20).[18] More detailed analysis of rice yields has been carried out by Ruttan on the basis of national and regional samples.[19] He classified farms by size and tenure, distinguishing share tenants and full owners, and presented separate yield figures according to whether the rice was irrigated or not, lowland or upland. From the national data it appears that yield per hectare bears no systematic relationship to farm size, though it tends to be lower on large farms (say 10 hectares and up) for most categories of farms.

Regressions on the grouped data underlying Table 4-18 show the following results, with values expressed in pesos:

$$\frac{VA}{A} = \underset{(5.04)}{14{,}557} - \underset{(-4.75)}{1{,}107 \log A} \qquad R^2 = 0.63$$

$$\frac{CVA}{CA} = \underset{(6.22)}{1{,}278} - \underset{(-4.46)}{76 \log CA} \qquad R^2 = 0.61,$$

where VA is value-added, A is area in acres, CVA is value-added in crops, and CA is cultivated area in acres. (The t-statistic is in parentheses; log refers to the natural logarithm.)

These results confirm that there is a statistically significant negative relationship between output per land area and farm size (or, for the second regression, between crop output per cultivated area and size of cultivated area).

Although no overall data are available on labor productivity by farm size, Ruttan's study of tenure and productivity in Bulacan province shows a sharp increase with size, corresponding to a sharp decline in the labor-land ratio (Table 4-24). Rough guesses as to the distribution of labor across farm sizes, based on the distribution of farm population by farm size and evidence on the importance of wage labor in agriculture, point in the same direction.

The composition of output varies less by size than is typical for Latin American countries. Apart from the concentration on poultry, hogs, and fruit characterizing the very smallest farms (under 1 hectare), the dominance of rice, coconuts, and corn, as a group, is evident at all farm sizes, although rice and corn are relatively more important on small farms and coconuts on large farms (Table 4-22).

Some of the decrease in land productivity with farm size is related to lower land quality. Although figures bearing directly on how land value or

Table 4–20. Philippines: Yield per Hectare by Size of Farm, Irrigated and Nonirrigated Land, 1960

Farm size (hectares)	Palay rice, 1st crop, lowland			Palay rice, 2nd crop, lowland			Sugar cane, Q/A	Coconuts, Q/A	Corn Q/A
	Q/A	QI/AI	QNI/ANI	Q/A	QI/AI	QNI/ANI			
	(1)	(2)	(3)	(4)	(5)	(6)	(7)	(8)	(9)
All farms	30.16	35.79	27.05	26.70	30.50	22.37	53.02	3,227	13.27
under 0.2	49.68	61.00	32.80	52.13	53.24	42.18	48.10	3,684	12.16
0.2 and under 0.5	34.35	41.28	26.40	34.40	38.00	22.52	43.72	3,485	9.60
0.5 and under 1	30.77	36.42	26.09	27.17	29.63	22.27	38.94	3,373	9.85
1 and under 2	31.19	37.61	27.29	28.77	32.00	23.75	41.14	3,512	11.85
2 and under 3	31.12	37.13	27.69	27.88	31.39	23.36	42.62	3,433	13.02
3 and under 4	31.31	36.61	28.22	27.06	30.79	22.79	44.43	3,515	13.29
4 and under 5	30.74	35.80	27.85	25.79	29.26	22.17	42.99	3,398	14.36
5 and under 10	28.97	33.62	26.64	24.68	28.34	21.72	43.75	3,180	14.75
10 and under 15	27.49	32.52	25.35	25.02	30.17	20.98	45.68	2,995	14.51
15 and under 20	26.61	31.92	24.28	25.02	29.64	21.38	50.41	2,879	13.82
20 and under 25	25.54	29.59	24.06	22.73	26.24	20.28	53.34	2,907	13.55
25 and under 50	25.00	31.13	22.39	21.82	26.06	18.02	53.69	2,870	12.86
50 and under 100	26.07	33.04	21.91	23.67	26.17	19.56	56.93	3,197	11.90
100 and under 200	28.41	33.92	25.15	28.16	31.94	20.33	57.48	2,855	11.36
200 and over	28.44	32.95	26.49	26.32	31.61	18.79	58.57	3,024	14.02

Notes: Q is the total production; A is total area planted; QI is production under irrigation; AI is area planted under irrigation; QNI is production not under irrigation; ANI is area planted not under irrigation. Units by column: 1 through 6, cavans/hectare; 7, metric tons/hectare; 8, nuts/hectare; 9, cavans/hectare.

Source: Philippines census of agriculture, 1960.

land prices vary with size are not available, the 1960 census data on average value of farm land per hectare show generally higher values for the provinces with low average farm size. (It also, not surprisingly, shows higher value of buildings per hectare in the provinces with low average farm size.)

Since 1960, Philippine agriculture has seen the advent of miracle rice, permitting much higher yields with appropriate use of water and fertilizer. No aggregate evidence is available on relative factor productivity by farm size for the late 1960s or early 1970s, but some sample data are; these suggest that the new varieties brought no lasting changes in the usual relationships between yield and farm size in rice. Table 4-23, based on a sample in Nueva Ecija, indicates that yield was substantially lower on farms above 4 hectares than on those below 2 hectares; the area sampled was one of relatively high use of HYVs. Other samples show that, as in Pakistan, large farms have tended to adopt new varieties somewhat ahead of smaller farms, but the lag is relatively short.

Tenure and Productivity   The effects of land tenure on agricultural productivity have been the topic of considerable discussion in the Philippines, partly because of the finding that land productivity on tenant farms frequently exceeds that on owner-operated farms, in contradiction of the common prediction (noted in section 2.4 above) that tenancy leads to low use of variable inputs and low productivity. Thus, Estanislao noted:

The University of the Philippines Survey in 1955 reported that for the crop-year 1954–1955, productivity per hectare of cropland was: P237.34 for owned farms; P307.44 for partly-owned farms; and P361.44 for tenant farms. Thus it appears that productivity per hectare of cropland moved inversely with the ownership of the farm.

This evidence in itself is not too meaningful because owned farms have much less capital than partly-owned tenanted farms. Average productivity of capital would therefore be a meaningful statistic in this case. The results are 0.973 for fully-owned farms, 1.105 for partly-owned farms and 1.125 for tenanted farms. It appears that the conclusion derived from computing productivity per hectare does not change at all.[20]

A similar picture came from a 1952 Survey in Central Luzon.[21] Ruttan concluded that "In situations characterized by static technology, static standards and levels of living, and low literacy and income levels, both total agricultural output and total marketable surplus can be maximized by a tenure system which forces the cultivator to produce beyond the level which satisfies his family consumption requirement. In this situation, share tenancy does not limit output but rather forces agricultural output above the level that would be achieved under a system of owner-partnership."[22]

A national survey by the Bureau of Agricultural Economics revealed generally higher yields on share-tenanted rice farms than on full-owner rice farms (Table 4-21). The 1960 agricultural census data also showed this pattern; for all area planted to rice, yield for full owners was 2.50 cavans (of 44 kilos), for part owners 2.65, for tenants 2.95, and for land operated by a manager 2.64. Pure cash tenancy was very rare and average yield was 2.72; for share tenancy it was 2.97 and for fixed amount of produce 3.00. Ruttan felt, however, that there might be serious difficulties in using the national data as a test of productivity hypotheses, since regions with good soil, climate, and locational characteristics might be atypical in their farm size or tenure structure. Accordingly, he organized data on irrigated rice farms producing two crops a year from five barrios in the province of Bulacan, where the physical environment is relatively homogeneous. Only share-tenant and lease-tenant farms were included, as Ruttan focused on the proposition that sharecropping would foster lower land and labor productivity and lower use of purchased technical inputs than would leaseholding. The results showed that land productivity was higher under share tenancy for smaller farms (less than 2 hectares) and for larger farms it was lower (Table 4-24).[23] Except for the smallest farms, a higher share of lease holders used fertilizer and insecticides.[24] The sharecropped farms under two hectares applied more labor per hectare, while the percent of available labor days spent working off the farm was lower than for leaseholders; these patterns were reversed for farms over two hectares. Recent data from Nueva Ecija showed no overall tendency to less labor application by share tenants.[25]

The University of the Philippines 1955 survey reported greater capitalization on tenanted than on owner-operated farms, a striking result in itself. Capital per hectare was 244 on owned farms, 278 on partly owned farms, and 321 for tenant farms.[26] One hypothesis suggested by the available information is that for small tenanted farms, the availability of capital, far from being a problem, was better than for owned farms. Since tenanted farms are, on average, considerably smaller than owner-operated ones, this could explain the higher average capitalization (on a per hectare basis) for the former; it could also play a role in the unusually high land productivity on small tenanted farms. The 1955 survey also

Table 4-21. Relationship Between Farm Size, Tenure and Yield on Rice-Producing Farms in the Philippines, 1962

	Size of farm in hectares									
	0.6-0.9	1.0-1.4	1.5-1.9	2.0-2.9	3.0-3.9	4.0-4.9	5.0-9.9	10.0-14.9	15.0-24.9	25.0-49.9
	Yield (0.44 kilo cavans per hectare)									
All rice-producing farms										
Share tenants	27.8	35.6	39.3	37.9	36.2	35.6	35.9	38.4	a	a
Full owner	33.4	27.8	27.5	26.6	28.7	28.1	25.5	25.5	19.6	16.6
Irrigated first crop										
Share tenant	41.1	36.1	46.5	44.6	41.4	44.2	40.1	a	a	a
Full owner	38.0	37.1	30.4	35.0	37.8	36.4	33.2	36.6	a	a
Irrigated second crop										
Share tenant	32.9	35.8	41.4	35.9	34.0	35.9	34.6	a	a	a
Full owner	37.1	32.9	33.6	29.9	36.4	29.5	30.7	30.2	a	a
Nonirrigated (rain-fed) first crop										
Share tenant	29.9	38.0	40.3	40.4	38.9	35.2	39.3	a	a	a
Full owner	24.1	26.0	29.9	27.9	30.2	27.3	27.0	26.1	26.0	13.9
Upland rice										
Share tenant	15.0	19.4	23.2	20.7	16.4	22.0	19.2	a	a	a
Full owner	32.5	19.7	15.2	17.7	18.9	24.3	17.7	19.1	14.8	15.7

[a]Less than five farms reporting.

Source: Vernon W. Ruttan, "Tenure and Productivity of Philippine Rice Producing Farms," *Philippine Economic Journal* 5 (1) (1966). Tabulated from data collected by the Bureau of Agricultural Economics, Department of Agriculture and Natural Resources.

Table 4-22. Output Composition by Farm Size, Philippines, 1960 (Percentages)

Farm size (hectares)	Palay (rice)	Corn	Coconuts	Other crops	Livestock
0 - 0.2	1.39	0.25	0.51	3.50	94.35
0.2- 1	15.12	4.73	6.54	14.19	59.42
1 - 3	32.16	6.52	13.46	9.26	38.60
3 - 5	36.42	6.23	20.03	9.84	27.48
5 - 10	28.50	6.72	25.51	18.66	20.61
10 - 25	21.62	5.51	30.10	26.95	15.82
25 -100	19.04	3.26	36.16	29.12	12.42
Over 100	18.35	3.00	34.76	24.18	19.71

Source: Calculated from agricultural census of 1960; these figures correspond to Est. 1 of total agricultural output by farm size, Table 4-18.

Table 4-23. Philippines: Yield per Hectare for Irrigated 2-Crop Farms, by Tenure and Farm Size, Gapan, Nueva Ecija, Wet Season, 1970

	Tenure classification			
	Lease-hold	Share tenant	Owner operator	All farms
Farm size				
Less than 2 hectares				
No. of farms	29	43	11	83
Yield/ha. (metric tons)	2.7	3.2	2.9	3.0
2-4 hectares				
No. of farms	97	103	21	221
Yield/ha. (mt.)	2.6	2.6	2.7	2.6
More than 4 hectares				
No. of farms	11	a	a	21
Yield/ha. (mt.)	2.3			2.2
All farms				
No. of farms	137	153	35	
Yield/ha. (mt.)	2.6	2.7	2.7	

[a]Average yield not calculated for categories with less than ten farms.

revealed that value of land per hectare was substantially greater for tenanted land,[27] possibly reflecting a disproportionate number of share tenants in the richer rice areas, and helping to explain their high land productivity and capitalization. More recently, a 120-farm survey by the Bureau of Agricultural Economics (BAECON) in 1970 found higher average investment per hectare on owner-operated farms (860 pesos per hectare), as contrasted with part-owners (727), share tenants (660), and lessees (523).[28] It remains to be seen whether or not these two contradictory results simply reflect different samples—and the fact that no

Table 4-24. Tenure, Productivity, and Farm Size on Irrigated Rice Farms Producing Two Crops per Year in Five Barrios in Bulacan, 1963–64

	Size of farm (ha.)				
	0.1–1.0	1.1–2.0	2.1–3.0	Above 3.0	Total
Land productivity (kg. of rough rice/ha./year)					
Share tenure	4,948	3,836	3,189	1,919	3,541
Lease tenure	4,748	3,013	3,522	5,964	3,738
Labor productivity (kg. of rough rice per day)					
Share tenure	4.67	7.70	8.49	9.12	7.15
Lease tenure	6.08	7.55	8.56	13.73	8.90
Percent of farms using fertilizer					
Share tenure	52.8	35.9	47.3	33.3	43.6
Lease tenure	45.5	75.0	75.0	60.0	62.5
Percent of farmers using insecticide					
Share tenure	38.9	20.8	21.0	21.9	24.8
Lease tenure	36.4	37.5	25.0	40.0	34.4
Percent of available labor days employed off farm					
Share tenure	12.7	13.3	12.7	29.6	13.8
Lease tenure	16.7	28.1	17.1	18.6	19.8
Labor (days)/hectare					
Share tenure	1,060	498	376	210	495
Lease tenure	781	399	411	434	420

Source: Vernon W. Ruttan, "Tenure and Productivity of Philippine Rice Producing Farms," Philippine Economic Journal 5 (1) (1966); originally from University of the Philippines College of Agriculture, Department of Agricultural Information Survey.

systematic relations exist between tenure and the variables under discussion—or changing relationships over time. In the latter case, the impact of the increasing mechanization of Philippine agriculture on the relative investment in and productivity of different tenure farms clearly warrants attention.

While it is not yet clear how all the pieces of evidence from the Philippines on the tenure-productivity relationship fit together, what seems well established is that the traditional view of share tenancy as an inefficient form receives no general support.[29] Better theories of how landlords and tenants interact are necessary and are gradually being formulated.[30]

4.4   (WEST) PAKISTAN[31]

Farm Size and Factor Productivity: Evidence.   Pakistan, like the Philippines, has been substantially affected by new crop varieties over

Table 4-25. Farm Size and Tenure, Pakistan, 1960

Farm size (Acres)	Number of farms (1000)	Percent of farms	Area (thousands of acres)	Percent of area	Number of farms by tenure of operator		
					Owner	Owner cum tenant	Tenant
	(1)	(2)	(3)	(4)	(5)	(6)	(7)
0.0- 1.0	742.2	15.28	334.4	0.68	466.0	35.48	245.8
1.0- 2.5	855.7	17.62	1,345.5	2.75	414.3	95.38	346.1
2.5- 5.0	806.0	16.60	2,911.1	5.95	327.5	145.4	333.1
5.0- 7.5	581.0	11.96	3,545.7	7.25	202.3	121.4	257.2
7.5- 12.5	758.7	15.62	7,357.0	15.04	231.8	171.2	355.7
12.5- 25	728.9	15.01	12,533.0	25.61	219.6	169.0	340.3
25 - 50	285.9	5.89	9,467.6	19.35	93.7	70.7	121.5
50 - 150	87.6	1.80	6,538.9	13.36	38.92	22.95	25.76
Over 150	13.98	0.29	4,896.4	10.01	8.85	2.71	2.42
All farms	4,856.0	100.0	48,929.6	100.0	1,997.7	834.3	2,028.0

Source: Pakistan, Ministry of Agriculture and Works, Pakistan Census of Agriculture, Vol. 2, Report 1 (Karachi, 1963).

the last 10-15 years; it also benefitted from a boom in the use of tubewells, beginning in the late 1950s and permitting a significant expansion of irrigable area. With better seeds and more water, parts of the country have indeed been undergoing a Green Revolution. Accordingly, it constitutes an interesting context in which to probe some of the effects of such rapid technological improvements on the relative productivity of farms by size.

Estimates of the relative productivity and employment generation in Pakistani farms of different sizes are based mainly on estimates from data provided in the 1959-60 agricultural census (before the rapid change just cited), on micro data from the Punjab Farm Accounts and Family Budget Surveys (hereafter referred to as FAFBS) of the middle and late 1960s, on a recent survey and analysis by M. H. Khan,[32] and on the 1972 agricultural census. Less can be said about the relationship between tenure and productivity.[33] The distribution of farms and area by size and tenure as of 1960 is presented in Table 4-25.

Both the 1959-60 agricultural census and micro evidence available from the Punjab FAFBS indicate a negative relationship between size of farm and value of output per acre (either land area or cultivated area). The 1972 agricultural census tentatively suggests a weaker negative relationship. The implications of Khan's more recent work (1974 and 1976) are not immediately clear, but it does raise the issue of whether or not there has been a significant change in recent years under the influence of the Green Revolution. We consider the census and FAFBS data first, then compare the 1972 census and the Khan results to it.

Our estimates of the relationship between farm size in acres and land and labor productivity as of 1959-60 are summarized in Table 4-26. The first estimate of land and labor productivity is based on the assumption of the same crop yields on all farm sizes; the second—more or less a best estimate—utilizes the scanty available evidence on yield differentials. With respect to value of product per acre of cultivated land, productivity falls sharply with farm size, being only about 45 percent as high for farms of 50 to 150 acres as for farms from 1 to 2.5 acres (according to Estimate 2).[34] As we see below, much of this inverse relationship must be attributed to a poorer soil-water combination on the larger farms.

The FAFBS samples done annually in recent years and periodically over several decades provide good micro data on land productivity by farm size, albeit on the basis of a small sample.[35] A distinction is made between big landowners, peasant proprietors and tenant cultivators. Table 4-27 summarizes the information on gross farm income and value-added per acre and per cultivated acre for the single crop year 1968-69. Table 4-28

Table 4-26. Output per Acre and Output per Worker by Farm Size—1959-60, Pakistan, Based on 1959-60 Census of Agriculture

Size of farm (in acres)	Output per unit of land								Output per worker	
	Estimate I				Estimate II					
	Output/ cropped area[a] (1)	Output/ net sown area[b] (2)	Output/ cultivated area[c] (3)	Output/ acre (4)	Output/ cropped area[a] (5)	Output/ net sown area[b] (6)	Output/ cultivated area[c] (7)	Output/ acre (8)	Est. 1 (9)	Est. 2 (10)
Less than 1.0	752.0	1,033.7	926.6	739.2	679.8	935.1	838.1	668.6	80.1	105.6
1.0 to less than 2.5	396.6	516.4	460.5	391.4	366.1	476.8	425.6	361.7	220.5	251.5
2.5 to less than 5.0	283.8	362.5	326.4	277.4	265.3	338.7	305.0	259.2	420.3	449.6
5.0 to less than 7.5	246.1	312.1	281.9	248.5	234.7	296.3	267.7	236.0	496.7	541.9
7.5 to less than 12.5	220.3	272.3	245.3	216.3	209.8	259.4	233.5	205.9	695.6	730.2
12.5 to less than 25.0	197.5	236.1	244.8	179.5	203.5	243.2	216.1	158.5	847.6	813.4
25.0 to less than 50.0	177.9	204.1	174.4	136.2	193.4	221.7	189.5	148.0	957.5	852.7
50.0 to less than 150.0	151.3	164.7	129.5	76.9	164.0	178.7	140.5	83.4	1,186.6	814.7
150 and over	143.1	154.8	82.3	28.4	153.1	165.6	88.0	30.4	998.8	614.1
All farms	214.9	257.1	220.9	168.1	214.8	257.1	220.9	168.1	643.2	643.2

[a]Cropped area is the aggregate area of crops raised in a farm during the census year, including the area under fruit trees. Figures here refer to nine major crops plus fodder.

[b]Net sown area is the cultivated farm area actually cropped during the census year, regardless of the number of crops raised, and it includes area under fruit trees for the same year.

[c]Cultivated area includes:
  (a) net sown area; and
  (b) current fallow (i.e., the cultivated area that was not cropped during the census year, but was cropped during the preceding year).
Uncultivated area includes:
  (a) culturable waste area;
  (b) area not available for cultivation; and
  (c) forest area.

Source: Calculations by the author on the basis of the 1960 Census of Agriculture. For details, see A. Berry, "Some Evidence on the Economic Potential of Small Farms in Pakistan" (mimeo), 1976.

Table 4-27. Land Productivity by Size of Farm, Punjab, 1968–69 (Based on FAFBS)

Size of farm (in acres)	No. of farms	Gross income per acre	Gross income per cult. acre	Value-added per acre	Value-added per cult. acre
	(1)	(2)	(3)	(4)	(5)
Total	53	198.9	244.85	179.0	220.39
0 - 7.4	0	—	—	—	—
7.5- 12.4	8	401.8	404.59	380.1	382.79
12.5- 24.9	25	281.6	314.82	269.4	301.16
25.0- 49.9	16	220.7	247.45	189.1	212.03
50.0-149.9	3	191.7	226.93	157.8	186.78
150.0 and more	1	22.9	43.29	20.2	38.05

Source: Board of Economic Inquiry, Punjab (Pakistan), *Farm Accounts and Family Budgets of Cultivators in the Punjab, 1968-1969,* by Zaheer Iqbal Qazi and Sardar Mohammed (Lahore: Syed Sons Printers, 1972), pp. 5-6.

Table 4-28. Land Productivity by Size of Farm, Punjab, 1966-67/1968-69 (Based on FAFBS)

Size of holdings	Gross income per acre cultivated[a]	Cultivated area as a proportion of owned area[b]	Income per acre owned = (2) × (3)
1	2	3	4
	Rs.	Ratio	Rs.
A. Irrigated area			
(i) up to 12.5 acres	467.78	.8759	409.33
(ii) 12.6-25.0 acres	391.51	.8545	334.55
(iii) 25.1-50.0 acres	258.99	.7802	206.40
(iv) above 50.0 acres	134.35	.4880	65.56
B. Barani areas			
(i) up to 12.5 acres	277.75	.8759	243.28
(ii) 12.6-25.0 acres	172.81	.8545	147.67
(iii) 25.1-50.0 acres	42.69	.7802	33.31
(iv) above 50.0 acres	40.45	.4880	19.74

[a]Represents a three-year average for the period 1966-67 to 1968-69.
[b]The same ratios are used for barani and irrigated areas, as separate figures were not available.
Source Ronald Herring and M. Ghaffar Chaudhry "The 1972 Land Reforms in Pakistan and Their Economic Implications," *Pakistan Development Review* 13 (3) (1974):263. The sources are Board of Economic Inquiry, Punjab (Pakistan), *Farm Accounts and Family Budgets of Cultivators in the Punjab,* 1966-67, 1967-68, and 1968-69.

relates to the three-year period 1966–67 to 1968–69 and distinguishes between irrigated and barani regions. The negative relation of size to productivity is clear in all cases, and there is a marked similarity between the rate of decrease of land productivity in the FAFBS and in the agricultural census estimates; a comparison is presented in Table 4-29. The FAFBS data indicate that the relationship is not a spurious result of lower irrigated land/total area ratios on large farms, since it appears almost as strongly in irrigated areas as overall.

The FAFBS data permit further probing of the effect of size and other variables on output by regression analysis. The simple association between gross farm income per acre and area (using 1968-69 FAFBS survey data) is:

$$\frac{Y_{GF}}{A} = \begin{array}{c} 663 - 281 \log A; \\ (6.28)\ (3.64) \end{array} \quad \overline{R}^2 = .191,$$

where Y_{GF} is gross farm income, A is area in acres, and t values are shown in parentheses. When regional dummies are included, the relationship is:

$$\frac{Y_{GF}}{A} = \begin{array}{c} 346 - 187 \log A + 317\,D_1 + 396\,D_2 + 59\,D_3 \\ (5.38)\ (-4.84)\quad (8.25)\quad\ (11.15)\quad (1.60) \end{array}$$
$$+\ 108\,D_4 + 279\,D_5; \quad \overline{R}^2 = .835,$$
$$(3.07)\quad\ (7.70)$$

where variables are as before, and D_1 through D_5 are regional dummy variables. Including dummy variables for tenure adds little explanatory power; relative to tenant-operated farms, both large owners and peasant-proprietor farms have lower gross income per acre, given size and region, but the level of significance is moderately high only for large owners.

$$\frac{Y_{GF}}{A} = \begin{array}{c} 294 - 136 \log A + 335\,D_1 + 405\,D_2 + 75\,D_3 \\ (3.68)\ (-2.59)\quad (8.28)\quad\ (11.35)\quad (1.96) \end{array}$$
$$+\ 116\,D_4 + 292\,D_5 - 54\,D_{LO} - 25\,D_{PP}; \\ (3.28)\quad\ (7.89)\quad\ (-1.73)\quad (-1.01)$$
$$\overline{R}^2 = .835.$$

(Variables are as before, with the addition of dummy variables D_{LO} and D_{PP} for large owners and peasant proprietors, respectively.)

The impact of farm size on gross farm income per acre is less negative when region and tenure are taken into account; this fact may be seen in the smaller absolute magnitude of the negative coefficient on logarithm of farm size in the last two of the three regression results.[36] The negative effect of farm size is also evident when the dependent variable is either net farm income per acre or value-added per acre. When the output

Table 4-29. Relative Land Productivity by Farm Size: Agricultural Census and FAFBS Survey-Based Estimates Compared

(Index = 100 for Size Category 7.5-12.5 Acres)

Farm size (acres)	Agricultural Census, 1959-60 — Value of production per:		Punjab: Farm Accounts Survey — 1968-69				Punjab: Farm Accounts Survey — Averages for 1966-67 to 1968-69[a]			
			Gross income per:		Value-added per:		Gross income per:			
							Cultivated acre		Acre	
	Acre (1)	Cultivated acre (2)	Acre (3)	Cult. acre (4)	Acre (5)	Cult. acre (6)	Irrigated (7)	Barani (8)	Irrigated (9)	Barani (10)
0 - 7.5	—	—	—	—	—	—				
7.5- 12.5	100	100	100	100	100	100	100	100	100	100
12.5- 25.0	77.0	92.5	70.1	77.8	70.9	78.7	83.7	62.2	81.7	60.7
25.0- 50.0	71.9	81.1	54.9	62.2	47.6	55.4	55.4	15.4	49.3	13.7
50.0-150	40.5	60.2	47.7	56.1	41.5	48.8	} 28.7	} 14.56	} 16.0	} 8.11
Over 150	14.8	37.7	5.70	10.70	5.31	9.94				
(50.0-150 & Over 150, combined)	} 29.5	} 52.12	} 21.1	} 32.6	} 18.6	} 28.7				

[a]In 1968-69 there were no farms of less than 7.5 acres in the sample; if this was true also in 1966-67 and 1967-68, the category 0-12.5 acres is the same as 7.5-12.5 acres, and the FAFBS index has in fact the same base (i.e., in the category 7.5-12.5) as the agricultural census data.

Source: Based on Tables 4-26, 4-27, 4-28. Data from the agricultural census are those of Estimate II, Table 4-26.

or income measure is divided by cultivated acres, the (negative) coefficient of the land variable is somewhat lower but still quite significant.[37]

It is clear, both from the importance of the regional dummies in the above equations and from the smaller decline in land productivity with increasing size in those equations than in the aggregate data from the Agricultural Census or the FAFBS, that much of the negative relationship observed in these latter (Table 4-29) is due to large farms being found predominantly in low productivity zones, where the low productivity is mainly the result of lack of water. Note that whereas the aggregate data of Table 4-26 (Estimate 2) imply an output/acre level 60 to 65 percent lower for farms of 50 to 150 acres (average size 75 acres) than for farms of 2.5 to 5.0 acres (average size 3.6 acres), the Punjab regressions with regional dummies imply a gross farm income per acre lower by only 39 percent (on a farm of 75 acres compared with one of 3.6 acres) in the region of highest productivity (Sahiwal) and 56 percent lower in a hypothetical region with productivity at each farm size half way between that of the lowest and highest productivity regions.[38] Without regional dummies (that is, based on the first equation) the differential is 73 percent. Perhaps one-quarter to one-half of that differential is explained by different land-water situations in the six regions distinguished. Were more subregions differentiated, one would expect still more of the differential to be explained. Since the land-water characteristics vary more across the country than within the Punjab alone, one might speculate that something on the order of one-half of the total differential of 70 to 75 percent identified in Table 4-26 could be explained in this way.

In summary, while it is clear that a substantial part of the negative relationship between farm size and land productivity emerging from these data is due to the aggregation process, there is no strong suggestion that it can be wholly explained in this way. Both the census data and the FAFBS data point to the same correlates of the lower productivity of large farms—lower cultivated area relative to total area, lower cropping intensity (cropped area/net sown area), lower share of output from livestock, and lower ratio of labor to land (Table 4-30). Broadly speaking, the region specific data is consistent with the aggregate information.

As of 1960, labor productivity (output per man-day) increased substantially with farm size, as indicated in Table 4-26, based on the agricultural census data. Between farms in the 1- to 2.5-acre range and those in the 50- to 150-acre range, it appeared to rise by three- to fourfold. Other sources, including the FAFBS, imply similar relationships.

Proximate Explanations of the Factor Productivity Differences by Size Revealed by 1959-60 Census Data and FAFBS Data of the late 1960s. A number of proximate causes associated with the higher output per cultivated acre observed on smaller farms in the above surveys can, as just noted, be identified fairly clearly; (they must in turn be explained in terms of more basic differences). Two such factors were the lower ratio of fallow to cultivated land on smaller farms and their higher cropping intensity (Table 4-31). Abstraction from these two factors can be achieved by considering the ratio of value of crop and livestock output to net sown area (where value-added in livestock is included in the numerator and fodder area in the denominator), as in column 4; the higher output per acre on the small farms results mainly from the much higher value-added in livestock per acre of fodder. Value of crops per net sown area is essentially constant (column 5), with the smallest size category being only about 40 percent higher than the largest, and with relatively little decline occurring until the quite large farms of 50 hectares and up. All of this moderate differential is related to different crop composition (since in the estimate an increasing relationship between yield and farm size was assumed). Fallow was a much higher share of cultivated area on the farms above 50 acres, being 21.4 percent for those in the 50-150 range and 47 percent for those over 150 acres. Both these figures, but especially the latter, are striking, in view of the high ratio of irrigated area to cultivated area on the largest farms, 58.4 percent, but much of this may have been run-off irrigation and therefore not equivalent to reliable canal or tubewell irrigation.

Within the category of crops, there is some tendency for the largest farms, specifically those above 50 acres, to have a composition of output weighted more heavily toward the low-value products. The medium-sized farms have about the same value per acre as the small ones. Reasonably contemporary figures on yield differentials by farm size[39] refer only to five crops: cotton, rice, maize, sugar cane, and wheat. Only in the case of sugar cane and maize were there substantial yield differentials by size, in both cases favoring the larger farmers. However, these crops were relatively unimportant in the overall acreage in 1959-60, so it would appear that yield differentials are less important in determining the relationship between value of crops and the cropped area than are differences in composition of output. In 1959-60, there were quite large differences among crops in average value of output per acre, with sugar cane and rice being substantially above maize and cotton, and with wheat still lower. Most of the lesser crops, such as jowar, bajra, and gram, were also low. The

Table 4-30. Evidence on Labor Inputs (Man-days per Cultivated Acre) by Farm Size, Pakistan

Farm size (acres)	Aggregate estimates based on 1959-60 Agricultural Census		Micro data from farm management projects[b]						World Bank Mechanization Study[c]	
	Est. 1[a]	Est. 2[a]	Kohat unirrig.	Kohat irrig.	Hazara	Muzaffargarh	Hyderabad	Gujranwala	Before mechaniz.	After mechaniz.
Less than 1.0	418	290	—	—	—	—	—	—	—	—
1–2.5	154	127	—	—	—	—	—	—	—	—
2.5–5.0	84	77	—	—	—	—	—	—	—	—
5.0–7.5	74	67	—	—	70.2 (7.5)	—	—	106.4 (7.14)	—	—
7.5–12.5	53	50	75.1 (7.9)	—	—	93.5 (9.2)	74.0 (8.4)	—	—	—
12.5–25	41 (17.2)	41 (17.2)	33.0 (20.8)	75.6 (17.6)	36.2 (16.5)	59.3 (22.1)	48.1 (12.9)	65.6 (18.0)	—	—
25–50	31 (33.1)	34 (33.1)	—	—	—	—	40.0 (24.5)	52.1 (37.1)	51 (26.4)	39 (45.3)
50–100	19 (74.6)	29 (74.6)	—	—	—	44.8 (71.0)	—	—	45 (36.3)	32 (86.0)
100–150	—	—	—	—	—	—	—	—	37 (50.6)	24 (145.8)
Over 100	14 (350.0)	24 (350.0)	—	—	—	—	—	—	26 (108)	26 (277.4)

Note: Figures in parentheses indicate the average farm size of the set of farms for which the labor/land ratio is reported.

[a] Workers per cultivated acre converted to days/cultivated acre, assuming 240 days per worker per year.

[b] Figures correspond to averages of categories, grouped as small, medium, or large. Source: Ronald Herring and M. Ghaffar Chaudhry, "The 1972 Land Reforms in Pakistan and Their Economic Implications," Pakistan Development Review 13(3) (1974): 261. These authors do not indicate the year to which the data refer, nor their sources, although the data were published between 1968 and 1973.

[c] Farm size measured in cultivated acres and therefore somewhat smaller than total farm size. Source: World Bank Staff Working Paper #210, "The Consequences of Farm Tractors in Pakistan," prepared by John P. McInerney and Graham F. Donaldson, February 1975, pp. 51–55.

Table 4-31. Factors Associated with Variations in Land Productivity by Farm Size (West Pakistan, 1959–60), Based on 1959–60 Census of Agriculture

Size of farm (acres)	Cropping intensity[a] (all crops) (Percent)	Irrigated area/cultivated area (Percent)	Fallow cultivated area (Percent)	Total value (crops & livestock) net sown area (Est. 2)	Total value of crops area cultivated (excl. fodder) (Est. 2)	Total value of crops[b] net sown area[b] (excl. fodder) (Est. 2)	Value added in livestock cropped area in fodder	Net sown area Total area
	(1)	(2)	(3)	(4)	(5)	(6)	(7)	(8)
Under 1.0	138	54.5	10.4	935.1	178.7	199.4	4,082.4	71.51
1.0 to less than 2.5	130	63.3	10.8	476.8	175.0	196.1	1,799.9	76.52
2.5 to less than 5.0	128	66.1	10.0	338.7	178.0	197.7	1,071.1	78.41
5.0 to less than 7.5	127	70.0	9.7	296.3	185.1	204.9	747.0	79.62
7.5 to less than 12.5	124	72.8	10.0	259.4	181.3	201.4	519.9	79.40
12.5 to less than 25.0	119	74.0	11.1	243.2	188.6	212.3	361.7	75.99
25.0 to less than 50.0	115	68.3	14.5	221.7	171.4	200.5	306.2	66.73
50.0 to less than 150	109	47.5	21.4	178.7	125.2	159.3	299.4	46.71
150 and over	108	58.4	46.9	165.6	78.5	147.7	284.8	18.38
All farms	120	67.8	14.1	257.1	170.7	198.7	534.2	65.42

[a]Intensity of cropping represents the ratio in which the total area of crops stands to the net sown area. It indicates the extent to which one and the same area was used for cropping. Thus, the percent cropping intensity would be determined as follows:

$$\frac{\text{Total cropped area} \times 100}{\text{Net sown area}}.$$

[b]Refers to nine major crops. See Berry, "Some Evidence on the Economic Potential of Small Farms in Pakistan" (mimeo.), 1976.

Sources: Columns (1)–(3) are from *Census of Agriculture* (see Table 4-25). Columns (4)–(7) are from Berry, ibid.

tendency for the medium-sized farms to have high crop value/crop acreage is related to their having a higher share of their cropped area under rice and sugar cane than do the smaller or (especially) the larger farms. Such differences in crop composition by size are mainly the result of aggregation across regions with different crop specialities (e.g., wheat vs. rice), and this contribution to the negative relationship between size and productivity must be removed before any efficiency comparisons can be made (discussion of preceding section).

The key feature in generating the high total value of output/total area on small farms is their higher production of livestock, despite their allocation of about the same share of cropped area to fodder. If one relates value-added in livestock to area in fodder (Table 4-31, column 6), the ratio falls sharply with farm size, even when poultry is excluded.[40]

Basic Explanations of Variations in Land and Labor Productivity by Farm Size Revealed in 1959–60 Agricultural Census and 1960s FAFBS.   The proximate explanations of factor-productivity differences across farm size discussed above leave unexplained why large farms had more fallow land, irrigated smaller shares of their area, produced a different product-mix, and so forth. For policy purposes, it is crucial to identify the more basic factors at work. Among the common propositions in this connection are: (a) land quality is lower on large farms; (b) the price of capital is lower to larger farms and the price of labor is higher than for small farms, leading to a preference for land- and capital-extensive production on them; (c) farm management is more often absentee on the large farms, implying a preference for low managerial input types of production. Limited information can be brought to bear on proposition (b), while only impressionistic evidence is available re (a) and (c).

Sample surveys, mostly taken in the last decade, suggest that the predicted effects of a higher price of capital (or lower accessibility) and lower price of labor are indeed making themselves felt. For most Pakistani farmers, the main source of credit appears to be friends and relations; in Naseem's study in Sahiwal district, for example, these groups provided 63 percent of loans; product buyers provided 18 percent and the Agricultural Development Bank 9 percent.[41] Lack of credit is mentioned more frequently by small operators as the reason they have not adopted such purchased inputs as fertilizer or, more generally, as an important constraint on production (see Tables 4-32 and 4-33 for the results of a survey by Azam in Harmoia Village, 1970-72).[42] At the same time Azam notes: "It seems that small farmers are able to offset the severity of these constraints, to some extent, by making changes in their input mix, relying to a greater degree on the resources available on the farm, i.e., farm labor and farmyard manure."[43] Data showing the higher labor/land ratio on smaller farms was presented in Table 4-30. In discussing M. H. Khan's recent results below, we return to the question of how adequately the smaller farmers have been able to offset their relative disadvantages in recent years.

Farm Size and Savings Behavior: Results Based on FAFBS. Measurement of savings in agriculture, and on small farms in particular, is notoriously difficult, partly because of the general difficulties in reporting output and income on small farms, and partly because in the case of savings in particular, a substantial share may be in the form of investment on the farm where a major, or the primary, input is labor. The Punjab family farm accounts are a useful source of information on savings, even though the sample is too small to permit any conclusions at a high level of confidence. But the careful reporting is a major advantage.

Information on the savings over 1965-70 of the various groups of farmers included in the FAFBS show the usual positive relation between family income and the savings rate.[44] Since family income is positively associated with farm size, families living on larger farms tend to have higher savings ratios.[45]

When savings per cultivated acre (S/CA) is regressed on number of cultivated acres (CA), either for 1968-69 or for 1965-70, the sign of CA is negative, but not significant at the 0.95 confidence level, and it explains almost none of the variance in S/CA.[46] The most relevant equations to show the association of S/CA with size for 1965-70, allowing for regional differences in land characteristics, are (t-values shown in parentheses):

$$(S/CA)_1 = 1.20 - 0.03CA + 127D_1 \qquad \bar{R}^2 = 0.652$$
$$(0.07) \quad (-.13) \quad (5.95)$$

$$+ 170D_2 + 83.8D_3 + 22.0D_4 + 81.5D_5$$
$$(8.32) \quad (3.82) \quad (1.02) \quad (3.84)$$

$$(S/CA)_2 = 5.51 - .122CA + 140D_1 \qquad \bar{R}^2 = 0.761$$
$$(0.36) \quad (-.57) \quad (7.56)$$

$$+ 187D_2 + 88.5D_3 + 21.5D_4 + 80.6D_5 ,$$
$$(10.55) \quad (4.65) \quad (1.15) \quad (4.38)$$

where the savings per cultivated acre variable is as defined in note 46. In

Table 4-32. Main Reasons for Not Using as Much Fertilizer as Desired by Various Categories of Farmers in Harmoia Village during Rabi 1970–71 and Kharif 1971–72

Size of holding (acres)	Cultivators reporting some difficulty	Main reasons for not using desired amount of fertilizer			
		Lack of credit	[a]Shortage of irrigation water	Nonavailability of fertilizer when required	Fertilizer sale point too far off[a]
			(percentage of fertilizer-users)		
Up to 6.00	100.00	94.12	20.59	2.94	2.94
>6.00 to 12.50	95.31	87.50	21.87	12.50	6.25
>12.50 to 25.00	60.09	56.52	17.39	4.35	8.70
>25.00	50.00	—	50.00	—	—
All sizes[b]	89.43	82.11	21.13	8.13	5.69

Note: The percentages in the rows may add to more than 100 because the farmers may have more than one reason for not using the desired amount of fertilizer.

[a]The nearest fertilizer sale point is at a distance of 12 miles.
[b]The percentage in the row "All sizes" have been weighted according to number of farmers in each category.

Source: K. M. Azam, "The Future of the Green Revolution in West Pakistan," *International Journal of Agrarian Affairs* 5 (6) (March 1973).

Table 4–33. Main Constraints on Farm Production Faced by Different Categories of Farmers in Harmoia Village, Lyallpur District, during Rabi 1970–71 and Kharif 1971–72

Size of holding (acres)	Irrigation water	Credit	Fertilizer	Improved seed	Plant protection
	(percentage of farmers)				
Up to 6.00	88.23	94.11	14.70	—	—
>6.00 to 12.50	92.18	62.50	25.00	6.25	7.81
>12.50 to 25.00	72.91	43.43	43.48	13.04	8.69
>25.00	50.00	—	—	50.00	100.00
All sizes[a]	86.99	66.66	25.20	6.50	7.31

Note: The percentages in the rows may add to more than 100 because farmers may have faced more than one constraint.

[a]The percentages in the row 'All sizes' have been weighted according to number of farmers in each category.

Source: K. M. Azam, "The Future of the Green Revolution in West Pakistan," *International Journal of Agrarian Affairs* 5 (6) (March 1973).

this case, too, no significant relation between farm size and savings per cultivated acre emerges, suggesting that a given amount of land tends to generate about the same amount of savings, whether operated in large farms or in small ones.

Farm Size and Technological Advance. Herring and Chaudhry, among others, have posed the question of whether or not land redistribution (i.e., a small-farm structure) would slow down the introduction of tubewells and tractors with negative-yield effects. The complementarity (via risk reduction) between the assured supplemental water from the tubewell and the growing of new varieties is noted. Considerable evidence suggests that larger farms are the first to adopt new technologies, which then spread to small farms, after benefits are demonstrated. A number of observers have felt that the record of small farmers in adopting the new seed-fertilizer technology is quite impressive, despite the resource constraints faced.[47] In any case, it is important to take note of the evidence on relative adoption and use of modern inputs by farm size.

As of 1960, smaller farms compared quite favorably in this respect. The 1959–60 agricultural census showed the use of fertilizers, both chemical and organic, to be much higher on smaller farms, the share of net sown area manured fell from 58 percent[48] on farms of less than 1 acre to 5 percent on farms with 50 acres and up; mounds of chemical fertilizers per acre of net sown area fell from 0.64 in small-size categories to around 0.1 for the category of farms above 12.5 acres (Table 4–34). The very small

Table 4-34. West Pakistan: Use of Fertilizers by Farm Size, 1960 and 1972

Farm size (acres)	Percent of farms reporting use of any fertilizer		Percent of cropped area fertilized	Percent of net sown area fertilized	Percent of farms reporting use of chemical fertilizer	Maunds of chemical fertilizer per acre of net sown area
	1960	1972	1972	1960	1960	1960
Less than 1.0	16.2	34	35	58	2.22	0.643
1.0 to under 2.5	25.4	44	42	30	4.18	0.387
2.5 to under 5.0	32.1	48	42	19	5.81	0.237
5.0 to under 7.5	36.6	51	42	15	7.16	0.169
7.5 to under 12.5	41.2	55	43	13	8.70	0.141
12.5 to under 25.0	44.0	58	43	10	9.90	0.113
25.0 to under 50.0	41.3	53	41	8	9.37	0.091
50.0 to under 150.0	26.6	45	41	5	6.48	0.091
150.0 and over	13.5	39	49	5	5.19	0.118
All farms	32.6	52	43	12	6.42	0.138

(continued on next page)

Table 4-34. (Continued)

Farm Size (acres)	Percent of farms reporting use of any fertilizer, 1960			Percent of net sown area fertilized, 1960			Maunds of chemical fertilizer per acre of net sown area, 1960		
	Owner	Owner cum tenant	Tenant	Owner	Owner cum tenant	Tenant	Owner	Owner cum tenant	Tenant
Under 1.0	14.98	24.16	17.44	59	51	57	0.574	0.526	0.764
1.0 to 2.5	24.39	34.35	24.19	30	31	29	0.327	0.423	0.440
2.5 to 5.0	31.94	42.94	27.60	21	22	17	0.230	0.259	0.233
5.0 to 7.5	37.40	48.59	30.32	17	17	13	0.190	0.182	0.150
7.5 to 12.5	41.32	53.01	35.36	14	14	11	0.192	0.148	0.132
12.5 to 25.0	43.97	52.50	39.42	12	11	9	0.150	0.113	0.091
25.0 to 50.0	38.93	53.43	40.73	10	8	7	0.122	0.092	0.070
50.0 to 150.0	23.45	28.42	29.77	7	4	5	0.126	0.079	0.064
150.0 and over	13.64	17.90	7.86	7	3	4	0.153	0.038	0.118
All farms	29.51	45.91	30.27	14	11	11	0.168	0.129	0.123

Sources: Pakistan, 1959–60 Agricultural Census and 1972 Agricultural Census.

farms of less than 2.5 acres formed a special category, with use much higher than that of intermediate-sized farms of 2.5 to 12.5 acres; intensity of this input did not decline for chemical fertilizers, but did for manure in the larger-size categories. Among tenure categories, with size held constant, differences were less noticeable, although owner-farms had the highest percent of net sown area manured, with owner *cum* tenant farms and tenant farms a little lower; the low figure for the owner *cum* tenants may reflect their having rented to a point where their land/labor ratio and land to other inputs ratio was atypically high—certainly higher than in the case of some other farms.

With respect to chemical fertilizers the most striking differences were at the larger-farm sizes, where application was highest on the owned-farms (Table 4-34). On small farms, by contrast, it tended to be somewhat higher on the tenanted farms and a little lower on the owned-farms, or owned *cum* tenanted farms. One wonders whether this reflected the involvement of the landlord in the case of sharecropping; possibly either credit or the fertilizer itself was supplied by him.

The 1972 agricultural census shows a markedly higher proportion of farms applying fertilizer (52 percent vs. 33 percent in 1960) and a higher share of cropped land receiving fertilizer (43 percent vs. 12 percent of net sown area in 1960 and an even lower share of cropped area). This dramatic increase is observed also in chemical fertilizer usage, estimated to have increased by about twenty-fold between these years.[49] The intercensal period saw a much faster growth in the usage of fertilizer on large farms than on small ones; whereas percent of net sown area fertilized bore a strongly inverse relationship to farm size in 1960, there was little relationship in 1972 (Table 4-34).

Recent sample survey data, focused especially on wheat areas, are instructive with respect to adoption of new seeds. They reveal, generally, a tendency for larger farms to adopt the new Mexican wheats earlier than small farms, but for the lag to be short. A survey by Lowdermilk produced the figures in Table 4-35. The striking fact is the high share of small farms adopting in the second year.[50] Azam cites other surveys in Pakistan, all of which found high adoption ratios on all farm sizes; even among *barani* (rain fed) farmers in the Hazara District, Rochen found in 1970 that 69 percent were adopters.[51] In a drier *barani* region, the Planning and Development Department of the Government of the Punjab carried out a survey and found only one of 43 farmers had tried the Mexican wheat. The main determinant of the adoption of these water- and fertilizer-responding varieties is thus the availability of water. Size and tenure *per se*

Table 4-35. Percentage of Sample Farmers Reporting Cultivation of Some Dwarf Wheat, by Rabi Season, and Percentage Expecting to Cultivate in 1970-71

Size of holding (acres)	1966-67 or before	1967-68	1968-69	1969-70	Expect in 1970-71
2.5 to <7.5	8	66	71	81	85
7.5 to 12.5	10	69	90	91	86
12.5 to 25	8	66	86	90	93
25 to 50	14	71	88	94	95
50 and above	39	88	95	99	99

Source: Max K. Lowdermilk, *Preliminary Report of the Diffusion and Adoption of Dwarf Wheat Varieties in Khanewal Tehsil, West Pakistan* (Ithaca: Cornell University, 1971, mimeo.), p. 4.

appear to have little to do with it; lack of credit accounts for part of the lag of smaller farmers, but does not hold them up for long if the pay-off is high.

The proposition that lack of funds, or possibly risk aversion, rather than lack of awareness explains any tendency for small farms to use less of such modern inputs as fertilizer is supported by the Harmoia sample, which shows high shares of all farm sizes applying fertilizers, but for some crops substantially lower quantities of nutrient per acre on the small farms.

With respect to the implications of the Green Revolution for small farmers in Pakistan, Azam felt:

The evidence of the present and other authors given above indicates that while the smaller farmers do face relatively more severe constraints of irrigation water and credit, the difference in the severity of these constraints is not serious enough to have caused any significant differences in the yields obtained by the small farmers as compared with larger farmers . . . . In view of the evidence presented above, we would tend to reject the hypothesis that small farmers have been unable to finance complementary inputs and that they need special price incentives and special credit and extension support in order to adopt the new technology. However, we are of the view that there is need for a more extensive survey before we are in a position categorically to reject this hypothesis.[52]

Technological Gap and the Weakening of the Inverse Relationship between Farm Size and Land Productivity.   The FAFBS data from the Punjab suggested that small-farm productivity still exceeded that on large farms as recently as the late 1960s. More recent evidence tends, by and large, to confirm this. The 1972 agricultural census results have not been analyzed in detail; one calculation of crop production measured in caloric equivalents, and assuming the same yields for all farm sizes, suggests a differential between farms of under 5 acres and over 150 of 30 percent (latters' productivity lower than that of the former). The differential in value of crop output in 1960 was much higher, probably 70 percent.[53]

Khan's recent (1972-73) survey in five districts of the Punjab and four of the Sind confirms the weakening of the inverse size/land productivity relationship and indicates a gap between large and small farms in the use of new inputs; it also permits separate consideration of relatively progressive areas. In most regions studied, Khan finds a *positive* relationship between value of output of five major crops per cropped acre (or net farm income per cropped acre) and size (Table 4-36) and concludes that it is the large farmers who have mainly benefited from the Green Revolution in various regions of Pakistan. Part of these disproportionate benefits he links to government subsidies for modern inputs (chemical fertilizer, pesticides, farm machinery, and water) and part to their better credit facilities.[54]

Khan's survey was designed to include some progressive districts and some backward ones; of the nine, six are described as progressive. A positive relationship between farm size and output/cropped acre emerged in all of the progressive districts and some of the backward ones. This result does not differ qualitatively from what we have estimated for 1959-60, when for the same five crops it appeared that value of output per cropped acre was 5-10 percent higher on farms above 50 acres than on those below 12.5 acres (though highest of all for the middle-sized farms), but the differential implicit in Khan's figures in Punjab and Sind is greater (about 18 percent)—see Table 4-37, columns (4) and (7). The data are, of course, not fully comparable, the 1959-60 data referring to all of Pakistan and Khan's to a sample of farms in two of the four provinces. But they suggest considerable relative gains by the larger farmers. Although Khan does not present data on value of output per cultivated acre, a rough estimate based on ratios of cropped to cultivated area in Punjab and Sind from the 1972 agricultural census suggests that the smallest farms maintained about a 10 percent differential over the largest in 1972,[55] down from a 60 percent differential in 1960.[56] Output per acre appears still to have been much higher on small farms in 1972, but, as before, most of this differential is presumably due to less irrigation and lower quality land on the large farms. In short, the comparison of Khan's 1972-73 findings and our estimates based on the 1959-60 Census of Agriculture indicates that, if his districts were reasonably representative

Table 4-36. **Indexes of Land Productivity, Punjab and Sind: Khan's Sample**

Farm size (acres)	Relatively backward districts			Relatively progressive districts					
	Jhelum	Rahimyav Khan	Average	Gujranwala	Sahiwal	Lyallpur	Average	Punjab	Punjab and Sind
Punjab: value of farm output/cropped acre, five major crops									
<12.5	104.2	94.3	99.3	86.3	89.5	56.0	76.4	86.1	86.4
12.5–25	90.6	99.6	93.6	92.0	92.9	65.3	83.4	88.1	91.5
25–50	67.5	103.8	85.7	96.8	97.7	89.8	94.8	91.1	91.3
>50	50.4	99.2	74.8	113.8	104.4	121.0	113.1	97.8	101.7
Punjab: net farm income/cropped acre, five major crops									
<12.5	102.6	103.0	102.8	94.6	87.1	57.5	79.7	89.0	89.2
12.5–25	100.0	111.4	105.7	98.1	92.6	66.9	85.9	93.8	94.0
25–50	70.0	111.4	90.7	97.7	97.5	90.7	95.3	93.5	92.4
>50	39.4	92.8	66.1	106.1	104.8	119.9	110.3	92.6	99.0

Sind: value of farm output/cropped acre, five major crops

	Relatively backward districts		Relatively progressive districts		Average	Sind
	Jacobabad	Larkava	Nawabshah	Hyderabad		
<12.5	86.5	84.6	79.8	96.2	86.9	86.8
12.5–25	86.6	96.0	102.1	98.7	98.9	95.8
25–50	86.6	93.5	95.2	91.3	93.3	91.6
>50	110.9	106.5	104.0	104.5	105.0	106.5

Sind: net farm income/cropped acre, five major crops

	Jacobabad	Larkava	Nawabshah	Hyderabad	Average	Sind
<12.5	88.4	81.6	87.4	100.4	92.4	89.5
12.5–25	86.8	94.5	95.1	100.9	96.8	94.3
25–50	89.2	92.4	93.1	89.8	91.8	91.1
>50	109.5	108.1	105.8	104.1	106.0	106.9

Source: Adapted from M. H. Khan, *The Economics of The Green Revolution in Pakistan* (New York: Praeger Publishers, 1975), p. 54.

Note: Averages are unweighted across the districts to which they refer.

Table 4-37. Relative Crop Land Productivity: 1959-60 Census of Agriculture and 1972-73 Survey by Kahn

| | Census of Agriculture (1959-60) | | | | Khan: 1972-73 | | | | | | | | |
| | Value of crops (excl. fodder) Total area (1) | Value of crops (excl. fodder) Net sown area (except in fodder) (2) | Value of crops (excl. fodder) Cultivated area (except in fodder) (3) | Value of five[a] crops Cropped area (4) | Value of output/cropped acre: five major crops | | | Estimate of value of crop output/cultivated acre: five major crops | | | Estimate of value of output/acre: five major crops | | |
Farm size (Acres)					Punjab (5)	Sind (6)	Punjab & Sind (unweighted average) (7)	Punjab (8)	Sind (9)	Punjab & Sind (unweighted average) (10)	Punjab (11)	Sind (12)	Punjab & Sind (unweighted average) (13)
<12.5	122.0	101.2	106.0	93.08	86.1	86.8	86.4	103.0	114.0	108.5	98.8	108.9	103.9
12.5-25	124.1	106.8	110.5	105.4	88.1	95.8	91.5	98.1	111.1	104.6	91.4	99.0	95.2
25-50	102.9	100.9	100.4	107.7	91.1	91.6	91.3	97.3	95.4	96.4	85.8	74.9	80.4
≥50	4.69	78.87	65.20	99.8	97.8	106.5	101.7	101.6	96.8	99.2	76.5	57.2	66.9
All farms	100.0	100.0	100.0	100.0									

[a] Wheat, rice, maize, cotton, and sugar cane. These crops accounted for 79 percent of total sown area in the Punjab and 77 percent in Sind. M. H. Khan, *The Economics of the Green Revolution in Pakistan* (New York: Praeger Publishers, 1975). p. 13.

Sources: Table 4-31 and the sources used in that table provide the 1959-60 estimate. Cols. (5)-(7) are from Table 4-36. The remaining columns are based on Cols. (5)-(7) and the data on the ratios of cropped/cultivated and cropped/total farm acres, by size groups, from the 1972 agricultural census. In other words, if Khan's sample farms were typical of the two provinces in respect of these ratios, then the last 6 columns would correctly reflect the productivity differentials in those farms. In fact, the cropping intensities (cropped area/cultivated area) presented by Khan (ibid., p. 16) are much higher than emerge from the agricultural census. Possibly Khan's districts were atypical in this respect, or possibly the five crops he considers were atypical. The interpolation of his table is difficult as for some districts the district average cropping-intensity ratios appear to be inconsistent with those reported for the various farm-size categories.

of Pakistan,[57] a considerable gain in the relative efficiency of the larger farms (especially those over 50 acres) has occurred, although the shift is less than might at first appear.

In 1959-60, the relative advantage of smaller farms was based on the high value of livestock products and the higher share of land placed under crops, not on higher value of crops per net sown area (Table 4-31). If value of other agricultural sales were added to Khan's crop output data, the relative position of the larger farms would presumably look worse. Since aggregation across districts in our 1959-60 census-based estimates presumably raised the relative productivity of small farms above the level of the typical district, some part of the difference observed in Table 4-37 between those estimates and Khan's may be due to the higher level of aggregation in the former. But it seems likely that the intervening period has indeed witnessed a substantial improvement in the relative performance of large farms. It is important to trace, to the extent possible, the factors that have contributed to this relative (and, of course, absolute) improvement. The relatively small size of Khan's sample in most districts means that, for a given farm size, the standard error of estimate with respect to the universe must be substantial; it is, nevertheless, worthwhile taking a tentative look at whether a comparison with the 1959-60 Agricultural Census gives clues as to what sort of evolution has been occurring.

Table 4-38 presents a comparison of cropping intensities in 1960 and 1972; it suggests considerable increases in cropping intensity in all size categories, with the biggest increases typically occurring on the large farms of 150 acres or more. Thus, while the ratio of cropped/cultivable land rose by 14 percent overall, it nearly doubled on farms of 150 acres or more.

Khan's data on yields for the major crops in 1972-73 are summarized in Table 4-39. Yield-farm-size relationships vary with the crop; the relationship tends to be positive for wheat, cotton, and sugar, and undefined (i.e., variable) for rice and maize. At least in Khan's sample, the relationship for a given crop can differ substantially by district. The generally positive association with size appears to be somewhat stronger than in the earlier survey in the 1960s. As noted earlier, the relative use of fertilizer by large farms (in terms of the percent of net sown area fertilized) rose between 1960 and 1972. Khan finds a higher application per cropped acre on larger farms, for the crops he studied in 1972-73.[58] These farms have a lead, although usually a rather small one, in the adoption of new varieties.

Only after further observation in the future will it become clear whether the improved relative performance of large farms in Pakistan is a perma-

Table 4-38. Changes in Intensity of Agriculture, 1960-72

Farm size (acres)	Cultivated Total		Cultivated Cultivable		Net Sown Cultivable		Cropped Net sown		Cropped Cultivable		Cropped Cultivated	
	1960 (1)	1972 (2)	1960 (3)	1972 (4)	1960 (5)	1972 (6)	1960 (7)	1972 (8)	1960[a] (9)	1972[b] (10)	1960 (11)	1972 (12)
<1	79.8	92	90.3	97.6	81	94.9	138	156.3	111.8	148.3	123	152
1- 2.5	85.8	91	91.7	97.3	82	93.5	130	143.0	106.6	133.7	116	137
2.5- 5	87.1	92	92.3	97	83	93.1	128	135.9	106.2	126.5	115	131
5- 7.5	88.2	93	92.8	97	84	92.8	127	131.1	106.7	121.7	114.5	125
7.5-12.5	88.2	93	92.3	96	83	94.1	124	124.5	102.9	117.2	111.3	119
12.5-25	85.5	90	90.1	94	80	87.6	119	118.6	95.2	103.9	106.3	111
25-50	78.0	84	84.0	89	72	80.8	115	114.2	82.8	92.3	98.0	103
50-150	59.4	71	69.3	79	54	57.8	109	112.5	58.9	65.0	85.5	97
≥150	34.6	46	50.6	61.32[c]	27	48.9	108	110.4	29.2	54.0	57.5	88
All farms	65.4	83	84.0	89	72	82.1	120	120.1	86.4	98.6	102.8	111

[a]Calculated as col. (7) times col. (5).
[b]Calculated as col. (8) times col. (6).
[c]The figure shown in page 8 of the census is 58, whereas our calculation comes to 61.32.

Source: 1960 Agricultural Census, p. 217. 1972 Agricultural Census, pp. 7, 13. Data refer to "private farms"; there were an insignificant number of government farms.

Table 4-39. Yield per Acre, Selected Crops, Punjab and Sind (in maunds, 82.28 lbs.)

District, Farm Size	Wheat		Rice			Cotton		Sugar-cane	Maize	
	Local	Mexi-Pak	Local	Basmati	IRRI	Local	Improved		Local	Improved
Punjab: Relatively Backward District										
Rahimyar	9.7	15.8	6.1*	22.5	54.0	7.9	11.0	41.8	9.3	
<12.50	9.2	15.6				8.1	10.2	37.2	6.0	
12.50–25.00	10.0	15.1	30.0		54.0	6.0	10.3	38.6	12.0	
25.00–50.00	9.2	13.7	12.5	22.5		9.0	10.4	44.0	12.0	
>50.00	12.5	16.8	3.5*			8.0.	11.6	41.9	8.0	
Punjab: Relatively Progressive Districts										
Gujranwala, Sahiwal, and Lyallpur	15.7	22.8	20.1	20.6	31.8	11.5	16.2	37.4	10.2	24.7
<12.50	13.7	19.1	21.6	20.3	31.9	9.0	12.8	36.5	10.0	18.1
12.50–25.00	13.8	21.7	20.2	18.8	29.8	7.9	14.4	33.7	10.8	24.2
25.00–50.00	16.0	23.0	19.1	21.4	30.1	11.8	15.7	36.8		25.6
>50.00	16.4	23.1	21.3	21.8	33.9	10.5	17.3	37.6		20.2

Table 4-39. (Continued)

District, Farm Size	Wheat		Rice			Cotton		Sugar-cane	Maize	
	Local	Mexi-Pak	Local	Basmati	IRRI	Local	Improved		Local	Improved
Sind: Relatively Backward District										
Jacobabad	8.7	8.4	17.7		23.6					
<12.50	7.7		18.1		30.0					
12.50–25.00	7.9	6.9	16.6		28.0					
25.00–50.00	5.8	6.8	18.0		23.9					
>50.00	10.0	9.2	17.8		22.9					
Sind: Relatively Progressive Districts										
Larkana, Nawabshah, and Hyderabad	12.0	26.6	19.2	19.1	29.7	14.9	16.6	641.6	27.5	
<12.50	7.3	27.1		17.0	32.8	11.8	15.0	643.8	40.0	
12.50–25.00	7.6	24.3			28.6	11.3	16.0	706.0	15.0	
25.00–50.00	7.8	23.7	18.5	18.6	29.3	11.5	16.1	643.2		
>50.00	9.3	28.9	19.2	20.0	30.9	19.2	17.1	625.7		

*This figure appears unrealistic.

Notes: The output of sugarcane has been expressed in *gur* form in the Punjab and in cane form in Sind.
Blank spaces indicate data not applicable.
Where figures refer to more than one district, they are unweighted averages of the district figures.

Source: Adapted from M. H. Kahn. *The Economics of the Green Revolution* (New York: Praeger Publishers, 1975), p. 17.

nent or a transitory phenomenon. It seems possible that there will be some tendency for the inverse relationship to strengthen again, as the rate of varietal and other types of technological improvement slows down and/or access to inputs becomes more evenly distributed. Varietal change is likely to slow down; even if it does not, smaller farmers may soon become accustomed to changing varieties quickly. But if such inputs as tubewells and mechanized cultivation have unavoidable indivisibilities, the size-productivity relation is unlikely to again become as negative as it was in 1960; for example, the greater profitability of cultivating marginal land will preclude the degree of underutilization characteristic of pre-Green Revolution years, while the tractor simplifies such cultivation and, in some cases, contributes to making previously uncultivable land usable.[59]

Effects of the Technological Gap on Income and Land Distribution. Between the two agricultural censuses, parts of Pakistan benefited substantially from new technology, including better varieties and the further spread of tubewells. And the availability of machines now makes it possible for them to dispense with the labor-intensive techniques previously used (and normally taking the form of share cropping arrangements with tenants). Many observers have argued that this growth process has worsened the agricultural income distribution, either by leading to a more concentrated land distribution and/or because large farmers have benefited disproportionately from yield increases, tubewells, etc. Tractorization and mechanization, part of government policy, is viewed with suspicion by many observers for the same reasons. Some of the evidence discussed above is consistent with the proposition that large farmers have raised the intensity of their cultivation more than have small farmers.

While the data on number and size structure of farms are not comparable between the two censuses, the distribution of farm area by form of tenancy shows a striking decline in the share of all land farmed by tenants with no land of their own—from 39 percent in 1960 to 29 percent in 1972. There was a moderate decline in percentage of land rented (49 percent to 45 percent), with the decline in area farmed by landless tenants being largely offset by an increase of renting by owner *cum* tenants. Among large farms of 50 acres and up, the increasing importance of the owner *cum* tenant category was especially in evidence, with the share of land in this category rising from 22.5 to 33.6.

Evaluating the causes and effects of the shift away from tenanted land must await further research. Since one possible explanation is that it is a result of the decision by large landowners to operate their own land on a mechanized basis, after evicting their tenants,[60] there are obvious grounds for concern. Those grounds are strengthened by the evidence that, despite their relative gains in the period in question, the large farms were still characterized by similar or lower land productivity than the small ones, so no output gains could be expected from the increasing size of operational units.

The effect of a decreasing share of land under tenancy is also ambiguous. There have been, to our knowledge, no studies of the relationship between tenure and productivity in Pakistan, although it is interesting to note that land utilization is generally a little higher on tenanted farms, given farm size, than on owner-operated farms or farms where part of the land is owned and part rented (Table 4-40). Of land that is cropped, a higher share tends to be irrigated and a higher share fertilized on tenanted land than on owned land (Table 4-41). These relationships may not be causal ones; it could be argued that there is a tendency for better land—that which can generate a surplus—to be rented out more than poor land. But the data certainly give no support to the various hypotheses that imply lower utilization on tenanted land than on owned land.

4.5   INDIA

Appendix A of this study presents a detailed analysis of the relationships between farm size, land productivity, and technical change for India. That investigation draws upon NCAER household survey data for the three years 1968-69 through 1970-71. These data provide important advantages over those used in most previous studies on India, because they are for all of India; they are at the farm level instead of being grouped into size-class averages, and they span an important recent period during the Green Revolution.

Analysis of the relationship of farm size to productivity has a long tradition in India, as does the central conclusion of most of that analysis: output per acre declines as farm size rises. Although there is extensive debate on the causes of this pattern, there is a general consensus that it exists—or at least that it existed prior to the Green Revolution of the late 1960s. Much of the empirical evidence on the relationship has come from the Farm Management Studies (FMS) of the 1950s, a series of farm surveys

Table 4-40. Relative Intensity of Land Use by Tenure and Size, 1972

Farm size (acres)	Owner		Owner *cum* tenant		Tenant	
	cultivated/culturable	cropped area/net sown area	cultivated/culturable	cropped area/net sown area	cultivated/culturable	cropped area/net sown area
<1	.97	1.51	.99	1.47	1.00	1.57
1–2.5	.96	1.35	.98	1.40	0.99	1.42
2.5–5	.96	1.27	.98	1.29	0.99	1.37
5–7.5	.95	1.20	.98	1.23	0.99	1.32
7.5–12.5	.93	1.15	.97	1.18	0.98	1.21
12.5–25	.90	1.09	.94	1.11	0.96	1.13
25–50	.86	1.02	.90	1.04	0.92	1.04
50–150	.76	0.97	.82	0.98	0.79	0.96
≥150	.57	0.86	.60	0.91	0.59	0.93
All farms	0.84	1.07	0.90	1.09	0.94	1.16

Note: Cultivated area includes net sown area and fallow area. Cropped area allows for the effect of multiple cropping by including a given plot of land each time it is harvested in the course of a year. A good overall measure of utilization would be the ratio of cropped area to culturable area, but data on fallow land are not shown by tenure classes in the source, making it impossible to calculate this ratio.

Source: Pakistan Census of Agriculture 1972: All Pakistan Report, Data by Provinces, pp. 7–9.

Table 4-41.   Percent of Cropped Area Irrigated and Fertilized, by Tenure and Farm Size, 1972

Farm size (acres)	Owner		Owner cum tenant		Tenant	
	Irrigated	Fertilized	Irrigated	Fertilized	Irrigated	Fertilized
1	60	33	72	39	82	44
1-2.5	67	39	73	46	84	50
2.5-5	71	41	72	41	81	45
5-7.5	74	43	74	39	81	44
7.5-12.5	75	41	74	39	85	47
12.5-25	79	43	75	39	87	47
25-50	77	43	70	39	82	42
50-150	70	42	63	39	73	42
≥150	70	47	74	51	81	57
All farms	74	42	72	40	84	46

Source: Pakistan Census of Agriculture 1972; All Pakistan Report, Data by Provinces, pp. 21-22.

that provided data by farm-size group averages on production and other economic variables.

Table 4-42 presents a review of regression results organized by C. H. H. Rao for three regions and a number of years, showing the negative relationship between gross value of output per acre and farm size, and a tendency for that inverse relationship to weaken between the 1950s and the 1960s. Table 4-43 presents data on gross output per acre by farm size from a number of different states.

In the Indian case, the causes of declining output per acre as farm size rises have been debated at length. One hypothesis has been that smaller farms have higher quality soil, for reasons such as past "forced sales" of lower quality portions of formerly larger farms; or, the Malthusian proposition that family size grew to larger proportions on farms with more fertile land, leading to greater fragmentation of those farms through inheritance. Another major hypothesis is that the labor market is dualistic and cheap family labor has led to greater output per area on smaller farms. In Appendix A, Surjit Bhalla reviews these and other arguments in the debate and presents the theoretical arguments he considers most relevant for India at this time.

While there has been general agreement that in the 1950s an inverse relationship existed between farm size and output per acre, there has also been a strong suspicion that this relationship weakened or even reversed itself during the course of the Green Revolution, in the late 1960s and

Table 4-42. Relationship between the Gross Value of Output Per Acre and Farm Size

Year		Muzaffarnagar (Uttar Pradesh)	
		Slope (b)	Coefficient of correlation
1955-56		-0.25^a	-0.46
1956-57		-0.17^a	-0.33
1966-67		-0.14^a	-0.25
1967-68		-0.09^b	-0.25
1968-69		-0.04^c	-0.17
		Ferozepur (Punjab)	
1955-56		-0.06	-0.09
1956-57		-0.17^b	-0.28
1967-68		-0.03	-0.05
1968-69		-0.03	-0.04
		West Godavari (Andhra Pradesh)	
1957-60			
	Output	-0.11^c	-0.62
	Labor	-0.13^b	-0.82
	Fertilizer	-0.05	-0.21
1969-70	Output	0.02	0.15
	Labor	-0.16^b	-0.86
	Fertilizer	0.10^c	0.77

[a]Significant at 0.1 percent level.
[b]Significant at 1 percent level.
[c]Significant at 5 percent level; the remaining coefficients are not significant at 5 percent level.

Source: C. H. H. Rao, Technological Change and Distribution of Gains in Indian Agriculture (Delhi: MacMillan Co. of India Ltd., 1975), p. 143.

Original Sources: (1) The results pertaining to Muzaffarnagar and Ferozepur are taken from N. Bhattacharya and G. R. Saini, "Farm Size and Productivity: A Fresh Look," Economic and Political Weekly, Review of Agriculture, 24 June 1972. (2) The results relating to West Godavari for the period 1957-60 are obtained by using the data contained in Directorate of Economics and Statistics, Ministry of Food and Agriculture. Studies in Economics of Farm Management, West Godavari. (3) The results relating to West Godavari for the year 1969-70 are obtained on the basis of the data contained in Waheeduddin Khan and R. N. Tripathy, Intensive Agriculture and Modern Inputs: Prospects of Small Farmers—A Study in West Godavari District, National Institute of Community Development (Hyderabad, 1972), pp. 13, 64, 76.

early 1970s, because of presumed advantages of the larger farms in access to and use of the new technologies. C. H. H. Rao noted this trend (Table 4-42). The data and analyses of Appendix A permit an evaluation of this possibility, since the underlying survey data span the critical period 1968-69 through 1970-71, when major changes due to the Green Revolution were taking place.

Table 4-43. Gross Output per Acre by Farm Size: India, Selected Regions, Farm Management Studies Data (Rs. per Acre)

Size group (acres)	Average size of farm	Gross output per acre
Uttar Pradesh		
Below 5	3.3	263
5-10	7.6	267
10-15	12.1	205
15-20	16.9	227
Above 20	27.6	259
Punjab		
Below 5	3.8	200
5-10	7.4	186
10-20	14.4	173
20-50	29.1	155
Above 50	78.8	142
West Bengal		
Up to 1.25	0.66	232
1.26-2.50	1.81	241
2.51-3.75	3.10	233
3.76-5.00	4.35	202
5.01-7.50	6.23	238
7.51-10.00	8.36	224
10.01-15.00	12.13	175
Above 15.00	23.23	189
Andhra		
Up to 1.25	0.72	470
1.26-2.50	1.81	433
2.51-5.00	3.54	376
5.01-7.50	6.15	307
7.51-10.00	8.97	326
10.01-15.00	12.33	379
15.01-20.00	17.01	401
Above 20.00	31.82	334
Madras		
Up to 1.25	1.54	267
2.5-5.0	3.59	237
5.0-7.5	5.93	198
7.5-10.0	8.66	193
10.0-15.0	11.64	125
15.0-20.0	16.93	74
20.0-25.0	22.07	90
Above 25.0	46.24	68
Madhya Pradesh		
Up to 5	2.95	102
5-10	7.35	87
10-15	12.45	89
15-20	17.05	80
20-30	24.25	79
30-40	34.65	81
40-50	44.25	90
Above 50	85.40	86

Table 4-43. (Continued)

Size group (acres)	Average size of farm	Gross output per acre
Bombay		
Up to 5	2.8	121
5-10	7.7	120
10-15	12.1	65
15-20	17.0	85
20-25	22.3	51
25-30	27.6	61
30-50	37.3	68
Above 50	66.4	42

Source: C. H. Hanuamantha Rao, *Agricultural Production Functions, Costs and Returns in India* (Bombay, Asia Publishing House), p. 11.

Tables 4-44 through 4-47 summarize some of the major empirical results of Appendix A. The principal findings are the following:

(1) The hypothesized inverse relationship between farm size and output per farm area is confirmed empirically. (Table 4-44, equation i, shows a highly significant negative coefficient of output per acre on the logarithm of farm size.)

(2) The relationship holds even when the influence of land quality (as reflected by land price) is removed (equation iii, Table 4-44). It holds even when an extreme test is made by removing the influence of irrigation as well (equation iv, Table 4-44).

(3) The relationship holds systematically at the level of the individual product sector, so that changing product-mix alone does not account for declining output per farm area (Table A-3, Appendix A).

(4) The inverse relationship persists in the third year, although its steepness is moderately reduced. This finding means that the Green Revolution has, at most, weakened somewhat the pattern of lower land productivity on larger farms. (Compare the coefficient on logarithm of farm size in Table 4-44 for equations i, 1970-71, and ii, 1968-69.)

(5) Regressions of inputs used on farm size confirm the hypothesis that factor combinations shift away from labor toward land and (to a lesser degree) capital as farm size rises. The elasticity of input use with respect to farm size (percent rise in input use per percentage rise in farm land area) is only 0.55 for labor, 0.74 for capital, and 0.77 for seeds, fertilizers, and insecticides (equations ii through iv Table 4-45).

Table 4-44. Selected Empirical Estimates of the Relationship of Farm Size to Productivity: India, 1968-69 and 1970-71

Regression parameters:						
Constant	Coefficients			$\overline{R^2}$	Year	Equation
a	b	c	d			
882 (41.6)	−130 (13.6)	—	—	.095	1970–71	i
918 (37.9)	−168 (15.6)	—	—	.120	1968–69	ii
663 (30.0)	−108 (11.9)	.07 (15.3)	—	.200	1970–71	iii
496 (22.0)	−92 (11.6)	.046 (11.0)	4.6 (23.8)	.393	1970–71	iv

Notes: Absolute value of *t*-statistic in parentheses.
Model: $y = a + b \log A + cP + dI$,
where y is output per farm area, A is farm area, P is price of unirrigated land, I is percent of land under irrigation.

Source: Appendix A, Tables A-2, A-13.

Table 4-45. Regression Results for Selected Tests on Factor Cost and Factor-Use Intensity by Farm Size, India, 1970–71

Dependent variable	Coefficients on: Constant	A	log A	P	I	$\overline{R}^2$	Equation
rental/acre	203 (5.2)	−4.9 (1.9)	—	.027 (1.98)	.46 (.76)	.19	(i)
log K	6.8 (110.3)	—	.74 (27.5)	—	—	.34	(ii)
log S	4.1 (55.1)	—	.77 (23.7)	—	—	.28	(iii)
log L	5.2 (127.9)	—	.55 (31.2)	—	—	.40	(iv)

Notes: A = farm area (acres); K = capital stock; S = expenses on seeds, fertilizers, and insecticides; L = labor input; P = price of unirrigated land; I = percentage of land under irrigation.

Source: Appendix A, Table A-4 and section A-3.4.

(6) Data for land rental prices (equation i, Table 4–45) and interest rates on borrowed capital (Table 4–46) support the hypotheses that these prices are higher for the smaller farmers and that they probably play an important role in (a) the declining output per land available and (b) the shift from labor to capital, as farm size rises.

(7) Total social factor productivity also declines as farm size rises (Appendix A, Table A–13 [b]). When a social wage of zero is applied for labor cost, total social factor productivity is 35 percent higher on farms under 5 acres than on farms over 25 acres. When one-half the market wage is used as the social cost of labor, total social factor productivity holds approximately constant over the two smallest size groups (up to 15 acres), at a level from 20 to 25 percent higher than that obtained on farms over 25 acres. Even when the full wage is used as the cost of labor, total social factor productivity declines as size rises (after initially rising from the smallest size group to the second group, 5–15 acres).

(8) For the range of larger farms (those above 30 acres) the inverse relationship between farm size and output per farm area is not found to be statistically significant, suggesting that in India the dominant influence on the overall size-productivity relationship is labor-market dualism—which phases out after a threshold size is reached above which primarily wage labor rather than family labor is employed. (See section A–3.3[d], Appendix A.)

(9) The data on adoption of high-yielding varieties indicate that the percentage of farm area under HYVs is approximately as high for small farms as for large farms (Table 4–47, column C), meaning that it would be inaccurate to depict small farms as laggards in the adoption of technological change.

(10) Nevertheless, during the period of the Green Revolution, larger farms do appear to have increased both output per acre and the fraction of their farm area under HYVs more rapidly than smaller farms (Table 4–47, columns D and E). Even so, the negative relationship between farm size and land productivity has changed relatively little (the absolute value of the coefficient of output per acre on the logarithm of farm size declined by one-quarter to one-third during the period 1968–69 to 1970–71). (Note that, as discussed above, the same relative change, perhaps to a more sizable degree, appears to have occurred in at least some regions of Pakistan, although the data available for the case of Pakistan are less reliable than those for India.) This phenomenon represented more a catching up by the large farms than a lagging behind by the small. The

Table 4-46. Cost of Borrowed Capital by Farm Size (Percent per Annum)

Farm size (acres)	Percent rate
Below 5	17.3
5-15	13.8
15-25	12.2
Over 25	11.8

Source: Appendix A, Table A-5.

Table 4-47. Indicators of Technical Change by Farm Size, India, 1968-69 to 1970-71

Farm size (acres)	Adoption of HYVs, 1970-71			Percent change, 1968-69 to 1970-71, in:	
	% of farms A	% of farms with irrigation B	% area of farm under HYVs C	income/acre D	fraction of farm area under HYVs E
Below 5	29.1	42.1	16.5	9.0	13.0
5-15	33.4	45.3	16.3	13.2	27.3
15-25	42.7	58.1	18.5	13.1	41.2
Over 25	36.7	44.4	18.1	42.4	63.1

Source: Appendix A, Tables A-14 and A-15.

relative change was probably facilitated by easier and cheaper access to credit for large farms than for small.

(11) Finally, regression analysis relating output per acre to farm size, price of land, percent of area under irrigation, and percent of land leased in shows no statistically significant effect of tenure condition (area leased in) upon land productivity. This finding tends to support the Cheung hypothesis that sharecropping need not reduce allocative efficiency, as opposed to the Marshallian approach, which predicts lower land productivity because of the disincentive to the use of variable inputs under sharecropping.

The main thrust of these findings is that India, like other countries considered in this chapter, possesses relatively underutilized land in its large-farm sector and a relatively high application of labor on its small-farm sector, so that land redistribution could be expected to raise agricultural output as well as agricultural employment. Moreover, this diagnosis, which is consistent with earlier evaluations for India, remains valid even at the present time, after a period of rapid technological change, even though this change has somewhat improved the relative land utilization of large farms. Furthermore, as the adoption of HYVs becomes more generalized over time, it is plausible that the small farms will regain their earlier, still wider margin of superiority over large farms in land productivity. This possibility is enhanced by the fact that the new technology of the Green Revolution is basically scale-neutral (improved seeds, fertilizer, insecticides). However, the natural tendency in this direction could be impeded by the lack of availability of credit to smaller farms. This consideration leads to the policy implication that, in the absence of land redistribution, an important measure will be the channeling of credit facilities toward the small-farm sector.

4.6   MALAYSIA, MUDA RIVER AREA

Farm Size and Productivity.   This relatively homogeneous agricultural area has been the subject of a careful recent (1972-73) survey; the detail available permits consideration of some issues that could not be dealt with in the other countries or regions discussed here. Muda River is of interest partly because of its relatively mono-crop character—rice is the dominant product, accounting for over 90 percent of total value of farm output. It is also characterized by rather smoothly functioning markets, as far as can be ascertained.[61] Large differences in land productivity by size are thus unlikely to arise as a result either of different output composition or of labor-market dualism in particular or differential input prices in general.

Table 4-48 presents data on factor productivity with double-cropping farms grouped, as usual, by size.[62] As between the smallest farms (less than 1.5 relongs[63]) and those over 10.5 relongs (among which there is no noticeable association with size) land productivity (value-added per relong) falls by about two-thirds. Very high land productivity is only characteristic of the smallest farms, however, so that by the range 1.5 to 3.5 relongs, productivity is only 50 to 60 percent above that of the large farms just cited. Farms of below 5 relongs have an average land productivity 32 percent greater than those above 5 relongs.[64] The data permit some judgment as to whether or not the decrease in productivity with size is associated with land quality; in fact, the opposite is the case, average stated value of land per relong being noticeably higher on the larger farms. Value of capital per relong, on the other hand, tends to be negatively associated with size, being something over twice as high on

Table 4-48. Factor Productivity of Muda River Farms by Size, Double-Croppers, 1972-73[a]

Area of farm at beginning of year (relongs)	Number of farms	Value-added in agriculture/ relong	VAA/ value of land	VAA/ value of land and capital	Value of land per relong	Value of capital per relong	Value of farm output /relong	Value of farm output/ Value of land	Value of farm output/ Value of land and capital
	(1)	(2)	(3)	(4)	(5)	(6)	(7)	(8)	(9)
<1.5	47	843 (764)	1.18	0.408	715	1353	883	1.24	.427
1.5-2.49	104	454 (457)	0.665	0.261	683	1056	535	0.784	.308
2.5-3.49	118	485 (488)	0.674	0.277	719	1033	570	0.792	.326
3.5-4.99	104	392 (395)	0.441	0.222	890	881	473	0.532	.268
5.0-6.49	176	378 (377)	0.362	0.215	1045	714	441	0.422	.251
6.5-8.49	88	378 (381)	0.354	0.216	1066	684	467	0.437	.267
8.5-10.49	58	325 (324)	0.296	0.181	1098	702	403	0.367	.224
10.5-14.99	37	302 (298)	0.212	0.169	1423	371	376	0.264	.210
15.0-19.99	20	312 (308)	0.247	0.183	1261	445	379	0.300	.222
20.0-39.99	10	287 (283)	0.270	0.158	1064	758	360	0.339	.198
All farms	762	370	0.451	0.223	1054	606	446	0.544	.269

[a]Use of area of farm at beginning of the year as the measure of farm-size biases the results somewhat in favor of small farms, though by no means enough to explain the observed differentials in columns (2) and (7). (See note 64 of text.)

Note: Columns are calculated by summing across all farms for the numerator and denominator. Figures in parentheses are means of the value of the ratio in question across farms. Given the small differences in size across farms in a given category, this difference in methodology is not of much significance.

Source: Muda River Survey, calculations by the author.

Table 4-48. (Continued)

VAA Labor Index	Purchased inputs Value of farm output	Purchased inputs Relong	Value of Padi rice as a share of value of farm output	Labor share of value-added	Hired labor share	Total factor productivity[b]
(0)	(11)	(12)	(13)	(14)	(15)	(16)
.734	.050	40	.834	.174	.049	1.65
.567	.151	81	.899	.196	.087	1.15
.627	.149	85	.920	.198	.097	1.20
.542	.171	81	.921	.224	.123	0.99
.553	.143	63	.893	.195	.116	0.99
.615	.191	89	.945	.226	.145	0.96
.537	.194	78	.961	.246	.170	0.83
.555	.197	74	.955	.302	.209	0.75
.645	.177	67	.958	.288	.211	0.80
.611	.203	73	.955	.332	.245	0.69
All farms .614	.169	75	.928	.212	.123	1.00

[b]Defined as the ratio of value-added in agriculture to the sum of labor costs (hired plus imputed family labor) and the value of land and capital times the estimated average rate of return of 17.6 percent.

Table 4-49. Family Income Structure by Farm Size, Double-Croppers, 1972–73

Farm size (relongs)	Value-added in agriculture/relong	Net income from agriculture/relong	Family income					Share in total family income of			
			Total	Net agricultural income	Nonagricultural	˙Wage	Miscellaneous	Agricultural income	Nonagricultural income	Wage income	Miscellaneous income
	(1)	(2)	(3)	(4)	(5)	(6)	(7)	(8)	(9)	(10)	(11)
<1.5	843	713.0	1132	620	512	340	172	.548	.452	.300	.160
1.5–2.49	454	363.7	998	669	329	218	111	.670	.330	.218	.115
2.5–3.49	485	392.8	1439	1139	300	173	127	.792	.208	.152	.093
3.5–4.99	392	300.0	1492	1211	281	144	137	.812	.188	.097	.095
5.0–6.49	378	295.9	1809	1577	232	113	119	.872	.128	.062	.069
6.5–8.49	378	271.8	2296	2014	282	110	172	.877	.122	.048	.082
8.5–10.49	325	215.1	2304	2078	226	50	176	.902	.098	.022	.079
10.5–14.99	302	191.7	2867	2420	447	66	381	.844	.156	.023	.139
15.0–19.99	312	217.4	3925	3579	346	143	203	.912	.088	.036	.063
20.0–39.99	287	185.4	5260	4701	559	208	351	.894	.106	.040	.070
All farms	370	272.5	1802	1499	302	149.5	161.8	.832	.168	.083	.090

Note: Because of slight ambiguities in the income statistics, cols. (10) and (11) do not sum exactly to col. (9), as in principle they should.

Source: Muda River Survey.

farms below 3.5 relongs as on those above 10.5 (though the largest farms are more highly capitalized than those in the 10.5- to 20-relong range). Thus, the ratio of value-added to value of land and capital is about 40 percent as high on farms above 10.5 relongs as on the smallest category, and about 60 percent as high on farms under 3.5 relongs. Value-added to value of land is only one-third as high on the former as on the latter.

In contrast to most other countries, labor productivity does not appear to increase systematically with farm size; based on our index[65] of labor inputs it is approximately constant (Table 4-48, col. 10), except for the smallest farms, where it is considerably above the average.[66] This approximate constancy suggests that there is no great difficulty for family members on small farms to hire out their services.[67] As Table 4-49 indicates, small-farm families do earn substantial shares of total income working for wages (30 percent for the smallest category), and allocate considerable time to this use. They also allocate relatively more time to home industry, the houselot, and fishing. Agricultural income (including livestock) is 90 percent of total income in the largest categories, but only 55 percent in the smallest. The fact that the larger farmers hire most of their labor clearly creates opportunities for the smaller ones. Differentials in income per farm across size are considerably greater than in income per adult, as larger farms correspond, on average, to larger families. While agricultural value-added on the 30 largest farms (top two categories) was about eight times that on the 47 farms in the lowest category, net income from agriculture was only about 6.4 times as high (Table 4-49) and total family income about 3.9 times as high. Meanwhile, the number of working adults was nearly twice as great on the larger farms, so the average income per working adult was only about twice as high. Most of this differential is simply explained by the difference in capital and land, assets that were clearly yielding high returns in this Green Revolution area.

The relatively higher labor productivity found on large farms in countries like Brazil and Colombia is due in part to an output composition calling for relatively little labor (e.g., cattle), partly to the use of labor-saving mechanization, and, in some cases, to the higher yields for specific crops on large farms. The other side of the coin is the impulse on small farms to use labor as much as possible, since it is of low opportunity cost. While there is some variation in agricultural product composition with size in Muda (Table 4-48, col. 13), it is very slight compared to most countries and to most of the countries or regions treated elsewhere in this study. And labor-saving mechanization has not proceeded too far, since most rice operations, except for land cultivation, are not mechanized. As a result the ratio of labor inputs/area in padi does not vary dramatically by size, being only 20 to 25 percent lower in the largest-farm category than in the smallest-farm categories (Table 4-50).

Although substantially higher in the smallest-farm category, yields vary little from the second category on up. Fertilizer and pesticide use is approximately constant on a per relong basis; purchase of seeds is higher on the smaller farms. Current costs for machinery use are about 65 percent higher on the largest than the smallest farms, and the ratio of current machinery costs to labor cost ranges from 0.14 for the smallest size group to 0.23–0.25 for the largest.

All in all, the picture seems to be one in which a relatively efficient labor market facilitates off-farm work for members of the small-farm families and the employment of labor by large farms. Most hired labor is of women, for the labor-intensive tasks.

Since, unlike most other cases studied, labor inputs per unit of output do not fall with increasing farm size, the relationship of total factor productivity with size (column 16, Table 4-48) is quite similar to that of land and capital productivity. Apart from the smallest category, the decline with size is gradual but systematic, with the categories between 1.5 and 3.5 relongs being about 50 percent more productive than those above 10.5 relongs. This is an impressive difference in the light of the apparently smoothly functioning labor market.

Although in this study we have not distinguished farms by tenure, a study by Huang has shown that in this area of Northwest Malaysia tenants and owner-tenants consistently have higher yields than pure owners. This result holds regardless of the nature of the rental contract; the differential is even greater after standardizing for farm size.[68] Together with the evidence from the Philippines presented in section 4.3, it highlights the need for revised hypotheses and for more empirical investigations to clarify the tenure-productivity relationship. At the same time, all the evidence indicates that this relationship is less important than the size-productivity one.

Measuring Size by Value of Land and Capital. The Muda data permit analysis in terms of alternative measures of size; Table 4-51 presents most of the same series as Table 4-48, but with farms classified by value of land and capital. Qualitatively similar trends emerge, though some interesting twists show up. When farms are classified by area (Table 4-48) value-added/hectare falls slightly more sharply with size than does

Table 4-50. Yields and Input Intensity of Rice Cultivation by Farm Size, Double-Croppers, 1972–73

Farm size (relongs)	Padi land (relongs) per farm			Labor use in rice per farm			Value of rice output per farm	Yield (value per relong)	Fertilizer used per farm	Fertilizer Padi area
	Beginning of year	End of year	Average	Total hours	Hired female equivalent hours	Hired female equivalent hours/relong				
	(1)	(2)	(3)	(4)	(5)	(6)	(7)	(8)	(9)	(10)
<1.5	0.86	1.28	1.07	753	898	839	699.7	654	21.21	19.8
1.5–2.49	1.84	2.04	1.95	1,478	1,756	901	881.4	452	48.28	24.8
2.99–3.49	2.90	3.56	3.23	1,932	2,693	834	1,512.9	468	69.87	21.6
3.5–4.99	4.03	4.34	4.18	3,030	3,565	853	1,751.3	419	80.62	19.3
5.0–6.49	5.27	5.51	5.39	3,890	4,509	837	2,107.7	391	104.85	19.5
6.5–8.49	7.11	6.90	7.00	4,865	5,710	816	3,238.3	463	148.23	21.2
8.5–10.49	9.23	8.78	9.00	6,404	7,496	833	3,752.4	417	203.29	22.6
10.5–14.99	11.74	11.13	11.44	7,571	8,759	766	4,585.2	401	259.30	22.7
15.0–19.99	15.19	14.24	14.72	9,408	10,959	745	5,993.9	407	324.40	22.0
≥20.0	22.11	21.65	21.88	13,094	15,320	700	8,727.1	399	467.10	21.3

Source: Muda River Survey.

Table 4-51. Factor Productivity of Farms, Classified by Value of Land and Capital, Double-Croppers, 1972–73

Value of land and capital (000 Malaysian dollars)	No. of farms	Average no. of relongs	Value-added in agriculture / Value of land and capital	Value-added in agriculture / Relong	Value of land per relong	Value of capital per relong	Value of farm output / Relong	Purchased inputs / Value of farm output	Purchased inputs / Relong
<2.5	70	1.31	.681	578	849	537	748	.227	170
2.5–4.5	117	2.24	.313	480	681	854	545	.119	65
4.5–6.5	146	3.65	.272	417	842	692	507	.178	90
6.5–8.5	103	4.76	.243	391	959	649	469	.166	78
8.5–10.5	85	5.31	.199	354	780	1,023	432	.181	78
10.5–14.5	91	7.07	.206	354	929	790	454	.220	100
14.5–18.5	61	8.23	.196	379	1,276	660	472	.197	93
18.5–24.5	48	11.10	.161	308	1,218	690	395	.220	87
24.5–30.5	20	14.84	.159	285	1,420	379	377	.244	92
30.5–78.0	21	18.60	.156	340	1,515	666	424	.198	84
All farms	762	5.50	.223	370	1,054	606	446		

value-added/value of land and capital; but when value of land and capital is the measure of size, value-added/relong falls less abruptly and value-added/value of land and capital more so. Thus, the largest farms in terms of value of land and capital have a value-added/relong ratio little below the overall average (10 percent), but a value-added/value of land and capital considerably farther (30 percent) below; land productivity is relatively high, because of heavy investment per hectare. A symmetrical difference appears at the small end of the spectrum.

With labor productivity not systematically related to farm size and land and capital productivity a decreasing function, the Muda River area seems to be a clear case of lower total factor productivity on the larger farms, whether size is defined by amount of land or by total value of land and capital.[69] The smaller farms not only achieve high productivity from the inputs used in agriculture, but receive a substantial share of their income from nonagriculture—30 to 35 percent for the smallest size groups—(Table 4-49). This share decreases fairly smoothly with size up to the largest category, where 20 percent comes from nonagriculture, possibly mostly from income on capital, in contrast to the smallest farms, where wage income is the bulk of nonagricultural income.

Savings Performance.   With a broad definition of consumption, including expenditures on housing purchases, additions, etc., the estimated savings rate ranges from negative for most of the smallest farm categories to very high for the largest two categories (Table 4-52); taken literally it suggests a marginal propensity to save (MPS) of 0.25 to 0.30 across these farm-size categories.[70] Allowance for life cycle and other factors would doubtless improve our interpretation of the determination of savings.

Their residual character makes savings estimates based on income minus expenditures highly sensitive to errors of observation;[71] such savings are also erratic in agriculture, due to the climate-induced (and price-induced) fluctuations in real income. The generally negative savings of the four smallest size categories may be due to atypically low incomes (or high expenditures) in the year in question (e.g., because of the sharp increase in expected future incomes due to the switch to double-cropping, or because life cycle[72] or other phenomena jointly caused a shift of those families to small size and to dissavings). Note that if small farms were small over a family's life cycle they could not dissave on a permanent or long-run basis.[73] There must, therefore, be something of a transitory nature in the behavior of these farmers, if the data are accurate. Alter-

Table 4-52. Savings Performance by Farm Size, Double-Croppers, 1972–73 (Ratios Expressed as Percentages)

Farm size (relongs)	Total income per family	S_1/Y (1)	S_2/Y (2)	D/Y (3)	Expenditures on housing[a] Y (4)	$\frac{S_1 + D + H}{Y}$ (5)	$\frac{S_2 + D + H}{Y}$ (6)	RI/Y (7)	$\frac{S_2 + RI}{Y}$ (8)
<1.5	1,132	1.54	1.83	3.02	2.22	6.78	7.07	2.75	4.58
1.5–2.49	998	−16.67	2.03	2.48	4.61	−9.58	9.12	2.54	4.57
2.5–3.49	1,439	−1.81	1.43	2.93	4.74	5.86	9.10	6.12	7.55
3.5–4.99	1,492	−8.55	2.06	3.76	7.61	2.82	13.43	8.94	11.00
5.0–6.49	1,809	4.77	1.42	2.46	4.99	12.22	8.87	5.16	6.58
6.5–8.49	2,296	9.30	3.34	2.51	3.52	15.33	9.37	8.98	12.32
8.5–10.49	2,304	8.12	4.38	6.46	2.95	17.53	13.79	6.91	11.29
10.5–14.49	2,867	9.85	4.27	3.14	5.05	18.04	12.46	8.30	12.57
15.0–19.99	3,925	21.77	0.97	1.72	2.93	26.42	5.62	19.59	20.56
20.0–40.0	5,260	20.03	4.94	2.59	6.35	28.97	13.88	9.88	14.82
All farms		3.65	2.46	3.10	4.64	11.39	10.20		

[a]Includes current and capital.

Symbols: S_1 = Gross income minus consumption expenditures.
S_2 = Institutional savings plus increase in jewelry plus loans to others, plus related categories.
Y = Family income.
D = Purchases of durable goods.
RI = Real investment in machinery, land, etc.

natively, of course, the negative savings rates may be due to errors of observation.

It is interesting to note that the overall estimated savings rate of 3.65 percent is not far above the estimated rate of savings in institutional assets, jewelry, loans to others, and such forms of wealth holding (2.46 percent). The difference includes real investment (machinery, land, etc.) minus build-up of debts to others. Savings in institutional assets, etc., together with real investment (col. 8) exceed the estimate of savings as a residual.

Expenditures on durable consumer goods and housing may also be viewed as part of savings, more broadly defined. Since current and capital expenditures on housing have not been distinguished, only a guess can be made at the capital component. For some size categories, it is clear that negative savings (in the narrow sense) may be partly accounted for by substantial expenditures along these lines. A plausible guess at savings of the sample families, including build-up of these forms of capital, would be 7 to 9 percent. When increase in real investment and decrease in debts to others are allowed for, it would more likely be in the range of 10 to 15 percent.

Unfortunately, our evidence on savings does not permit useful conclusions as to their relationship with farm size; although both total savings and savings per unit of land are a clearly increasing function of farm size (over most of the range), with plausible assumptions about how much of a family's savings are based on agricultural income, the presumably transitional character of dissaving on small farms rules out any meaningful assessment of the long-run relationship.

4.7   CONCLUSION

The empirical tests of this chapter generally support the hypotheses stated in Chapter 2. For all six countries with intensive data sets (from farm surveys or censuses), the statistical tests of this chapter confirm the negative relationship between farm size and output per unit of land area available. This negative relationship holds, even when removing the influence of land quality (either directly through the inclusion of land price in the analysis, as is done for Brazil, Colombia, India, and Malaysia, or indirectly by considering patterns on irrigated versus unirrigated land for the case of the Philippines).

The countries examined in this chapter vary considerably in regard to the degree of change over time in this inverse relationship between farm size and land productivity. During the decade of the 1960s, there appears to have been little change if any in Brazil (at least in the Northeast). In Colombia, large farms raised their land-use intensity proportionately more than small farms, but the large farms started from such a low base that by the end of the decade their degree of land utilization was still far below that of small farms. In Pakistan, there appears to have been a greater improvement in relative land productivity on large farms over the decade. In India, there was also an improvement. The somewhat greater improvements in Pakistan and India than in Brazil and Colombia presumably reflect the much greater impact of the Green Revolution in Asia than in Latin America. Despite these improvements, land productivity of large farms still remained below that on small farms in Pakistan and, especially, India, by the early 1970s.

Estimates of total social factor productivity generally confirm the conclusion of declining economic performance as farm size rises that is found on the basis of land productivity. For Brazil and Colombia, the largest-farm sizes have lower total social factor productivity than the medium and small-farm sizes. At an intermediate social price of labor, however, the very smallest farm sizes are found to be less efficient (in total social factor productivity) than the moderate-size groups. In Malaysia, total social factor productivity declines systematically as farm size rises. In India, total social factor productivity also declines as farm size rises. The decline is the most extreme and systematic when a zero social cost is imputed to labor. When alternative labor costs are imputed (ranging from half the market wage up to the full market wage), total social factor productivity holds approximately constant for the smaller-farm size groups (up to 15 acres) and then declines for larger-farm size groups.

In the area of tenancy, evidence for Brazil, the Philippines, and India fails to show any support for the hypothesis that sharecropping reduces land productivity. Therefore, there appears to be no strong case for practical importance of the argument that sharecropping lowers efficiency by causing the tenant to use inadequate levels of variable inputs per unit of land area (because he equates only his share of marginal product with full marginal cost). However, the absence of statistical significance for the sharecropping variable in explaining land productivity does not necessarily constitute empirical support for the contrary hypothesis, advocated by Cheung and others, that sharecropping causes no distortions in the production process.

FIVE

Conclusion and Policy Implications

The previous chapters of this study have considered the relative productivity of small and large farms from both theoretical and empirical standpoints and reached the general conclusion that the former normally generate higher land productivity and total social factor productivity (excepting the very smallest farm size groups in some countries, for the latter measure). From these results it follows that agricultural strategies focusing on small farms start with a major advantage: the demonstrated capacity to achieve high productivity of what is usually the scarcest resource, land (especially in Asia), largely through greater application of the abundant resource, labor. One such strategy has as its central feature redistribution of land from large farms into smaller ones; another, where little land is currently found in large farms, where it is not possible for political reasons to redistribute land, or where large farms are unusually productive, involves improving the access of small farms to credit and new technology, investing in infrastructure that helps to raise their productivity, and so forth. Both, clearly, are expected to lead to a more equal distribution of income than would pro large-farm strategies. Our results suggest that they can also be "efficient" policies, in the sense of leading to high total output levels. The data presented earlier in this study do not permit a quantitative comparison of the relative merits of "small-farm" vs. large-farm policies in the context of a given land distribution. They do provide some guidance with respect to the output implications of the distribution of land, and under stronger assumptions, the possible effects of land redistribution.

128

5.1   PROSPECTIVE IMPACT OF LAND REFORM ON PRODUCTION

The data presented in Chapter 4 on the farm-size–productivity relationship in the "data-intensive" countries provide the basis for a simple estimate of the potential for total increase in agricultural production from an equalizing redistribution of land, under the assumption of availability of such additional inputs of capital and seeds-fertilizer as the more intensive land-utilization patterns of small farmers would require, and assuming that new farms of a given size will be of the same efficiency as existing ones, and that there are no lasting output losses due to the turmoil, conflicts, and confusion accompanying land redistribution. These last two assumptions imply that in some contexts the estimates may more appropriately be described as medium or long-run than short-run. To the extent that the assumptions are not valid, the results must be adjusted. In countries where agricultural goods are not exported (or, alternatively, where their increased availability could not be used to reduce imports), not all of the total income gains would accrue to the farmers themselves, since some downward pressure on agricultural prices would be expected from land reform's output gains, although this tendency would be at least partially offset by the tendency for land reform beneficiaries to raise their own consumption of their produce (and, therefore, for the marketed surplus to rise less than total output).

In this benchmark calculation of the potential effects of an equalizing land redistribution on production, two steps are involved. The first is computation of the average parcel size that would result from such a reform, by dividing the total number of families in the rural labor force into the total farm land available. The second is to apply the statistical estimate of output per area currently achieved on that farm size (that is, the parcel size) to obtain an estimate of the production per area that would be expected on the postreform farms. Comparison of this output per farm area to the current average output per farm area then provides a first approximation of the potential percentage increase in production from total, equalizing land redistribution. This procedure makes the reasonable assumption that the input-output characteristics observed at present on family farms of the size that would prevail after land reform provide the best guide to the characteristics of production that would exist on postreform parcels.[1] In short, the calculation of an equalizing farm size, combined with the production characteristics observed for that size, provide the basis for predicting the effect of complete land reform on output.

This estimate abstracts from temporary disruption due to structural change and refers to the long-run "comparative static" change in the potential for agricultural production. The nature of existing physical infrastructure and other like rigidities implies that in practice the changes will be less than indicated by such estimates.

The calculation of a similar estimate for the change in employment to be expected from land reform would be more ambiguous. Two types of predictions could be of interest: first, the change in the number of person-hours that could be worked at or above a certain level of productivity, and, second, the amount of involuntary unemployment that would exist. With respect to the second question, the plausible proposition (consistent with empirical evidence) is that after complete reform labor would be fully employed in moderate-sized family parcels. If total useful hours of work per farm were low, there would be fairly low hours worked per family member, with considerable voluntary leisure-taking. Changes in the number of person-hours of work at certain levels of productivity could be predicted if one had good data on labor use by farm size. Estimates of this nature are not contained in the empirical analysis of this study. But the low labor use on large farms means that considerable employment creation would normally occur when their land is broken into smaller parcels.[2]

Table 5-1 presents estimates of the potential percentage gain in output from totally equalizing land redistribution into family farms for the countries examined in Chapter 4, following the methodology just discussed. The details for the calculations are set forth in the notes to the table. In determining the number of family parcels, it is assumed that each family has 2.5 workers. For Brazil, two sets of results are reported; the first refers to all of Brazil and is derived from the earlier study on potential effects of land reform based on 1962–63 farm survey data.[3] The second estimate is based on the SUDENE–IBRD data for 1973 and refers to an equalizing redistribution in the Northeast of Brazil only. The former estimate is much more conservative in concept than the other estimates reported in the table, because, to avoid possible overestimation in view of possibly differing land quality across sectors, the output calculations in this estimate are limited to land redistribution *within* individual product sectors, thereby ruling out the potentially important gains from changes in the product-mix (especially through the conversion of pasture land into cropped area).

The most striking production gains are those for Brazil's Northeast on the basis of the 1973 survey data.[4] The potential rise in output of about 80 percent is much larger than the earlier estimate of 25 percent output gain for Brazil as a whole. This divergence is attributable to two factors: first, the calculation for the Northeast does not impose the constraint of holding product-mix constant; second, a higher proportional output gain for the Northeast alone is consistent with the results found in the earlier study of product sectors throughout Brazil.[5]

The most important general result is that *all* six countries show potential output gains, and in all but Pakistan these are about 20 percent or greater, including such land-scarce countries as India and the Philippines. This finding provides further support for the hypothesis of section 2.3 and Appendix C of this study, that for a given level of concentration of land among operators, potential output gains from land redistribution may be almost as high in land-scarce as in land-abundant countries.

The specific results for India, with prospective output gains on the order of 19 percent, indicate a substantial scope for land reform's productive effects (although the result could be overestimated if no more land can be brought under irrigation, even though the incentive to irrigate is increased through the redistribution of unirrigated land). However, the other policy goal to be obtained through land reform, the attainment of substantially fuller employment in the countryside, would represent a crucial achievement, even if output increases were modest.

It is beyond the scope of this study to estimate the investment and recurrent costs that might be required to carry out the thoroughgoing land redistributions implied by these results. It is likely, however, that the benefit-cost ratios of these reforms would be positive and relatively high, compared with those of most development projects (and excluding any special weighting of social benefits associated with the equity impact of reform). The major productive inputs, land and labor, would already be available in the agricultural sector. The principal investment costs would arise in the form of additional requirements of capital and intermediate inputs. Simulation exercises for Brazil suggest that these additional costs would be limited. In the more conservative estimate whereby Brazilian agricultural output would rise by 25 percent from land redistribution (as discussed above), total capital inputs (buildings, equipment, animal stock) would need to rise by only 11 percent, and inputs of seeds, fertilizers, insecticides, feed, and vaccines would actually decline by approximately 13 percent, given existing small farm techniques.[6]

5.2   OVERVIEW

The general conclusion of this study is that the small-farm sector makes better use of its available land than does the large-farm sector,

Table 5-1. Potential Effects of Land Redistribution on Agricultural Production in Five Developing Countries

Variable / effect:	Brazil 1962–63	Brazil Northeast 1973	Colombia 1960	India 1970–71	(West) Pakistan 1960	Philippines 1960	Malaysia: Muda River 1972–73
A. Agricultural labor force (1,000)	11,720	7,815	2,781	146,491	8,000[h]	9,617	—
B. Total farm area (1,000 ha)	249,862	79,840	27,338	131,873	19,810	7,772	—
C. Equalizing parcel size, hectares (= $B/[A/2.5]$)	—	25.5[a]	24.6	2.25	6.19	2.02	0.80[n]
D. Output per hectare on parcel size	—	49.4[b] dollars	610[d] pesos	659[f] rupees	458[i] rupees	407[k] pesos	1,660 M. dollars
E. Overall average output per hectare	—	27.5[c] dollars	477[e] pesos	555[g] rupees	415[j] rupees	331[m] pesos	1300[o] M. dollars
F. Ratio, D/E	—	1.795	1.28	1.19	1.10	1.23	1.27
G. Percentage increase in output from total land							

[b] Weighted average. By zones, A through G, respectively: $18.02, 14.57, 30.09, 31.25, 177.7, 303.2, 91.46$. Computed by applying each zone's parcel size to regression number 4 of Table 4-2 (including application of regional intercept and slope dummy variables).

[c] Weighted average. By zones, A through G respectively: $6.22, 7.44, 13.67, 19.86, 29.95, 261.7, 36.43$.

[d] Value-added per effective hectare. Based on interpolation between midpoints of size groups (Table 4-8).

[e] Value-added per effective hectare.

[f] From equation (2), Appendix A.

[g] Calculated by applying weights of percent of total land in each size group (Table A-10) to regression-based estimate of output per farm area (Appendix A, equation 2) as applied to average farm size by class in Table A-10.

[h] Rough estimate. The 1961 population census figure was 7,644, but that census suffered from very considerable underenumeration.

[i] Based on interpolation within the size category 12.5–25 acres, Table 4-26. An average of the output/acre estimates I and II.

[j] Table 4-26, cols. (4) or (8).

[k] Based on estimate 1, average between 1 to 2 and 2 to 3 hectare size-group figures, Table 4-18, adjusted for differing value of land per acre (which tends to be lower on larger farms).

[l] Total based on specific calculations by state-product sectors. See W. R. Cline, *Economic Consequences of a Land Reform in Brazil*, p. 153.

[m] Table 4-18.

[n] Estimated on the assumption that postreform average farm size would bear a relation to existing average farm size equal to the ratio of labor of current operator families applied in agriculture to all labor applied in agriculture. In other words, farm size would fall, so that with the same total labor input it could come from operator families of the same average size as the existing ones.

The survey showed that 58 percent of labor inputs were hired. Meanwhile, 20 percent of family labor inputs are recorded as having been applied on other farms. (In this estimate, we assume labor is more productive when applied on other farms, due to timing, in the same proportion as hired labor is assumed to be more productive than family labor in general.) Since operators and their families are estimated to contribute half of total labor inputs at present, farm size is assumed to be halved in the reform, from its initial level of 1.6 hectares.

[o] From Table 4-48, interpolating in col. 2.

Source: A. Agricultural Labor force: Food and Agriculture Organization, *Production Yearbook 1973*, Table 5.
B. Total farm area: F.A.O., Report on the 1960 World Census of Agriculture, Table 2.10.

largely through applying higher levels of labor inputs (family labor) per unit of land. This conclusion is supported both with extensive cross-country data (on cultivation rates by farm size) and with statistical tests on intensive data sets for six major developing countries. Moreover, for those countries with sufficient data to permit analysis of total social factor productivity (Brazil, Colombia, Malaysia, and India), this broader measure of performance confirms the tendency for productivity to decline as farm size rises (at least above the very smallest size groups). The theoretical bases for expecting these patterns are outlined in Chapter 2 and generally supported by the empirical tests in Chapters 4 and 5. It is worth noting that the small farm's higher land productivity does not normally result from higher yields of specific crops, though in some countries this is a factor; often, however, average yields are higher on large farms. But small farms are almost universally characterized by higher land utilization, usually showing up in the form of high multiple-cropping ratios in land-scarce countries, where little land is uncultivated even on large farms, and in higher shares of total land cultivated in more land-abundant countries (where large farms often use much of their land quite extensively, e.g., for cattle grazing). A significantly higher intensity of livestock operations contributes importantly to the high land productivity of small farms in many countries (e.g., Pakistan, the Philippines, Mexico). The overall pattern can be best described as one that reflects the reasonable success of small farmers in using the available labor to raise output, whether this entails a move to double-cropping, investment in small animals, or whatever. The case of Japan, no longer characterized by an inverse relationship between size and land productivity, suggests that when enough lucrative off-farm employment becomes available, the pressure to use labor intensively on small farms diminishes. In other words, when a country is developed to the point where the opportunity cost of labor is relatively high, the special efficiency advantages of small farms tend to disappear. The other side of this coin is that as long as a country is underdeveloped, and excepting the unusual circumstances of very abundant land, the small farm will remain an important and even crucial element in an efficient agricultural sector.

The central policy implication of the analysis is that land redistribution into family farms is an attractive policy instrument for raising production and for improving rural employment and equality of income distribution. Fears of inefficient production on small farms are contradicted by widespread findings of constant, not increasing, returns to scale in agriculture. Concerns about losses of dynamic growth influences through land reform are cast into doubt by (1) the absence of any evidence for a positive influence of farm size on agricultural growth rates across countries, and (2) evidence that in the Green Revolution in Asia small farmers have quickly achieved adoption rates of high-yielding varieties nearly as high as those on larger farms. Finally, both the theoretical analysis and the empirical results contradict the notion that land reform could have substantial impact only for Latin American countries with enormous landed estates, but would necessarily have minimal impact in land-scarce Asian countries. Thus, the policy of land redistribution warrants consideration even in land-scarce countries.

The analysis of this study is prospective rather than historical, and it is beyond the scope of this volume to examine in detail past experiences with land reform.[7] Nevertheless, a summary review of major land reforms is useful in order to identify certain themes about the conditions for successful reform. In Latin America, significant land reforms have occurred in Mexico, Bolivia, Cuba, Chile, Venezuela, and Peru. A recent World Bank survey of land-reform experience in these countries[8] (excluding Cuba) concludes that the effects of reform on agricultural production were generally positive, with the possible exception of Peru. Moreover, in all cases the effect of reform was to make the distribution of income more equal.

In Bolivia, reform in the mid-1950s broke up large, traditional *haciendas* and created small family farms, with a major positive impact on the level and growth of production (according to the World Bank review). In Mexico, land reform dates from the 1910 Revolution and, especially, from the phase of active redistribution of land in 1934–40. After initial disruption, agriculture grew at an impressive rate. However, in present-day Mexican agriculture it appears to be the large commercial farms, especially those on irrigated land, that constitute the dynamic sector. The reform sector of *ejidos* appears to be relatively backward, although at social factor prices (with a low shadow price on labor) they are probably more efficient than the large commercial farms. The divergence in dynamism between the two sectors may be attributed in large part to more favorable access to credit and modern inputs on the large farms, and perhaps to the fact that within the *ejido* sector small farmers do not have the stimulus of incentives provided by direct ownership. Reforms in Chile and Venezuela also appear to have stimulated production. In Peru, the apparent stagnation of production after the ambitious land reform program begun by the Velasco government in 1969 may be attributable to the attempt to impose the structure of state cooperatives upon the postreform sector, thereby creating lack of incentives to farmers. In addition, land reform in Peru (as well as Chile) fell considerably below its potential in improving rural equity. The beneficiaries of land reform were primarily limited to former workers on the reformed estates, a limited minority of the rural labor force. (The equity effects of reform in Chile were limited still further by the partial reversal of reform after the military regime took power in 1973.)

In Asia, land reform in the early 1950s proved extremely successful in Japan, Taiwan, and Korea, where land was turned over to former tenant workers. These reforms led to impressive equality in the distribution of land and rural income. Moreover, subsequent technical change and productivity growth have been rapid in these countries. Extensive land reform in Iran in the 1960s was successfully implemented,[9] while total agricultural production was increased. However, there were short-run adverse effects on investment, because of uncertainty and problems with the maintenance of irrigation services; and because the reform was limited to workers residing on reformed estates, it failed to reach landless workers.[10]

In Algeria, nationalization of lands formerly in French estates led to large state farms that suffered from limited direct incentives to workers, while at the same time representing an enclave of a somewhat privileged rural class.[11]

Experience with land reform in many other countries, including India, Morocco, and a number of Latin American countries, has been a tale of ambitious legislation but minimal implementation in the face of powerful political opposition. Indeed, past experience with land reform shows that its most important precondition is a strong political basis for breaking the opposition of landlords. For example, in the case of Japan, postwar occupation forces imposed reform; and in Mexico and Bolivia, land reform followed social revolution.

The economic effects of land reform have been mixed. The reason appears to be primarily that the types of postreform structures and the nature of implementation have differed across countries. Generally, economic results have been more favorable where implementation has been swift, avoiding long periods of uncertainty. Economic results also depend on the extent to which governments provide the necessary infrastructure, extension services, and improved inputs, replacing the network for these services previously provided by large farmers, as well as increasing their availability to accompany increasing land cultivation by new smallholders. The various experiences with land reform also appear to show a pattern of greater production success where postreform organization is based upon direct ownership in small family farms rather than upon state and cooperative farms (although this issue is highly debatable).

Rather than historical precedent, however, the best guide to potential output effects of land reform is a careful empirical analysis of the existing structural features of agriculture within a given country. Simple extrapolation of the historical experiences of other countries is clearly inadequate.[12]

Because large-scale redistribution of land usually has severely limited political likelihood, it is important to consider alternative policy options as well. The chief implication of this study is that in the absence of land reform, governments can still work effectively toward the joint objectives of production and equity through measures aimed at the small-farm sector. The expansion of facilities providing improved seeds, fertilizer, and other modern inputs (and corresponding agricultural credit) is one such measure. The mounting evidence of high efficiency on small farms generally and a high return to these inputs in particular should provide assurance that such actions will be productive. Alternative measures warranting consideration are the initiation or expansion of credit for land purchases by small farmers and the implementation of progressive land taxation, in order to achieve gradually through the capital market and fiscal structure the objectives of redistribution of land ownership where, for political reasons, this goal cannot be addressed more directly through land reform.

A related policy implication concerns regulations on tenancy. In situations where the redistribution of land ownership is politically infeasible, it will be especially important to preserve for small farmers and landless workers at least that degree of access to land which they already have through land rental. Therefore, greater caution is called for with respect to imposition of rental and sharecropping restrictions that can lead to the eviction of tenants, rather than to a shift in income shares from landlords to tenants.[13] In the case of sharecropping, the theoretical ambiguity of any distortion to incentives, and the absence of empirical evidence of such distortions, means that the academically fashionable critique of the mechanism should not be considered sufficient grounds for the imposition of legal restrictions limiting or proscribing sharecropping—unless policymakers are prepared to provide alternative access to land through land redistribution. Instead, the results of this study suggest that government policies toward land rental should encourage large landowners to rent out their land in small operational units.

The partial (or even complete) exemption of large owners from land reform if they cultivate their own land, a feature of some land reform programs, seems in this light particularly misguided, unless it can stipulate a reasonable level of productivity by the rules it sets up. The landlord is likely to make a greater contribution to both output and income distribution by renting or sharing the land out in small parcels than by operating it himself.

An equalizing land reform of the type considered in the above calculations would leave neither very large farms nor very small ones, so both the inefficiency of the former and the sometimes nonviability (inability to provide a living for a family) of the latter would be avoided. In many other contexts, it is often argued that very small farms are not viable and should be consolidated into larger units, or that breakdown of existing units below a certain minimum size should be avoided. On inspection, the arguments for this sort of government intervention appear to be, in general, very weak. Where the argument rests on the need for some minimum size, if economies of scale are to be achieved, it is contradicted by the evidence from most countries that land productivity is highest on the very smallest farms; this would suggest that consolidation of tiny units would be more likely to lower output than raise it. A more serious argument is that even if their land productivity is very high the smallest farms are not a viable economic base for a family, since they provide too little income. But to take away the land of one small holder to bring another one up to the "viability" threshold is a dubious policy at best. In any case, if the smallest farms are truly too small to produce a living, it must be hypothesized that the families involved earn off-farm income, as is increasingly evident from data on income sources. If all families are surviving on a combination of farm and off-farm income, there is no "viability" argument for intervention, and there is certainly no inefficiency argument when these very small farms are highly productive.[14]

The advent of rapid varietal change, subsidized imports of tractors and other machinery, and substantial public investment in infrastructure, such as irrigation systems, has accelerated the rate of agrarian change in many developing countries. It has greatly increased the actual or potential profitability of large farms, which can take advantage of the machines more than small farms and are in a better position to adopt new inputs, direct public investments their way, and so on. This new situation creates a real danger that countries will pursue a large-farm, capital-intensive agricultural strategy that is unlikely to be in the long-run interest of the country as a whole. But the profitability of large farms creates a political force favoring this option. And the earlier adoption of new inputs by large farms—their "dynamism"—is likely to create the impression that they have general productivity advantages over small farms.

As we have argued above, especially in the context of Pakistan, these productivity advantages are sometimes partly illusionary (as where yields are the basis of the comparison, without allowing for differences in crop composition and land utilization) and usually partly transitory. Small farms, with the capital and risk constraints they face, usually lag somewhat in adoption of new inputs; but the lag is not normally long, and can undoubtedly be shortened by effective public policy toward these units. The danger is not that small farms are irremediably traditional, nonusers of modern inputs—a perception quite at variance with the facts. The danger, rather, is that the large farmers' accurate perception of their own self-interest and the policy-makers' inaccurate perception of the national interest will combine to assist the large farmers to expand at the expense of the smaller ones; by the time the latter have overcome the barriers to increasing productivity the resources under their control, especially land, may be seriously reduced, and the mass of landless workers in agriculture and low-productivity workers elsewhere correspondingly expanded.

The increasing productivity of large-scale agriculture can thus be a threat to small farmers at the same time that it raises the overall performance of the agricultural sector. For large farmers are likely to have the political influence to do what they want. Large owners have the option of releasing share-tenants; evidence from Pakistan shows that purchasers of large tractors over the last decade have tended both to expand the area they cultivate and to decrease the number of share-tenants on their land.[15] There is an issue in countries like Pakistan of whether or not, before their productivity regains its normal advantage relative to large farms, the area operated by small farmers will be reduced and many of them be pushed into other activities.

Kanel contrasts the experience in nineteenth-century European development where urbanization and attractive opportunities in industry, commerce, politics, and education drew the elite (as well as new classes) to nonagricultural opportunities, leaving agriculture to the peasants, with current opportunities for the corresponding rural elite in the LDC's.

At a time when nonagricultural opportunities are still limited, the Green Revolution has brought sudden and dramatic increases in income. On larger farms, the income of the landowner can be increased by mechanization, by displacement of tenants and hired workers, and by active management. ... In addition, at a time when government agencies, cooperatives and private marketing firms serving small farmers are poorly developed, actively managed farms can assume the role of providing services and infrastructure, and can expand aggressively into new markets as opportunities develop. ... Under these circumstances, with attractive income opportunities in agriculture and active management on large farms, private operators of large farms will be making crucial decisions about how agriculture is to be modernized. Development is more likely to proceed along a capital intensive, labor saving path, increasing the employment problem and concentrating the benefits of development in a few hands. These patterns are directly opposed to the requirements of a situation characterized by much more rapid population growth and more deficient employment opportunities in industry than those which characterized XIX century European development.[16]

The juncture of agrarian evolution at which countries such as India and Pakistan find themselves is, in short, a particularly delicate one; it requires unusually sophisticated analysis of the forces at work for change to steer a wise course that neither discourages large farmers from raising their productivity nor permits them to encroach on the future of the usually more productive small farmers.

Farm Size, Productivity, and Technical Change in Indian Agriculture*

Surjit S. Bhalla

A.1 INTRODUCTION

It is now almost a decade since the introduction of high-yielding varieties (HYVs) of foodgrains in Indian agriculture. There is considerable interest in an understanding of this technical change and its effect on production and employment. Of special interest is the effect of the seed and fertilizer (or Green) revolution on the so-called 'inverse' relationship between farm size and productivity. Does the relationship still exist in the post-Green Revolution years, and if it does, what are its causes? Are noneconomic or economic factors responsible for small farmers producing more output/acre than the large farmer? And what has been the contribution of HYV technology to farm productivity differences? Has it weakened the traditional "advantage" of the small farmer?[1] If it has, and if the distribution of income has shifted in favor of the large farmer, what policies are then desirable to redress the presumed imbalance?

These and other questions are examined for the 1970–71 agricultural year in India. Most, if not all, of the prior empirical studies that have dealt with agriculture in its Green Revolution phase have been based on extremely disaggregated data—village and/or district—and a disproportionate number of them have been based on the showcase areas of the

*I would like to thank William R. Cline for his help and encouragement.

Green Revolution—wheat in Punjab and Haryana and, to a somewhat lesser extent, rice in Tamil Nadu. The local nature of these studies has natural advantages—concentration on a homogeneous area allows them to adequately control for exogenous factors that affect farm productivity, e.g., soil quality, cropping patterns, and cultural environment. However, the dispersion in time, space, and methodology of these studies makes them unreliable for extrapolation to conditions prevailing in agriculture in general.[2] And it is knowledge about the behavior of agriculture on an all-India basis that is crucial for agricultural policies concerned with land reform, income redistribution, and fertilizer and credit distribution.

A unique feature of this study is that it analyzes data for all of India. As its source, it uses the data collected by the National Council of Applied Economic Research (NCAER) for the periods 1968-69, 1969-70, and 1970-71. The sample consisted of some 3,000 cultivating households who were interviewed in *each* of the three years. This data set, although not as intensive as some of the sources analyzed in the literature (Bardhan 1973*c* and Siddhu 1974) is, nevertheless, comprehensive in that it has data on farms dispersed throughout India. Thus, since local factors can be expected to average out, the general pattern can be observed by analysis of the NCAER data.

The data set is described in detail in section A.2. Noneconomic and economic causes of the inverse relationship are examined in section A.3—land quality and irrigation differences, and imperfections in the land, capital and labor markets are discussed in detail. Section A.4 examines the impact of the Green Revolution on farm productivity, and section A.5 contains a summary of the major results of this discussion. Annex A.1 lists in detail the procedure used for selecting the farms for analysis, and Annex A.2 describes the methodology used in constructing the synthetic figure for family labor input in farm production.

A.2   THE NCAER DATA

The NCAER undertook a survey (known as the Additional Rural Income Survey [ARIS]) of 5,115 households in 1968-69 to gather data on the type and distribution of income, and the pattern of consumption, savings, and investment of these households. The sample was selected according to a multistage, stratified probability design in order to provide a representative cross section of the rural Indian population. Higher-income households were oversampled. The survey was repeated in

1969-70 and 1970-71 on the *same* households and the final version of the data refers to a core sample of 4,118 households.

The NCAER data describes in detail the age-sex composition of households, the composition of income (by sources and occupation), the consumption pattern, the stock and flow of selected assets (farm land, farm equipment, irrigation, consumer durables, livestock), and the production behavior (if any) of the household. The latter includes crops grown, techniques used, costs incurred by category, etc. Detailed data relating to transactions in the capital market are available for the third year only, though a figure for net borrowing is available for each of the three years. In addition, "background" data on the villages where the households reside are also available.

The data came from a panel study for the three years and, as such, combine elements of both a time-series and cross-section nature. Surveys are often susceptible to measurement error, a form of which is individual response error. To the extent these errors are significant, a panel study should minimize them, since the respondents should get used to the questions over the years. Consequently, the data for at least the last year of the survey, 1970-71, is perhaps more reliable than that obtained if no previous surveys had been undertaken. At the same time, one should be aware that the data for the later years may suffer from bias due to the conditioning of the respondents, and the net effect on the reliability of the data is therefore uncertain. Nevertheless, third-year data has been chosen here as the primary unit for study and hypothesis testing, though the other two years are also analyzed whenever appropriate.

The NCAER data have a number of advantages for use in an analysis of farm production behavior. The oversampling of high-income households allows the data to be used for the study of the production behavior of large (over 15 acres) and very large (over 25 or 30 acres) farmers—a procedure not possible with most previous data sources in India. Also, its extensive coverage means that all of the major crops grown in all regions of India can be analyzed, and the different stages of adoption of the new technology meaningfully studied. Moreover, the analysis can be conducted on the basis of individual-farm data, unlike the Farm Management Studies of the 1950s, which were based on group averages.

Out of a total sample of 4,118 households, 2,532 were cultivators for all three years and 790 had the status of noncultivator for each of the three years. Noncultivator households and those that changed status during any of the three years of the survey are not analyzed in this study. Out of the 2,532 permanent cultivators, 1,772 were selected for analysis. Annex A.1

spells out in detail the procedure used for selecting a household as a unit for analysis.

A.3   THE INVERSE RELATIONSHIP OF FARM SIZE TO LAND PRODUCTIVITY

Causes and Consequences. The Farm Management Studies (FMS) of the 1950s covered approximately 3,000 farms in six states of India—Maharashtra, Madhya Pradesh, Tamil Nadu, Punjab, Uttar Pradesh, and West Bengal. The results of these studies were published in the form of cross-classification tables, with farms classified according to size groups. (Though preferable, disaggregated data on a per farm basis were generally not available to the researchers.) Although classification by size groups varied from state to state, a consistent pattern was nevertheless observed for all the states: there existed a negative relationship between farm size owned and production per acre owned.

Analysis of the FMS data was constrained to be on the basis of published aggregate tables; nevertheless, a vigorous debate ensued over the possible causes of this statistical finding.[3] Similar results were observed for other countries and, over the years, the 'inverse' relationship has almost achieved the status of a stylized fact of peasant agriculture. It has been extensively documented for countries in Latin America (Berry 1973 and Cline 1970), and Asia (Griffin 1974).

Although the derivation of policy implications from this relationship may be subject to the criticism that it is partial and concerns only one factor of production—land—there are strong reasons for attaching importance to this partial relationship. First, although land is not the sole factor, it is perhaps the most scarce factor in labor-abundant countries. Differences in per farm land area are therefore meaningful from a social point of view, since these variations may reflect differences in social efficiency. This is likely to be true if the reason for the higher productivity of the small farms is the application of more labor—a factor generally presumed to be in surplus in a country like India. Second, and more important, the inverse relationship has been observed in conjunction with generally constant returns to scale in agriculture. In the polar case of perfect competition and a linearly homogeneous production function for agriculture, output per acre should be *constant* across farm sizes; it should be independent of the size of a farm. If there is a systematic relationship between the two, positive or negative, there is an anomaly to be explained.

Given that there is a strong negative relationship, the question of a proper functional form to approximate it needs to be answered. As shown in the previous paragraph, theory dictates no relationship and therefore no estimating form. Alternative hypotheses about the causes of this relationship will dictate different estimating equations. The dual labor-market hypothesis (section A.3.3[d]) will dictate a two-step pattern of output per acre and farm size. According to this hypothesis, small farms are at one extreme and produce output with family labor; at the other extreme, large (capitalist) farms produce output with hired labor. Differences between the two are observed because the opportunity cost of labor is lower for the family farm, which consequently uses more labor to produce more output. (For the intermediate farms, output/acre declines as the proportion of the hired labor force increases from 0 to 100 percent). Land-market imperfections, i.e., a lower cost of land for the large farms, might dictate a continual decline in output/acre (section A.3.3[b]), but these individual hypotheses are not enough to dictate an estimation form, since imperfections in at least two markets are necessary for farm-size productivity differences to be observed. (See p. 156 for a discussion on this point.) An estimating form has therefore to be chosen on the basis of which form best describes the data; the basic forms that have been tried in the literature are three: the linear, log–log, and semi-log. The form preferred here is the semi-log (model 1); that is,

(1) $y = R/A = a + b \log A,$
       where y = production (or value-added) per acre of land in operation, A
          R = production (or value-added) in revenue or physical terms[4]
          A = land in operation; usually equal to land owned, but in the case of rentals, equal to land owned + land leased in—land leased out. (For purposes of convenience, A is referred to as land owned in the rest of this appendix.)

This form differs from the log–log form in which:

(1′) $\log y = a + b \log A,$

in that for the former (Equation 1) the elasticity of output/acre with respect to farm size is not constant, but is dependent on y (the elasticity for the semi-log form is b/y). Thus, at lower levels of yield/acre (larger farms) the decline is more rapid than at higher levels (smaller farms) for the semi-log form.

The measure of farm productivity, y, needs to be closely examined. The purpose of this paper is to study differences in farm productivity. Ideally, one would like to have estimates of *physical* output, rather than an estimate of *value* of output, R. A measure of value of output would be adequate if all farmers received the same price for their crops. Such may not be the case, and, indeed, it is likely that small farmers actually receive lower prices for their output than large farmers. If so, then use of R understates the productivity of the small farmer. Since physical output estimates cannot be derived from the NCAER data, one can only note the direction of the bias—since the measure understates it for the small farmer, the inverse relationship, if observed, is likely to be even stronger with an accurate measure of output.

The denominator, area cultivated, is deficient in that it does not control for soil quality differences between farms. Only if a systematic relationship existed between the size of a farm and its soil quality would the measure be in error. This problem is taken up in more detail in section A.3.2, but it should be noted that the direction of the bias due to noncorrection is likely to be in favor of the small farmer, i.e., they are presumed to have better quality land. Thus, the net effect of using $y(=R/A)$ as a measure of farm productivity is ambiguous.

The caveats having been noted, estimation of Equation 1, for the 1970-71 agricultural year, yields the following result:

$$(2) \qquad y = \quad 882 \quad - \; 130 \log A$$
$$\qquad\qquad (41.6) \quad (13.6)$$

$$R^2 = .09 \qquad N = 1772 \text{ obs.,}$$

where y values are in rupees per acre, and A is in acres. (The absolute value of the t-statistic is in parentheses.)

As can be noted, the inverse relationship between farm size and productivity is confirmed and, indeed, appears to be quite pronounced, as shown by the high degree of statistical significance of the relationship (high t-statistic). The low R^2 may be objected to, but it should be mentioned that Equation 2 includes farms from all of India, with differing quality of land and growing different crops. Unless it is assumed that larger farms have consistently lower quality land and/or consistently grow low yield/acre crops, the estimate of b in Equation 2 should be unbiased. (In section A.3.2, both of these assumptions are examined in detail.)

When this 'inverse' relationship was first observed in India, it was extensively analyzed for its causes. Proper understanding of these causes is crucial for policies such as land reform. If output/acre is higher on smaller farms, the relevant question is whether *increases* in output will result with land redistribution. Because of its policy relevance, the relationship has generally been explained with reference to either exogenous (that is, natural) factors or endogenous (that is, economic) factors. The classification is based on the premise that in the former case there is no implication that output increases would result if land were redistributed, but in the latter case production gains could be expected from land redistribution. In the sections that follow, the various hypotheses about the cause of the inverse productivity-size relationship will be critically examined on the basis of the results from the NCAER data.

A.3.2(a) *Noneconomic Factors—Land Quality.* Farms differ in soil quality and, naturally, this has an effect on the potential output of a farm. An explanation of productivity differences in terms of soil quality has, therefore, to be supported by the observation that soil quality worsens with farm size and that these differences account for *all* the variation in output/acre. In the following discussion, the various arguments for quality differences are considered and incorporated into the framework of the basic "model" (Equation 1) of the previous section.

One variation on the theme of land quality differences is that the "usable" land on a farm decreases with the size of the holding. Using portions of the FMS data, Rao (1967) found no inverse relationship when he adjusted the acreage for fallow land and irrigation. It is questionable whether endogenous factors like irrigation should be adjusted in order to explain farm-productivity differences (see p. 152). Regarding fallow land, if large farms do have a greater percentage of unusable land, then a lack of adjustment will understate the productivity of the large farmer.

The assumption that larger farms have proportionately more fallow land is questionable. Nevertheless, there is an easy test of this hypothesis: acreage may be defined in terms of usable area rather than actual area owned. Even if one makes the *extreme* assumption that the only usable area is the actual area cultivated, statistical tests with the NCAER data reconfirm the negative relationship. Equation (3) presents regression results with y = income per net cultivated area and A = cultivated area, rather than total farm area.

(3) $y = 1127 - 218 \log A$
              (32.5)   (13.5)

        $R^2 = .093$ (*t*-statistic in parentheses).

The relationship is about as strong as the case where A is defined as total land owned. The higher intercept is obtained because net cultivated area is always less than or equal to the area owned. The reason there is little difference with correction for fallow land is that farms in India vary much more in their cropping intensity than in their share of land held in fallow. Cropping intensity is the number of times the same piece of land is cultivated during the year, whereas land-use intensity is the ratio of net cultivated area (physical area cultivated regardless of number of times per year) to area owned.

Availability of irrigation is a prime determinant of differences in cropping intensity. If water is not available for the dry season, the land is left uncultivated, thus resulting in a cropping intensity of one. Higher intensities will result with more irrigation. This pattern is confirmed by the figures of Table A-1, which show a close relationship between cropping intensities and irrigation. It is also evident that although the land-use figure stays approximately constant at 90 percent, the figure for cropping intensity decreases as farm size rises. Thus, it is differences in cropping intensity rather than land-use intensity that help explain the differences in income/acre for the different-sized farms.[5]

Another variation on land quality differences is the argument that large farms have inherently lower quality land. Sen (1962) and Bhagwati-Chakravarty (1969) have offered alternative scenarios that might possibly bring about this curious result. Sen postulates a Malthusian process whereby families with better quality land are richer and therefore become larger; their farms eventually become fragmented into smaller holdings than those that evolve from holdings with lower quality soil. The Malthusian premise as well as the implicit constraint of no migration of family members are questionable aspects of this hypothesis.

Bhagwati-Chakravarty offer a "distress sales" hypothesis to explain the differences in land quality. Large farms, according to them, may result from the acquisition of land from distress sales on the part of the small farmers, with the latter generally parting with lower quality land. A corollary to this hypothesis is the contention that the resulting fragmentation of large holdings adversely affects the average productivity of land. The rationale for the first part of the hypothesis is provided by consideration of the subsistence requirements of the poor, small farmer. Even if the land market were perfect, and land prices fully captured productivity differentials, the small farmer may still be averse to selling his better quality land. Regarding fragmentation, Bardhan (1973c), in his analysis of farms during both the pre- and post-Green Revolution phase, found that fragmen-

Table A–1. Technical Characteristics of Sample Farms: All India, 1970–71

Farm size (acres)	Average farm size	Land-use intensity	Cropping intensity	Percentage area irrigated	Income per acre	No. of observations
0-5	2.95	94.3	1.38	46.4	737	621
5-15	9.3	93.1	1.26	45.3	607	734
15-25	19.5	90.8	1.15	35.3	482	248
Over 25	42.6	85.2	1.00	24.6	346	169
All	11.4	89.9	1.15	35.8	499	1772

tation did indeed have a negative influence on output. According to Bharadwaj's (1974*a*) analysis of FMS data, "the number of fragments per holding increases with size of holding, (but) the number of fragments per acre invariably decreases with size of holding" (p. 16). It is the latter figure that is more relevant for farm productivity, and it operates against the small farmer.

Lack of data prevents any test of the fragmentation hypothesis; some tests, however, can be conducted on land quality differentials, since the NCAER survey collected data on the prices of land (irrigated and unirrigated) that were prevailing in the village.[6] If these prices are accepted as proxies for land quality, then they can be used to adjust the raw acreage figures. This adjustment will only be meaningful on an interregional basis, since all farms within a village reflect the average price of land. Regarding the two prices, the price of irrigated land reflects, in addition to soil quality, differences in methods of irrigation (canals, wells, tubewells, etc.). The unirrigated land price presumably does not suffer from this drawback and is therefore preferred as an index of soil quality.

If price of unirrigated land, P, is accepted as a measure of soil fertility, then the NCAER data does suggest that at an aggregate level there is a negative relationship between farm size and soil quality. The correlation coefficient between farm size A, and price, P, is $-.017$, which is highly significant at the 1 percent level of confidence (1,772 observations).[7] This correlation (and the general use of a price term to adjust for quality differences) should be interpreted with caution, because of the danger of circularity in using a *price* term as an index of quality. The village price reported in NCAER, or the land revenue index used by Khusro (1964) as a proxy for quality, may do no more than reflect the superior productivity of the small farmer. If prices reflect expected output and these expectations are based on past output levels, then a higher output/acre will result in a higher price. Only adjustment by an exogenous index of soil quality is appropriate for testing for differences between farms. Lack of such an index forces one to use the stated price of unirrigated land, but it should be remembered that adjustment by P may bias the result in favor of the large farmer.[8]

In any case, omission of a quality term from Equation 1 biases coefficient b and, given the observed correlation between size and quality, it is likely to overstate the decline in farm productivity. The proper incorporation of price/acre differences into model 1 (Equation 1) is, however, difficult and dependent on one's assumptions about the nature and consequences of such (price) differences. Two methods of incorporating price differences will be discussed—each represents 'polar' assumptions, and the distinguishing factor between them is that one emphasizes the differences in physical size among farms, while the other emphasizes differences in scale.

Model 2, Equation 4, introduces the price term in an additive manner:

(4) $y = a - b \log A + cP,$

i.e., unit increases in price/acre result in constant additions to output/acre. Such increases are equal to c and are independent of land area A and price P. In this model, increases in price always result in increases in output/acre. The model makes the important assumption that P captures differences in land input quality, so that the same amount of physical land input results in higher output when land price is higher.

Alternatively, model 3 (Equation 5) introduces price in a multiplicative form, and here the emphasis shifts from the size of a farm in terms of physical area to the value of the land endowment of a farm, where that endowment is represented by the total value of farm land $(P.A)$:

(5) $y' = y/P = R/AP = a' - b' \log (AP)$
(5')   or $y = P(a' - b' \log P - b' \log A)$

Model 3 treats physical size and price in a symmetric manner. In this model, if b' is negative, the implication is that a larger value of land endowment leads to lower output per unit of land value, regardless of whether the land endowment is large because of high land price (quality) or because of large physical area. Moreover, increases in price P in model 3 do not necessarily result in increases in y.[9] Rather, if size of farm is held constant, successive increments in P not only result in diminished increases in y but also in a decline in y, after a point of maximum is reached.

The rationale underlying this behavior is plausible. Increases in P and A are not distinguished by the model—either increase implies an increase in the economically meaningful land asset of the farm. Thus, the same factors that cause a decline in productivity, if physical area of the farm is increased and quality (P) held constant, should also imply a decline if P is increased and A is held constant.

Perhaps the best interpretation of the choice between models 2 and 3 is that model 2 considers physical area per se to be of importance, whereas, model 3 concentrates on land value regardless of area. Now, from the standpoint of some farm operations it is important to consider physical area as meaningful irrespective of land value. In particular, some operations, such as plowing, are proportional to physical area whatever the land quality (or may even be inversely related to land quality—more intensive plowing may be necessary to break up lower quality hard-pan soil, for example). On the other hand, other activities are much more related to output than to physical area (harvesting, weeding, animal care), and because land quality will influence the amount of output per area, from the standpoint of these operations it is quality adjusted land size, or total land value, that is the relevant definition of farm size. Considering the alternative cases in support of the two approaches, it is useful to examine empirical estimates for both.

Results for the two models are presented in Table A-2. In either case, declining productivity is observed with respect to size (or scale). The explanatory power of the basic model is considerably increased (R^2 increases from 0.095 to 0.20 [model 2] and 0.16 [model 3]), and model 2 is seen to perform better than model 3. (The land value coefficient b' is, however, more significant than the area coefficient b.) Even when the data were disaggregated by major crop grown (section A.3.2[d]), Model 2 performed consistently better in statistical terms. Since qualitative results are unaffected by the nature of the model used, only results for model 2 are presented in the following discussion.

The introduction of a price term in models 2 and 3 has only accounted for exogenous differences in soil fertility—differences in quality due to irrigation are ignored. It has been observed with Indian data that small farmers have a greater percentage of land under irrigation, and this tendency is confirmed by the results reported in Table A-1. Thus, it can be argued, that the introduction of a price term does not adequately control for quality differences, since 'inherent' differences in irrigation have not been controlled for—consequently, a negative coefficient of b may reflect irrigation (and cropping-intensity) differences rather than differences in farm productivity.

It cannot be denied that inherent differences in soils do exist, and that they should be accounted for in any explanation of farm productivity. However, exogenous and endogenous determinants of soil fertility are difficult to separate. Man-made improvements in the form of irrigation and fertilizer application can affect the fertility of the soil and, in such a circumstance, it is improper to explain productivity differences after controlling for irrigation. If small farmers have a greater percentage of land under irrigation, then a prior question needs to be asked—Why do small farmers irrigate more?

An *extreme* test of the inverse relationship can be conducted by estimation of model 4:

Table A-2. Quality of Land, Irrigation, and the Inverse Relationship between Land Productivity and Farm Size. All Farms, 1970–71 (1,772 Observations)

Constant	Coefficients			$\overline{R}^2$	Equation
a	b	c	d		
882	−130			.095	1
(41.6)	(13.6)				
663	−108	.07		.200	2
(30.0)	(11.9)	(15.3)			
496	−92	.05	4.6	.393	3
(22.0)	(11.6)	(11.0)	(23.8)		
0.55	−0.12			.160	2′
(41.0)	(18.4)				
0.49	−0.13		0.0018	.208	3′
(33.8)	(20.0)		(10.4)		

Notes:
 a. Absolute value of the t-statistic is in parentheses.
 b. The equations represent model 4 in the text, of the form:
 $y = a + b \log A + cP + dI$
 where y is output per farm area, A is farm area, P is price of unirrigated land (land quality) and I is percentage of land (net) under irrigation.
 c. Equations 2′ and 3′ represent a "standardized acre" model of the form:
 $y' = a' + b' \log A' + d'I$
 where A' is value of land ($=$ Acreage, A, times price, P), and y' is output divided by land value.
Source: Calculated from NCAER Survey.

(6) $y = a + b \log A + cP + dI.$

Irrigation differences in this model are introduced via I—percentage of (net) area under irrigation. The model essentially answers the question: given differences in irrigation and land prices, does one still observe a significantly negative coefficient for b.[10]

Equations 3 and 3′, Table A-2, present results for models 2 and 3, when a term I, representing irrigation differences, is introduced. Coefficient b is reduced in size with its introduction, reflecting the negative correlation between farm size and irrigation. The explanatory power of the model is considerably improved (R^2 increases from 0.2 to 0.393), reflecting the important contribution of irrigation differences to variations in output.

In sum, the results of Table A-2 suggest that land-quality differences, whether in endogenous (irrigation) or exogenous (soil quality) form, do not explain the negative relationship between farm productivity and farm size. The next section investigates the contribution, if any, of cropping patterns to the observed negative relationship.

A.3.2(b) *Cropping Patterns*   The analysis so far has been conducted at the aggregate level; any differences that are presumed to exist among farmers in the crops grown have been ignored. It is doubtful whether this aggregation has in any way affected the results; unless large farmers consistently grow low-valued crops, the estimate of b (and the inverse relationship) should be valid, even with crop composition held constant. However, risk considerations, differences in labor requirements, and access to intermediate inputs may dictate a nonrandom relationship between size of farm and the product-mix.

The NCAER data allows only a partial test of the inverse relationship for individual crops. Identification is only available for the major crop grown by the farmer, i.e., the crop that occupies the most area of the total land cultivated. If farmers grow only one crop, then this identification is not a disadvantage. However, cropping combinations are quite common among Indian farmers. Rice is often combined with jute in West Bengal, and wheat (which is only a winter crop) is often grown with maize and jowar. Thus, a complete segmentation of crops grown is not possible with NCAER data. The following analysis of data by crop is justified if it is assumed that, given the major crop grown, there is no relationship between the cropping combination and farm size.

Table A-3 presents the results for models 2 and 4 at the individual crop level. Except for jowar and sugar cane, which are major crops for only 3 percent of the sample of farmers, the coefficient b is significantly negative at the 1 percent level (and the 5 percent level for maize) for all crops grown.[11] Controlling for irrigation, which as argued in the previous section is not entirely appropriate, causes the coefficient b in the regression for maize to be significant at only the 15 percent level of confidence. The results remain quite similar for the other crops, though the magnitude of b diminishes slightly.[12]

The results of this and the previous sections establish that there is a negative relationship between farm size and productivity at the aggregate level, and that this relationship remains significant even after differences in land quality, irrigation, and cropping patterns are allowed for. In section A.3.3, the analysis proceeds to an examination of the endogenous economic factors that might cause an inverse relationship to be observed.

Table A-3. Regression Results: Land Productivity in Relation to Farm Size, by Individual Crop, 1970-71

Crop	Constant	Coefficient on: logarithm of farm size, A	Price of land, P	% area under irrigation, I	$\overline{R}^2$
	a	b	c	d	
Rice ($N = 761$)	698 (21.8)	−115 (8.5)	.06 (9.8)		.190
Rice ($N = 761$)	596 (18.8)	−105 (8.16)	.046 (8.16)	2.8 (9.91)	.282
Wheat ($N = 389$)	1,021 (15.8)	−147 (6.28)	.025 (2.33)		.104
Wheat ($N = 389$)	605 (9.55)	−128 (6.47)	.021 (2.32)	6.06 (12.7)	.367
Maize ($N = 220$)	343 (4.8)	− 39.6 (1.77)	.098 (4.3)		.105
Maize ($N = 220$)	199 (3.33)	− 17.8 (.96)	.079 (4.2)	5.45 (10.4)	.400
Cotton ($N = 122$)	410 (4.33)	− 83 (2.95)	.17 (7.80)		.371
Cotton ($N = 122$)	399 (4.24)	− 76 (2.66)	.13 (4.5)	1.7 (1.64)	.380
Jowar ($N = 37$)	168 (1.36)	0.78 (.014)	.14 (4.04)		.285
Jowar ($N = 37$)	46.2 (.47)	− 6.62 (.15)	.08 (2.71)	5.5 (5.07)	.586
Sugarcane ($N = 13$)	1,630 (2.85)	−242 (1.24)	.005 (.05)		−.02
Sugarcane ($N = 13$)	1,446 (2.29)	−228 (1.14)	−.0008 (.008)	3.19 (.77)	−.06
Combination, two of above	708 (9.14)	−158 (5.81)	.10 (6.6)		.383
Combination, two of above ($N = 169$)	462 (6.79)	−122 (5.44)	.05 (3.97)	5.5 (9.39)	.595

Notes:
   a. The farms are classified into crop categories, according to the major crop grown. The major crop is one having a greater percentage of gross cropped area than any other crop.
   b. Model of the form:

$$y = a + b \log A + cP + dI$$

is estimated for each crop category, using output value for all crops on the farm.
   c. The absolute value of the t-statistic is in parentheses.
Source: Calculated from NCAER survey data.

A.3.3(a) *Farm Size and Productivity—Economic Explanations.* If the exogenous element of land quality is ruled out, then different farms producing the same product will have different factor combinations and output-input ratios, if:[13] (a) they differ in economic efficiency. Differences may be due to technical efficiency, price efficiency, or both; (b) they face different factor prices.[14]

The studies that have dealt with the question of differences in economic efficiency between large and small farms have generally come up with conflicting results. Lau-Yotopoulos (1971), in their analysis of FMS data for the fifties, found small farmers to be technically more efficient than large farmers. Siddhu (1974), using post-Green Revolution data for the Punjab, found no differences in economic efficiency for the two sets of farmers.

On *a priori* grounds, one would expect that large farmers are not at a disadvantage in terms of allocative efficiency. Better education, easier access to inputs, and connections with extension agents all argue in favor of productivity advantages for the large farmers. Unless land is being held for prestige or speculative reasons, of which there is not much evidence for India, large farmers should be at least as "rational" as small farmers. Whether they are is an empirical proposition which, unfortunately, is not testable with the NCAER data. The survey did not collect any data on family labor input in farm production—lack of this important input prevented a rigorous test of allocative efficiency.

If differences in economic efficiency are ignored, then the only hypothesis left to explain the relatively larger output/acre of small farmers is that concerning factor prices. Different factor prices imply different factor combinations, at least under the assumption of profit maximization. That farmers face different input prices is not a new proposition; nevertheless, it is controversial, because it asserts that factor markets are imperfect and the proof of such an assertion can be difficult.

The major factors of production in agriculture are land, labor, and capital. In the following discussion, each of the factor markets will be examined and, whenever possible, empirical evidence will be offered to support the assertions about imperfections. It should be pointed out that imperfections are necessary in at least two of the markets for factor combinations to be different. For instance, if only labor-market dualism were present, and this resulted in higher productivity of small farms, then land leases could still occur, until there was no difference in the marginal product of labor across farms. Along these lines, it has been erroneously stated by Bharadwaj (1974*b*) that under conditions of 'fixed' land for each holding, *ceteris paribus*, large farmers would choose a higher land/labor combination. In fact, if this were the only imperfection in the system, then land/labor, output/acre, and other ratios would be identical on all farms, for a linearly homogeneous production function.[15]

A.3.3(b) *Factor Markets—Land.*   The *a priori* expectation is that large landowners effectively face a lower price per acre of land owned. This imperfection results even after allowing for land leases. The general arguments are as follows. (a) Institutional factors, such as maximum rent chargeable, regulations on tenancy, etc., might cause the opportunity cost of land to be lower on larger farms. (b) If credit is available at cheaper rates to the larger farmer, then credit-supported purchases of land will effectively mean a lower price per acre for the large farmer. (c) If fragmentation of property is undesirable or inconvenient, then large farmers might prefer to sell their land as a continuous whole, rather than to parcel it out in small parts. "Package" selling and buying (lower transaction costs) might thus result in a lower price per unit of land.

The nature of these imperfections makes it difficult to test directly the hypothesis that large farmers face a lower price for a unit of quality-adjusted land. Indirect tests, however, are possible. Differences in cost of long-term borrowing can be observed and any systematic relationship between landownership and cost noted. (The discussion on credit markets (see p. 160) establishes that large farmers do indeed face a lower price of credit.) An alternative method is to study the lease market for land; if rental/acre is observed to have a negative relationship with farm size, then one would have partial support for the contention that large farmers face a lower price of land. The latter method, however, is not without its pitfalls. Observed rental/acre values may reflect tenancy arrangements as well as the 'price' of land. It is a moot question whether tenancy arrangements—sharecropping, fixed rentals, etc.—do affect static efficiency[16] (see Bardhan–Srinivasan 1973 and Cheung 1970, for differing views on the subject of tenancy and static efficiency). If output effects are present, then the tenancy factor should first be removed before conclusions about land prices are drawn.

In an analysis of FMS data, Bennett (1967) showed that rental/acre did decline with farm size. It is possible that this decline reflects tenancy effects as well as the price of land. Lack of data on tenancy arrangements prevented their incorporation into the analysis. The NCAER data suffer from the same failing. Tenancy arrangements are not identified; only the proportion of land leased in is known. If tenancy arrangements are ignored (a strong assumption, but see section A-3.6), the null hypothesis is

Table A–4. Regressions of Rental/Area on Area Rented: 1968-69 (Landlord) and 1970-71 (Tenants)

Year	Coefficients:				$\overline{R^2}$	Equation
	Constant	Area, A	Price of land, P	% age area under irr., I		
	a	b	c	d		
1968-69	208	−23.5	.027	0.39	0.14	1
(N = 36 obs.)	(4.3)	(1.2)	(1.8)	(.63)		
	203	−4.9	.027	0.46	0.19	1′
	(5.2)	(1.9)	(1.98)	(.76)		
1970-71	231.5	−50.1	.002	1.80	0.15	2
(N = 104 obs.)	(4.54)	(1.91)	(.23)	(3.91)		
	211.4	−7.84	.0008	1.82	0.14	2′
	(4.36)	(1.50)	(.77)	(3.93)		

Notes: 1. For description of model, see Table A-2, note b.
2. Equations 1 and 2 have land area expressed in log form and equations 1′ and 2′ have land area expressed in linear form. The dependent variable is equal to rental/acre.

Source: Calculated from NCAER data. See text.

that rental/acre is invariant with land leased. Two tests were conducted on this hypothesis with the data: (a) rental income as received by the landlord is compared to the land leased out for the first year of the survey 1968-69, and (b) rent paid by a lessee is compared to the land leased in during 1970-71. Thus, the data allow one to test for declines in rental/ acre for both landlords and tenants.

In either case, if R_e represents rent and L the leased out/leased in land, then R_e/L should be independent of L. Equations 1-2 and 1'-2' in Table A-4 represent the results for 1968-69 and 1970-71 and two functional forms—semi-log and linear. Even after controlling for land quality (variable P) and irrigation, the unit rental cost per acre decreases by Rs. 5-Rs. 10 for each additional acre of land rented. The significance of the results depends on the functional form adopted, but the general conclusion that emerges is that rental/acre declines with farm size. Though not conclusive, the results support the hypothesis that large farmers face an effectively lower price for land. Ideally, one would like to disaggregate by both the crop grown and 'type' of tenancy; the former was not possible due to degrees of freedom and, as mentioned earlier, no data was available to test for tenancy arrangements.

A-3.3(c) *Factor Markets—Capital.* Though often hypothesized, there has been little evidence to support the assertion that the cost of borrowing varies systematically with landownership. Numerous factors are expected to act against the small farmer obtaining credit at the same interest rate as the large farmer. The small farmer has fewer assets to offer as collateral. Moreover, his 'discretionary' income is smaller and his needs for consumption funds disproportionately greater. These conditions result in his paying a higher price for borrowed funds. The fact that observed interest rates might reflect risk considerations on the part of the lender does not affect the conclusion that the cost of capital is likely to be higher, and the use of capital different, for the small farmer.

The NCAER survey collected data on the source, volume, and cost of borrowed funds on the part of the individual households. A direct test of systematic differences in the price of borrowing is therefore possible, and the results presented in Table A-5 support the assertion that the interest rate on borrowing (cost of capital) declines as farm size rises.[17]

The traditional source of credit in the rural sector of India is the money-lender. Over the years, the institutional sources—government, cooperatives, and the commercial banks—have started making inroads into the rural capital market. In 1970-71, these sources handled 30 per-

Table A-5. Cost of Capital by Farm Size and HYV Classification

Farm size (acres)	HYV growers %	Non-HYV growers %	All %
0–5	13.9	18.6	17.3
5–15	12.3	14.8	13.8
15–25	11.6	12.7	12.2
>25	9.7	13.0	11.8
All	12.4	15.8	14.5

Notes: In these caluations, all farms that had a marginal cost of borrowing equal to 0 percent because of borrowing from 'friends and relatives' are excluded.

Since most (78 percent) of the 'friends and relatives' funds are concentrated in the large-size groups (over 15 acres), this means that the estimates presented are upper bounds for the group above 15 acres.

Source: Calculated from NCAER survey. See text.

cent of the total lending compared to 19 percent in 1961–62 and 7 percent in 1951–52 (see Table A–6). The money-lenders share declined from 75 percent to 50 percent over the same twenty-year period. Apart from considerations of infrastructure development, identification of the source of funds is important, because it is indicative of the interest rates charged. The government and cooperatives charge an interest rate 8 to 9 percent while the money-lender charges an (average) rate of 22 percent (Table A–7).

These institutional sources are heavily biased toward the HYV growers. As Table A–8(a) shows, only 18.6 percent of government lending and 38 percent of cooperative lending went to non-HYV growers. The commerical banks lent about 65 percent to the non-HYV sector, and it is indicative that most of their loans went to the large farmers. Considerations of default risk undoubtedly play a role in this pattern, with the HYV growers presumed to be a better credit risk.

As part of its campaign to increase production, the government of India has launched programs over the years to disseminate knowledge about HYVs and help farmers with inputs of fertilizer, etc. Tied funds for fertilizer and HYV use are often made available at low rates of interest to encourage growth of HYV production. Interest-free loans are also given by the agencies to farmers for the purpose of purchasing shares in cooperatives. Consequently, the bias toward HYV growers observed above is not accidental. In this regard, the bias of 'friends and relatives' (a source with presumably easier terms of credit) toward HYV growers is also relevant—only 15 percent of their loans went to the non-HYV growers. Stated differently, the money-lender accounted for only 29 percent of the

Table A-6. Proportion of Agricultural Borrowings from Different Agencies, According to Various Surveys (Percentages; All Cultivating Households)

Agency	AIRCS (1951–52)	AIRDIS (1961–62)	NCAER (1970–71)
Government	3.3	2.6	3.6
Cooperatives	3.1	15.5	22.7
Commercial banks	0.9	0.6	4.0
Money-lenders, traders, and commission agents	75.2	58.0	49.6
Friends and relatives	14.2	8.8	18.8
Landlords and others (including unspecified)	3.3	14.5	1.3
Total	100.0	100.0	100.0

Note: AIRCS and AIRDIS refer to two surveys, conducted by the Reserve Bank of India; All India Rural Credit Survey, 1951–52; and All India Rural Debt and Investment Survey, 1961–62.

Source: NCAER, *Credit Requirements for Agriculture*, 1974.

loans to HYV growers and 69 percent to non-HYV cultivators (see Table A–8[b]).

Access to institutional credit diminishes the cost of credit for all HYV farmers, and the greatest decline is observed for the smallest farmers—from 19 percent to 14 percent. For the largest farmers (>25 acres) the decline is small—from 13 percent to 10 percent. (The variability across farms is also diminished with HYV cultivation.) Interest rates range from 10 to 14 percent for HYV cultivators, and from 13 to 19 percent for households employing the traditional technology. These results suggest that increased access to institutional credit has the greatest impact on the small farmer. In other words, the 'element' of subsidy contained in institutional credit is largest for the small farmer.

The following conclusions emerge from the discussion of the rural capital market: (a) small farmers pay a higher interest rate for funds borrowed than do large farmers; part of this higher cost may be due to the relatively fixed costs of administration of loans by banks; (b) cultivation of high-yielding varieties improves access to institutional credit and thereby diminishes the cost of credit—this decrease is most pronounced for small farmers; (c) there is less variation in the cost of credit for HYV farmers than non-HYV farmers.

A–3.3(d) *Factor Markets—Labor.*   Of all the factor markets, it is the labor market that has attracted the most attention among analysts of agrarian structure and productivity in developing countries. Since Lewis's

Table A-7. Average Rates of Interest on Borrowings by Various Size-categories of Farmers from Different Sources (Percent per Annum)

Size of holding (acres)	Government	Cooperatives	Commercial banks	Money-lenders, etc.	Friends and relatives	All sources[a]
0-5	8.9	8.9	7.2	22.5	0.0	16.0
5-10	9.0	9.1	8.1	20.9	0.0	14.3
10-15	8.3	9.0	9.4	23.3	0.0	14.9
15 and above	8.4	9.0	9.2	16.3	0.0	9.0
All holdings	8.8	9.0	8.4	21.8	0.0	14.8

[a]Including landlords and others.

Source: NCAER, Credit Requirements for Agriculture, 1974.

Table A–8(a). Percentage Distribution by Sources of Loans among Different Farm Categories

	Type and size of holding (acres)									
	HYV					Non-HYV				
Source	0-5	5-10	10-15	15 and above	All holdings	0-5	5-10	10-15	15 and above	All holdings
Government	17.0	34.0	15.1	15.3	81.4	9.4	2.5	0.7	6.0	18.6
Cooperatives	10.9	15.7	9.3	26.1	62.0	11.8	11.2	5.6	9.4	38.0
Commercial banks	9.0	18.4	0.2	7.1	34.7	2.9	5.9	28.6	27.9	65.3
Money-lenders, etc.	7.6	8.5	8.5	4.7	29.3	33.3	21.1	6.7	9.6	70.7
Friends and relatives	9.6	3.4	1.3	70.8	85.1	9.4	3.0	0.4	2.1	14.9
All sources[a]	9.0	10.4	7.1	22.8	49.3	21.7	13.9	6.5	8.6	50.7

[a]Including landlords and others.

Source: NCAER, Credit Requirements for Agriculture, 1974.

Table A-8(b). **Borrowings from Different Agencies**

Source	HYV cultivators	Non-HYV cultivators	All
	%	%	
Government	5.9	1.4	3.6
Cooperatives	28.6	17.1	22.7
Commercial banks	2.8	5.2	4.0
Money-lenders, etc.	29.3	69.2	49.6
Friends and relatives	33.1	4.9	18.8
Total[a]	100.0	100.0	100.0

[a]Including landlords and others.

(1954) article on surplus labor, a considerable literature has been generated on the question of a dual labor market in developing countries. Though originally couched in terms of the industrial/agricultural sectors, the arguments apply equally to dualism *within* the agricultural sector, as long as a distinction is maintained between the traditional and modern methods of production. The modern sector is capitalist and hires workers to maximize profits; the traditional sector is a subsistence sector, where households use mainly family labor for production. The general presumption is that in this dual market the marginal product (wage) of the capitalist sector is approximately equal to the average product of a worker in the traditional sector.

Sen (1966) presents a formal, theoretical model, explaining labor-market dualism in agriculture. The basic assumption in his model is that the small farmers maximize utility in a trade-off between output and leisure within the confines of their limited land and family labor resources, whereas the large farmers maximize profits. Also, the small farmers use primarily family labor and large farmers hire labor for purposes of production.

Whether differences in objective functions are assumed or not, the question still has to be answered as to why the small farmers do not hire out their labor until the marginal products of labor are equated in the two sectors. Studies on Indian agriculture have consistently observed that small farms both hire in and hire out their labor. Table A-9 seems to bear this out for the NCAER data. Among the smallest category of farmers, 52 percent of the units had nonfarm earnings. For this same group, 83 percent hired labor at one time or another during the agricultural year. At an aggregate level, the percentage of farms hiring in and hiring out labor was 89 percent and 33 percent respectively.

The fact that a large number of small farms hire in and hire out their

Table A-9. Pattern of On-Farm, Off-Farm Employment

Farm size (acres)	Percent of farms hiring in labor (%)	Percent of farms hiring out labor (%)	Hired labor/acre
0-5	83	52	20.5
5-15	90	27	18.4
15-25	97	15	17.0
>25	95	12	15.5
All	89	33	18.7

Source: Calculated from NCAER survey. See text.

labor is not inconsistent with labor dualism. Agriculture is seasonal, and during peak periods, like harvest time, extra labor is needed to harvest the crop optimally. Both Cline (1970) and Mazumdar (1965) discuss in detail the likely reasons for labor dualism in such a context, and it would be repetitive to detail the arguments here. Instead, the major arguments for labor-market dualism will be outlined.

a) Dualism implies that the marginal product of labor is higher on the larger farm. It would appear that family income would be maximized by movement of labor outside the family to work where the wage was higher. This hiring-out process comes to an end when the marginal products on the farms are equated. Employment outside the farm, however, implies a loss to the individual worker in so far as he loses the higher income (average product) on the family farm.

The question arises: Why doesn't the family supplement the worker for the difference between the average and marginal products? An assertion of dualism boils down to an explanation of this phenomenon. If the outside work is adjacent to the farm, the hiring-out process might indeed take place until the marginal products were equalized. If not (as may often be the case), then the family may be unable to compensate the hired-out worker, because income earned on the farm was in kind, or because family income could not be pooled before distribution, or because it was simply unwilling to do so.

b) Another explanation of dualism is the assertion that the probability of outside employment for a family worker is less than 100 percent. In this case, the expected wage on the capitalist farm is equated to the family farm marginal product, thus resulting in a divergence in the respective costs of labor for the two groups—surplus labor is implicitly assumed, and this may indeed be true for the "slack" period of agricultural production. During "peak" periods, even small farms hire labor, and surplus labor is

no longer a valid assumption. However, to the extent the demand for labor is complementary over the different seasons, a wage gap in only one period is enough to assure a difference in labor costs for the two sets of farmers.
c)To be assured of employment during the peak season, large farms may prefer to hire a worker on a contractual basis. The small farmer would in this case be unable to make optimal marginal adjustments to his labor supply.

Researchers have used various techniques in their attempt to prove the existence of labor dualism. Yotopoulos et al. (1970), for instance, estimate different production functions for large and small farms and compare the marginal products at the geometrical means of the variables involved. If these estimates are significantly different, and higher for the larger farmer, then this is offered as evidence for labor-market dualism. Another method is to impute market wages to family labor input and compute accounting profits. When this procedure was used with the FMS studies, small farmers consistently showed negative profits. Moreover, accounting profit/acre increased with farm size. Though causes other than dualism may have been responsible for this phenomena, the results, nevertheless, are consistent with dualism in the labor market. Yet another approach to dualism is to observe factor inputs and factor combinations and determine whether they fit the theory. With differences in labor costs, large farms should have a higher capital/labor ratio than small farms, and the relative use of labor (and its complementary inputs) should decline as farm size rises. This phenomenon is used to identify imperfections in the factor markets in the analysis presented in the next section.

Lack of direct data on family labor input prevents a "production function" test of labor-market dualism. However, the NCAER data has the advantage that, due to oversampling of the rich households, it allows a test of dualism that has generally not been possible with other sources of data. This is a test of output/acre variation for the large-farm group by itself. According to theory, if labor-market dualism were the dominant influence in peasant agriculture, then among large "capitalist" farms there should be no variation in land productivity—because the entire range of such farms would be using hired labor, not family labor. (If capital market imperfections were dominant, then one would observe output/acre to *increase* with farm size; and if land imperfections were dominant, then output/acre should continue to decline with farm size.)

Identification of large farms who face the same market conditions, and particularly the ones pertaining to the labor market, is difficult in practice. This is because large farms in India are small enough to depend to a significant extent on family labor input. Large farms of the kind observed in Latin America (and the U.S.A.), and ones that would be ideal for such a test, are not common in India.

Table A-10 shows the distribution of land in India in 1960. The average Indian farm is observed to be 6 acres. Large Indian farms account for a very small proportion—only 4.7 percent of farms are above 25 acres. And even a sample of the largest Indian farms may not be appropriate for a test of the dominance of labor-market dualism, family labor input being a significant proportion of total labor input for these farms. Roy's (1974) study for the Punjab shows this ratio to be 25 percent for the > 30 acre farms. However, the differences in family labor among large farms may not be large enough to negate the proposition that these farms face essentially the same price for labor. Thus, a test based on them may provide meaningful results on the effects of dualism.

Models 2 and 4 are reestimated for large farms (>30 acres):

$$\text{(7a)} \quad y = \underset{(1.75)}{410} - \underset{(1.04)}{63.5 \log A} + \underset{(6.85)}{.11 P} \qquad R^2 = .28$$

$$\text{(7b)} \quad y = \underset{(1.6)}{308} - \underset{(.93)}{46.4 \log A} + \underset{(4.0)}{.06 P} + \underset{(7.45)}{4.8 I} \qquad R^2 = .517$$

$$\text{(number of observations} = 116)$$

Farm size turns out to be an insignificant variable in both the equations (as shown by the low t-statistics in parentheses). It would be desirable to conduct this test for the different crops grown; however, cell sizes become too small for hypothesis testing.

These results tend to confirm the presence of dualism. (To reiterate,

Table A-10. Land Distribution in India, 1961-62

Size of farm (acres)	Number of farms (%)	Area operated (%)	Average size of farms
0-1	18.3	1.3	0.5
1-5	44.1	17.7	2.6
5-10	19.3	20.3	6.9
10-15	7.8	14.0	11.8
15-25	5.9	16.8	18.6
25-50	3.6	17.9	32.9
>50	1.1	11.9	74.2
All	100.0	100.0	6.2

Source: National Sample Survey, 16th & 17th rounds, 1961-62; reported in B. Sen (1974).

equations identical to 7a and 7b for the entire sample of farms did result in a significantly negative coefficient for land.) Though a significant coefficient for land in Equations 7a and 7b would not necessarily have negated the hypothesis of dualism (this due to a sizable presence of family labor input on these farms), an insignificant coefficient does lend it strong support. That is, once a threshold size is reached on which hired labor predominates, the argument of a dichotomy between cheap family labor and expensive hired labor no longer applies. Thus, there would be no reason to expect continued decline in output per farm area over the remaining range of farm sizes, and, in fact, the statistical tests for large farms suggest that there is no significant continued decline in productivity as farm size rises.

A-3.4   *Intensity of Input Use and Factor Combinations.*   In the previous section, it was established that (a) output/acre declines significantly with farm size, and (b) that imperfections in the factor markets, and especially the labor market, may be causing this result. If differences in efficiency are ruled out, and the same production function is assumed for all farmers, then to achieve higher output per acre, small farmers must be using more inputs/acre. (Table A-1 showed that these farms also had more irrigation and a greater cropping intensity). The intensity of individual factor use, and its variability with farm size, is explored in this section. Also, differences in factor combinations observed are compared with predictions from theory.

If a linearly homogeneous production function is assumed, then for each input I, the elasticity of its use with respect to farm size should be unity. That is, if an equation of the form:

$$\log I = a + In \log A$$

is estimated for each input—labor, capital, and intermediate inputs (seeds, fertilizers, pesticides, and manure)—the coefficient "In" should not be significantly different from unity. Since the small farmers probably face a much lower price for labor, the relative use of this factor, along with other complementary factors should decrease with farm size. Consequently, one might expect all elasticities to be less than unity.

Estimation of the log–log form is not feasible when any of the inputs are zero. The equations presented below are estimates of the inputs when they are positive. The difference of this estimate from that representative of the entire group of farmers will be dependent on whether usage of the input was related to farm size. If, for instance, a smaller proportion of small farmers than large use any fertilizer whatsoever, a regression of fertilizer-users only will overstate the relative use of intermediate inputs on small farms and, consequently, bias downward the coefficient with respect to farm size.

The definitions and estimations for the inputs involved are as follows:

a) *Capital*. Data on the value of assets owned—farm equipment, irrigation, livestock, and farm machinery—are available for each household. The flow of capital services in the form of expenses for tractors, threshers, irrigation equipment, etc. is converted into stock by assuming a discount rate of 10 percent. The amount of capital used by each farm is indicated by the addition of these two stocks.

b) *Seeds, Fertilizers, etc.* Expenditures on seeds, fertilizers, pesticides, and manure, individually, were obtained by the NCAER survey. Farms are expected to differ in the use of this component not only with the use of other factors but also with the extent of involvement of the farm with HYVs. Though only the result for all farms is presented, it should be mentioned that farms separated into HYV/non-HYV growers did not show much difference from the aggregate estimate.

c) *Labor*. Labor costs are by far the dominant cost in peasant agriculture, often accounting for about 75 percent of total costs. Expenditure on hired labor is available for each farm, but an estimate for the most important component—family labor—is not directly available. An indirect approach was therefore used to arrive at an estimate of family labor input. Annex A.2 outlines in detail the methodology used and the assumptions made in arriving at this synthetic figure. Addition of this constructed cost of family labor with hired labor costs provides one with an estimate of L^*—total labor input on each farm. This representation of labor cost assumes that there is no difference in the quality of hired and family labor.

It should be mentioned that the estimate of family labor input has deliberately been made a "worst case" estimate from the standpoint of labor-market dualism; that is, it tends to impute to the small farmers less labor than might be used in fact. The worst case approach was chosen because the interest in the exercise is not to obtain exact estimates of labor input, but rather to observe differences in the use of this input across farm sizes.

Nevertheless, reliability of L^* would be enhanced if it were shown that its values paralleled closely those obtained from direct measurement. This, unfortunately, is not an easy task. Few published studies on Indian agriculture list variations in labor input/acre. Moreover, studies differ in coverage (farm sizes, crops), methodology, and region—factors that can drastically affect the estimates obtained. However, some comparison is desirable, and estimates presented in Table A-11 fulfill this need. The results are from diverse studies, and it is hoped that taken together they convey a picture that is representative of conditions prevailing in India.

Given the synthetic nature of L^*, it performs surprisingly well. Its 'average' estimate of 82 days/acre falls well within the range of the other studies. The values for labor/acre given in the table are averages and strongly dependent on the composition of the adoption pattern of the farmers. The averages can thus be expected to vary with cropping combinations and HYV adoption. This expected variability notwithstanding, it is gratifying to note that L^*, an indirect estimate, compares favorably with direct estimates of labor inputs.

The favorable comparison of L^* suggests that the tests based on it may be reliable. The first test is the estimation of Equation 8 for labor and other inputs. The results for each of the inputs are the following:

(8a) $\log K = 6.8 + 0.74 \log A$ $R^2 = 0.34$
              (110.3)   (27.5)

(8b) $\log S = 4.1 + 0.77 \log A$ $R^2 = 0.29$
              (55.1)   (23.7)

(8c) $\log L = 5.2 + 0.55 \log A$ $R^2 = 0.40,$
              (127.9)   (31.2)

where K is capital; S is the expenditure on seeds, fertilizers, insecticides, and manure; and the number of observations is 1,443.[18]

The null hypothesis is that all the estimated input elasticities should not be significantly different from 1—this in the case of perfect competition and a linearly homogeneous production function for agriculture. The elasticities reported in Equations 8a–8c are significantly different from 1, and it appears that labor use declines the most with regard to farm size (i.e., its elasticity with respect to size is the lowest). These results provide a strong explanation for the inverse relationship—a considerable portion of the difference in output/acre by farm size is due to different intensity of inputs.

Further support for this result is revealed by the pattern of factor ratios for the different-sized farms. According to theory, if capital and land are cheaper for the large farms and labor more expensive, then the following pattern of factor combinations should result: capital/labor ratio should increase and labor/land ratio should decrease as farm size rises. The

Table A-11. Comparison of Labor/Acre Estimates

Study	State	Major crop	Avg. farm size (acres)	Labor days/ acre
NCAER	All-India	All (1970-71)	11.4	82
Acharaya (1973)	Rajasthan	Wheat & maize (1971-72)	9.6	84
Roy (1974)	Punjab	Wheat (1971-72)	20.5	56
T. K. Pal[a]	Orissa	Rice (1971-72)	1.5	142
J. S. Sharma[a]	Uttar Pradesh	Rice & wheat (1971-72)	7.1	93
V. Rajagopalan[a]	Tamil Nadu	Rice (1971-72)	6.6	83
G. Pathasarathy[a]	Andhra Pradesh	Rice (1971-72)	11.8	142

Note: In the case where studies reported separate figures for cultivators of improved and local varieties, a simple average of the two is reported.

[a]These studies are taken from International Rice Research Institute, *Changes in Rice Farming in Selected Areas of Asia* (*1975*). Some of the articles reported separate estimates for regions within states. In such a circumstance, a simple average of the regions is reported.

Table A-12. Input Factor Combinations by Farm Size

Farm size	Labor/acre (days/acre)	Seeds etc./acre (Rs./acre)	Capital/acre (Rs./acre)	Capital/labor ratio	Number of obs. N
0-5	122	55	914	12.2	558
5-15	70	51	738	13.8	734
15-25	51	48	600	14.1	248
>25	47	36	459	11.7	169
All	82	51	748	13.1	1,709

Note: Averages are based on 1,709 farms rather than 1,772. Sixty-three farms had to be excluded due to construction of a "synthetic" figure for labor inputs. (See Annex A.2.)

Source: Calculated from NCAER survey. See text.

prediction for the capital/land ratio is ambiguous, since both inputs are cheaper for the large farmers.

The observed combinations (reported in Table A-12) follow the expected pattern; labor/acre declines with increase in farm size, with the small farmers using almost twice as much of the relatively cheaper labor as the large farmers. The capital/labor ratio increases with farm size, thus reflecting the substitution of the cheaper capital for the relatively more costly labor.[19] Capital/acre declines with farm size, as does the use of seeds and fertilizers—this result possibly occurring due to the complementarity of these inputs with the greater labor input on small farms.

In summary, the results of this section suggest that the observed 'inverse' relationship between farm size and productivity is not due entirely to exogenous differences in land quality, but is a result also of real differences in factor prices. And these systematic differences lead to different combinations of input and output ratios. Though imperfections in all markets are responsible for this phenomenon, the nature of the results suggest that dualism in the labor market is the most important factor.

The data used were for the 1970–71 agricultural year—a year some six years after the introduction of the high-yielding varieties. The Green Revolution has, therefore, not qualitatively affected the inverse relationship. However, explicit differences in HYV adoption were not introduced into the analysis. This is done in section 4, along with an analysis of changes in the inverse relationship from 1968–69 to 1970–71 and the causes thereof.

A-3.5   *Total Factor Productivity.*   Sections A.3.3(a) through A.3.3(d) have examined economic efficiency in a partial context; individual factor markets were analyzed for their impact on resource allocation. From the standpoint of the overall economy, it is the total social factor productivity that is relevant. The important question is whether differences in total resource usage can be observed across farms.

The important calculation of total factor productivity cannot be done properly with the NCAER data. As mentioned and discussed in the previous section, no direct data are available for family labor inputs. Some estimates of labor input were, however, calculated and presented. If these estimates are accepted, then a statistical exercise of productivity calculations can be conducted. A strong caveat, however, is in order; this exercise is at best a crude attempt at an assessment of total factor productivity differences. However, given that sensitivity tests are carried out, and that the labor input calculation is a "worst case" version, the exercise is not without some merit.

Table A–13(a) shows the relevant statistics for the different farm-size groups, and Table A–13(b) the total social factor productivity (TSFP) under different assumptions of factor cost. TSFP is simply defined as the ratio of value-added per acre (income/acre minus seeds and fertilizer costs per acre) to resource costs per acre (capital assets/acre plus labor/acre).

For the Lewis assumption of surplus labor (zero social cost), TSFP declines uniformly with farm size for both sets of assumptions about the

Table A-13(a). Data for Total Factor-Productivity Calculations (Rs. per acre)

Farm size (acres)	Labor (Rs.)	Capital	Land value	Assets	Income	Seeds, fertilizers	Value-added
	A	B	C	D = B + C	E	F	G = E − F
0–5	122	914	3,992	4,906	737	55	682
5–15	70	738	3,652	4,390	607	51	556
15–25	51	600	3,375	3,975	482	48	434
Over 25	47	459	2,541	3,000	346	36	310
All	82	748	3,534	4,282	499	51	448

Sources: Tables A-12, A-16, and NCAER data.

Table A-13(b). Total Social Factor Productivity: Sensitivity Analysis

Farm size (acres)	0-5	5-15	15-25	Over 25	All
I. Interest rate on capital = 10% Labor cost at:					
A) Zero	1.39	1.27	1.09	1.03	1.05
B) ½ wage	1.00	1.01	0.91	0.83	0.81
C) ¾ wage	0.88	0.92	0.84	0.76	0.72
D) full wage	0.79	0.84	0.78	0.70	0.66
II. Interest rate on capital = 15% Labor cost at:					
A) Zero	0.93	0.84	0.73	0.69	0.70
B) ½ wage	0.74	0.72	0.64	0.59	0.58
C) ¾ wage	0.67	0.67	0.61	0.55	0.54
D) full wage	0.61	0.63	0.58	0.52	0.50

Note: Wage is average market wage as calculated from "Agricultural Wages in India, 1971." The average wage was calculated to be Rs. 3.11/day. Also see Annex A.2 to this Appendix.

opportunity cost of capital (10 percent and 15 percent). At the other extreme, if labor is valued at its market wage, then only slight differences are observed in productivity for farms of 0 to 15 acres; however, a decline is still obtained for larger farms. The intermediate sensitivity tests (labor at 50 percent and 75 percent of market wage) generally confirm the impression that small farms have greater total factor productivity than large farms.

These results supplement the earlier results on dualism. Not only is there an "inverse" relationship between farm size and land productivity, but also between farm size and total social factor productivity.

A-3.6 *Tenancy.* One of the recurring themes in discussion of farm productivity is the effect of tenancy per se on output. The traditional conclusion, rooted in Marshallian logic, is straightforward: if output is to be shared, then a sharecropper will have an incentive to use variable inputs less intensively; hence, he will obtain a lower output. Alternative tenancy arrangements (e.g., fixed-rent or cost-sharing) may not necessarily have this negative effect.

This conclusion was effectively challenged by Cheung (1969) who contended that the nature of tenancy would have no effect on output, provided the landlord was in a position to dictate the intensity of variable in-

Table A-14. Tenancy and Its Effect on Output per Acre, 1970-71

Constant	Coefficients on: Logarithm of farm size, A	Price of land, P	% area under irrigation, I	% area leased in, PL	$\overline{R}^2$
878.2	−129.5			0.76	0.095
(40.9)	(13.6)			(1.1)	
663.1	−107.8	0.071		−0.17	0.199
(26.9)	(11.9)	(15.2)		(.26)	
495.8	− 91.7	0.046	4.6	−0.14	0.393
(22.0)	(11.5)	(11.0)	(23.8)	(.24)	

Note: Number of observations is 1,772. Absolute value of the *t*-statistic appears in parentheses.

puts. This neoclassical assertion has not gone unchallenged (Bardhan-Srinivasan 1971).

Only limited data are available in the NCAER survey to examine this important question. No information is available on the type of tenancy arrangement; all that is known is whether a farmer was a tenant and the extent of the land leased in. Thus, a rigorous test of the Cheungian assertion is not possible. However, given that as much as 47 percent of tenancy in India was of the share-cropping type (Lakshminarayan-Tyagi 1977) in 1971-72, some negative effect of tenancy on output, if it exists, should be observed.

Table A-14 presents the results for the 1970-71 agricultural year. Tenancy is measured as the percentage of operated land that is leased in, *PL*. No specification of the model yields a significant effect for tenancy. Model 1 yields the result that tenancy has a slightly positive effect; the coefficient is 0.76, though the *t*-statistic is only 1.1. Adjustments of quality of land and irrigation do lead to tenancy having a negative sign; however, the *t*-statistics are very low (0.26 and 0.24).

The results of Table A-14 reinforce the Cheung conclusion that tenancy has a zero effect on output. However, the data limitations are an important qualification to the observed results.

A.4   TECHNICAL CHANGE AND THE FARM SIZE-PRODUCTIVITY RELATIONSHIP

The preceding analysis has shown that the inverse relationship between farm size and productivity still holds for the post-Green Revolution period of 1970-71. Though the analysis included HYV farms, adoption differences and the effect of the new technology on output was never explicitly discussed. Nor were changes in farm productivity over the years 1968-69 to 1970-71 analyzed.

Prior to the introduction of the new varieties, long-run implications could easily be drawn from static, one-period observations. The dynamism implicit in technical change can be expected to change productivity relationships, and it is by no means obvious that the small farmers would continue to produce more output/acre in the Green Revolution era. However, unless all imperfections are removed, or the advantages made compensating, some differences in productivity would still be observed; and the analysis for 1970-71 indicates that the small farmers continue to produce more output/acre. It can be argued that this is not a good test of the impact of the Green Revolution, since high-yielding varieties accounted for a relatively small proportion of total acreage in 1970-71. The terminal effect may be simulated by observing areas where the effects of the new varieties are most pronounced. This procedure is not without its drawbacks, but if such areas continue to sustain the inverse relationship, then a similar pattern can also be expected to prevail in Indian agriculture in the future.

The two major crops in India are rice and wheat, and, by all accounts, Tamil Nadu (rice) and Punjab-Harayana (wheat) are the most progressive areas. Adoption of the new technology in these areas has been rapid and pronounced. According to the NCAER data, 79 percent of farmers in Punjab-Haryana, and 59 percent of farmers in Tamil Nadu had adopted the new technology. The all-India figures (NCAER data) are 35 percent and 26 percent for wheat and rice, respectively.

The results for model 4 for the two areas are as follows:[20]

Punjab-Haryana (wheat):

$$(9a)\ y = 991 - 220\log A + .02P + 5.8I$$
$$\quad\quad (5.9)\quad (4.5)\quad\quad (1.2)\quad (6.9)\quad\quad R^2 = 0.5.$$

Tamil Nadu (rice):

$$(9b)\ y = 687 - 162\log A + .03P + 6.1I$$
$$\quad\quad (2.8)\quad (3.2)\quad\quad (1.1)\quad (2.8)\quad\quad R^2 = 0.26.$$

Equations 9(a) and 9(b) indicate that for both Punjab-Haryana (wheat) and Tamil Nadu (rice) the inverse relationship appears to be quite strong. Both states have had the active support of the government (extension agencies) and have witnessed a rapid spread of the new technology. The persistent negative coefficient of the land variable indicates that the small farmer is likely to retain his traditional advantage vis-à-vis the large farmer, even after the new technology has settled down.

This analysis for Punjab and Tamil Nadu, although useful, does not contain information on the "dynamic" effects of technical change. In particular, one needs to know whether introduction of the new technology has weakened (or strengthened) the inverse relationship.[21] And if it has been weakened, is it because small farms lag significantly behind large farms in adoption behavior? If so, then in terms of innovation, growth, and investment, land redistribution to small farmers could be undesirable for reasons of dynamic growth potential, even though favorable to production in terms of static optimal resource use.[22] If adoption of the new technology is not specific to farm size, then, *ceteris paribus,* the inverse relationship should remain constant. If it does change, a reasonable explanation must be offered.

The dynamic behavior of farm production is explored in Table A-15—the results for model 4 are presented for each of the years, 1968-69, 1969-70, and 1970-71. Comparing the equations for each year, it is observed that the inverse relationship has weakened somewhat over time. The absolute magnitude of the coefficient on the logarithm of land area declines by 34 percent over the three-year period.[23] Nevertheless, a strong

Table A-15. Farm Productivity Regressions for 1968-69, 1969-70, and 1970-71

Year	Constant	Coefficients: logarithm of farm size, A	Price of land, P	% area under irr., I	$\overline{R}^2$
	a	b	c	d	
1970-71	882 (41.6)	−130 (13.6)			.095
	496 (22.0)	−92 (11.6)	.046 (11.0)	4.6 (23.8)	.393
1969-70	925 (43.2)	−168 (17.2)			.143
	558 (24.9)	−128 (16.1)	.028 (6.66)	6.2 (28.5)	.454
1968-69	918 (37.9)	−168 (15.6)			.120
	607 (22.07)	−139 (14.1)	.052 (10.1)	4.1 (15.3)	.292

Notes: 1. For description of model, see Table A-2, note 2.
   2. Absolute value of t-statistic is in parentheses.

Source: Calculated from NCAER survey. See text.

negative relationship persisted in 1970-71 and remained highly significant in statistical terms. Table A-16 adds further support to this conclusion on the basis of group averages. Small farmers' incomes increased by only 9 percent over the three years, whereas, large farmers (>25 acres) income increased by 42 percent. Thus, it appears that the large farmers are reducing the gap in productivity. An understanding of this result is helped by knowledge of the nature and diffusion process of the new technology.

The basic requirements for HYV adoption are irrigation, new seeds, and fertilizer. These inputs are highly divisible. If access to information and inputs were equal, small farms should share to the same extent in proportionate gains as the large farms; their traditional advantage should remain, and the output/acre relationship should not necessarily change over the years. The 'neutrality' of technical change will depend on which of the following causes was dominant:

a) *Irrigation*: This is the most important determinant of adoption. Irrigation is necessary for successful application of the new technology. Given that small farmers have 'inherently' a greater percentage of land under irrigation (Table A-1), they are best placed to adopt the new technology.[24]

b) *Labor Demand*: The new technology places an increased demand on labor inputs. If unemployment or underemployment were present on the small farms prior to the Green Revolution, this fact should be to the advantage of the small farmer. The large farmer, primarily dependent on hired labor, does not enjoy this benefit. Mechanization, however, can help the large farmer, especially if he has access to it on a subsidized basis.

c) *Risk and Information*: Adoption of the new technology requires knowledge and entails risks. The large farmers' education, connections with extension agents, and wealth all make him a better candidate for adoption than the small farmer.

d) *Working Capital*: HYV adoption requires a significant increase in working capital. Operating costs in terms of seeds, fertilizer, and labor can more than double with the new technology. If access to credit is unequal, small farmers might be severely constrained in their desire to innovate. (This argument is independent of any additional consideration of risk that might be involved.)

Since conflicting results are predicted, it is difficult to forecast *a priori* the adoption rates by the different categories of farmers. Nevertheless, there is a strong expectation that causes (c) and (d) are the most important ones for the explanation of adoption.

The results of Table A-17 bear out this expectation. The percentage of

Table A-16. Average Income per Acre and HYV Area, 1968–69 to 1970–71

Farm size (acres)	HYV area %, 1968–69	Income/acre 1968–69	HYV area %, 1970–71	Income/acre 1970–71	% change in HYV area	% change in income/acre
0–5	14.6	676	16.5	737	13.0	9.0
5–15	12.8	536	16.3	607	27.3	13.2
15–25	13.1	426	18.5	482	41.2	13.1
>25	11.1	243	18.1	346	63.1	42.4
All	12.8	426	17.4	499	35.9	17.1

Source: Calculated from NCAER survey. See text.

Table A-17 Characteristics of Technology Adoption, 1968–69 to 1970–71

Farm size (acres)	1968–69				1970–71			
	% of all farmers who are adopters	% of all farmers with irrigation who are adopters	Area under HYV %	HYV area as % of irr. area	% of all farmers who are adopters	% of all farmers with irrigation who are adopters	Area under HYV %	HYV area as % of irr. area
0–5	21.6	34.7	14.6	33.6	29.1	42.1	16.5	29.3
5–15	26.7	37.5	12.8	32.1	33.4	45.3	16.3	29.3
15–25	28.2	46.7	13.1	39.6	42.7	58.1	18.5	40.7
>25	30.2	46.5	11.1	35.9	36.7	44.4	18.1	48.7
All	25.5	38.7	12.8	34.8	33.5	46.5	17.4	36.4

Notes: Only figures for *net* irrigated area are available for 1968–69. Gross irrigated area figures (used for computation in cols. 5 and 9) were constructed by imputing a cropping intensity equal to that employed by the farmer in 1970–71.

Source: Calculated from NCAER survey. See text.

farmers adopting the new technology increased with farm size in 1968-69, with 30 percent of the large farmers (>25 acres) and 22 percent of the small farmers (<5 acres) adopting the new technology. The differences hold up even when the proportions are stated in terms of adoption rates for the subclass of irrigated farms (col. 3)—46 percent of the irrigated large farms and 34 percent of the irrigated small farms grew HYV varieties in 1968-69. The difference between the two sets of farmers is small, especially given the resource constraints of the small farmer. Initially, therefore, the small farmers seem to have done better than might be expected. They did not lag behind significantly in innovation; indeed, as Table A-17 shows, they had a greater percentage of their area under HYVs than the large farmers.[25] (This is partly an illusion—small farmers also have a greater percentage of irrigated area. Column 5, Table A-17 suggests that farms of all sizes have an approximately equal proportion of irrigated land under HYVs.) Though different farm groups progressed differently in terms of adoption, the data for 1970-71 show that the small and large farmers are almost on equal ground. Then why the observed decline in the relative advantage of the small farmer? Table A-16 contains the explanation for this decline—the large farmers have increased their area under HYV the most—63 percent compared to 13 percent for the small farmers. It is this percentage that is the most important indicator of changing relative group performance. *Ceteris paribus,* output/acre should be proportional to area under HYVs; and if this increased the most for the large farmers, their proportionate gains in output should also have been the highest. This is apparently why output/acre does not decline as rapidly with farm size in 1970-71 as it did in 1968-69.

Because aggregate patterns of changes in HYV adoption by farm size may represent changes in crop composition rather than underlying trends related to farm size, it is useful to examine the trends separately for farms specializing in wheat and rice. Table A-18 presents data on HYV adoption by wheat and rice farms in 1968-69 and in 1970-71. These data make it clear that the greater proportionate gains in overall area under HYVs during the period were in wheat, probably because of its greater profitability than that of rice. Indeed, for rice the fraction of area under HYVs actually fell during the period for farms under fifteen acres, although this apparent decline may be attributable to a change in the definition of varieties classified as HYVs between the two surveys. In any event, it is evident that the main surge from a low base of percentage of area under HYVs occurred on large wheat farms. This increase was sufficient to reverse the 1968-69 pattern of a greater percent of area under HYVs on

Table A-18. Adoption of HYVs and Area under HYVs: Rice and Wheat Farms (Percentages)

Farm size (acres)	Number of farms	1968-69		1970-71		1968-69 to 1970-71 percent increase in:	
		Adopters	Area under HYVs	Adopters	Area under HYVs	Adopters	Area under HYVs
Rice							
0-5	352	23.9	18.8	28.4	15.6	18.8	−17.0
5-15	305	23.6	15.6	26.2	14.2	11.0	− 9.0
15-25	74	31.1	19.4	37.8	20.4	21.5	5.1
>25	30	50.0	21.3	43.3	26.0	−13.4	22.1
All	761	25.5	17.8	29.0	17.9	13.7	0.6
Wheat							
0-5	94	24.5	12.6	42.6	21.3	73.9	69.0
5-15	195	40.5	12.9	53.8	24.3	32.8	88.4
15-25	60	38.3	13.1	60.0	25.0	56.7	90.8
>25	40	27.5	9.1	57.5	25.5	109.1	180.2
All	389	35.0	12.0	52.4	24.6	49.7	105.0

Source: NCAER Survey data.

small wheat farms than on large. A similar but less dramatic relative gain by large farms (based on area, not percent of number of farms) occurred in rice, although in this crop the percent of area under HYVs was already higher on large than on small farms in the base year. In sum, details for wheat and rice farms show similar trends in HYV adoption with respect to farm size as do the aggregate data on adoption.

As with any technical change, the 'pioneers' are likely to be a select group, and in the case of the new varieties, these consisted of progressive farmers with readily available irrigation. The latecomers are the marginal farmers (and marginal units of irrigated land). If adaptability is equally distributed across farms of all sizes, and inspection of 1968-69 data suggests that this is the case, then the area under HYVs should increase equally for all sets of farms. But as Table A-17 indicates, there is a greater increase in adopters among small farmers, but it is the large farmers who increase the HYV area the most. Thus, backwardness on the part of the small farmer is not a likely explanation for the distribution of income changing in favor of the large farmer.

Differential risk aversion on the part of small and large farmers may be responsible for the observed result. HYV cultivation is not a risk-free occupation, and the allocation of crops to the different varieties can be viewed as a portfolio choice problem. It may be that the small farmer's 'quota' of HYV area is less than that of the large farmer—thus, the observed difference.

Inspection of cols. 5, 9, Table A-17, indicates that this is not a likely explanation. Portfolio considerations dictate that the relevant variable is not percentage of HYV area, but rather the percentage of irrigated area devoted to the modern varieties. This figure declines for the small farmer (from 34 percent to 29 percent), but increases for the large farmer (from 36 percent to 49 percent) over the three-year period. It is highly unlikely that the small farmers had "overshot" their portfolio equilibrium in 1968-69 and thus had to decrease the HYV area in 1970-71.

An alternative and likely explanation is a relatively simple one: the irrigated area devoted to HYVs declines because the marginal small farmer, being in a disadvantageous position, does not adopt the new technology to the same extent as the marginal large farmer.

The lower resource base of the small farmer is an obvious disadvantage; but, more importantly, it is the higher cost of funds (section A.3.3 [c]) that he faces that makes his adoption pattern predictably different from that of the large farmer. The importance of the cost of borrowed funds is enhanced by HYV cultivation; the new varieties drastically increase the level of operating expenditures, and by necessitating an assured water supply increase the demand for irrigation (long-term credit). In this regard, it is interesting to note the different reasons offered by small and large farmers for not using fertilizer in 1970-71 (Table A-19). Lack of credit was mentioned as a major constraint by 48 percent of the small farmers and only 6 percent of the large farmers; and, as a contrast, 32 percent of small farmers and 84 percent of large farmers mentioned irrigation as a major limitation. These survey responses, though not definitive, add support to the hypothesis that access to credit may be responsible for the gains in income (and HYV area) made by the large farmers.

A.5   SUMMARY AND CONCLUSIONS

The NCAER survey, which canvassed farm households on an all-India basis, was used in this study to examine the relationship between farm size and productivity and the impact of the Green Revolution on such a relationship. The major conclusions of this study are as follows.

It was found that the inverse relationship was still significant during the Green Revolution years of 1968-69 to 1970-71, though there was a moderate tendency for this relationship to weaken over time. Differences in land quality and irrigation did not fully explain the negative relationship that continued to hold, even after the removal of their influences in the regression estimates. Alternative hypotheses on the cause of this phenomenon were critically examined and it was determined that the most likely cause of the inverse relationship (land quality and irrigation held constant) was the imperfections in the factor markets—in particular, the labor market.

The cost of capital was also found to significantly decline with farm size, as was the cost of land as measured by unit rental cost relative to size of area rented. Tests relating factor use to farm size revealed that the input of each factor rises by less than the percentage increase in farm size. Moreover, the relative decline is most rapid for labor, tending to confirm the dominance of labor-market dualism as a determinant of land use. The fact that the measured decline in land productivity is very weak when only a range of large farms (using mainly hired labor) is examined adds further support to the importance of labor-market dualism, which is premised on a higher effective cost of wage labor than family labor. (This lower cost of labor on family farms induces them to achieve a higher cropping intensity and a greater output/acre than the large farmer.)

Table A-19. Reasons For Not Using Fertilizers during 1970–71 by Land-Owned Group

Land owned (hectares)	Percentage of households giving the particular reasons								
	Fertilizer not available either in sufficient quantity or in time or both	Inadequacy of funds and credit	Inadequacy of water	Excessive rains	High cost of production due to fertilizer input	Susceptibility to pests and diseases	Risk	Averse to change	Other unspecified reasons
0–2.5	4.13	47.88	32.63	0.66	1.60	—	0.91	0.65	23.45
2.5–8.5	2.11	38.74	45.96	0.39	0.92	—	3.06	—	17.26
8.5 and above	0.09	6.30	83.80	0.47	—	—	0.61	—	8.81
All classes	3.48	43.17	38.78	0.60	1.36	—	1.26	0.49	21.28

Source: NCAER, *Fertilizer Use on Selected Crops in India* (New Delhi, India, 1974).

The effect of the new technology was also examined and it was observed that adoption rates among small and large farmers were similar. Further, more, approximately the same proportion of farm area was under the high-yielding varieties on small as on large farms. The rates of increase of both these variables (adoption and area) for the small farmer has, however, lagged behind those for large farmers, with the consequence that differences in output/acre are greater in 1968–69 than in 1970–71. Lack of credit for capital improvements and fertilizer use might have caused the small farmers to lag behind, but the main phenomenon occurring was a relative improvement by the large farmer rather than a lag by the small farmer. Despite this improvement, the negative relationship between farm size and land productivity remained strong in 1970–71—some six years after the advent of the Green Revolution.

The nature of these results are suggestive of the following policies:

a) *The desirability of land reform.* Given the imperfections in the factor markets, and particularly the labor market, a policy like land reform would not only lead to greater equity but also, in all likelihood, to greater output (with output per land endowment rising) and higher efficiency (with factor prices tending to equalize across farms).

b) *Credit policies in favor of the small farmer.* The analysis suggests that small farmers are progressive and quick to adopt the new technology, but that they are often constrained by lack of credit for their investment and operating expenses. Relaxation of this constraint should speed the spread of the new technology and also tend to diminish the trend of in- creasing inequality in farm incomes.

REFERENCES

Acharaya, S. S. 1973. "Green Revolution and Farm Employment." *Indian Journal of Agricultural Economics* (July–September).
Bardhan, P. K. 1970. "Green Revolution and Agricultural Laborers." *Economic and Political Weekly* (July):1239.
_____. 1973a. "On Factors Affecting Agricultural Wage Rates," *Economic and Political Weekly* (June 30):A–57.
_____. 1973b. "Variations in Agricultural Wages." *Economic and Political Weekly* (May 26):94
_____. 1973c. "Size, Productivity and Returns to Scale: An Analysis of Farm Level Data in Indian Agriculture." *Journal of Political Economy* (November–December): 1370–86.

Bardhan, P. K., and Srinivasan, T. N. 1971. "Cropsharing Tenancy in Agriculture: A Theoretical and Empirical Analysis." *American Economic Review* (March).

Bennett, R. L. 1967. "Surplus Agricultural Labor and Development—Facts and Theories: Comment." *American Economic Review* (March).

Berry, R. A. 1973. "Land Distribution, Income Distribution, and the Productive Efficiency of Colombian Agriculture." *Food Research Institute Studies* 12 (3).

Bhagwati, J. N., and Chakravarty, S. 1969. "Contributions to Indian Economic Analysis: A Survey." *American Economic Review* (Supplement) (September).

Bharadwaj, K. 1974*a*. *Production Conditions in Indian Agriculture: A Study Based on the Farm Management Surveys*. Cambridge: Cambridge University Press.

Bharadwaj, K. 1974*b*. "Notes on Farm Size and Productivity." *Economic and Political Weekly* (March 30):A-63-72.

Chaudhri, D. P. 1974. "Factors Affecting Productivity on Different Size Class of Farm Holdings in India." Unpublished manuscript.

Cheung, S. 1969. *A Theory of Crop Sharing Tenancy*. Chicago: University of Chicago Press.

Cline, W. R. 1970. *Economic Consequences of a Land Reform in Brazil*. North Holland.

Griffin, K. 1974. *The Political Economy of Agrarian Change: An Essay on the Green Revolution*. Cambridge, Mass.: Harvard University Press.

International Rice Research Institute. 1975. *Changes in Rice Farming in Selected Areas of Asia*. Los Banos, Philippines.

Jose, A. V. 1974. "Trends in Real Wage Rates of Agricultural Laborers." *Economic and Political Weekly*. (March 30).

Khusro, A. M. 1964. "Returns to Scale in Indian Agriculture." *Indian Journal of Agricultural Economics* (July-December).

Lau, Lawrence J., and Yotopoulos, P. A. 1971. "A Test for Relative Efficiency and Application to Indian Agriculture." *American Economic Review* (March): 94-107.

Lakshminarayan, H., and Tyagi, S. S. 1977. "Interstate Variations in Types of Tenancy." *Economic and Political Weekly*. September 24.

Lewis, W. A. 1954. "Economic Development with Unlimited Supplies of Labor." *Manchester School of Economic and Social Studies* (May).

Marbro, R. 1971. "Employment and Wages in Dual Agricultures," *Oxford Economic Papers* (November).

Mazumdar, Dipak. 1965. "Size of Farm and Productivity: A Problem of Indian Peasant Agriculture." *Economica* (May).

———. 1975. "The Theory of Share-Cropping with Labor Market Dualism," *Economica* (August).

National Council for Applied Economic Research. 1974. *Credit Requirements for Agriculture*. New Delhi, India.

Paglin, M. 1965. "Surplus Agricultural Labor and Development: Facts and Theory." *American Economic Review* (September).

Rao, A. P. 1967. "Size of Holding and Productivity." *Economic and Political Weekly* (November 11).

Roy, Shymal. 1974. "Effects of Farm Tractorization on Productivity and Labor Employment on Punjab Farms, India." Ph.D. dissertation, University of Missouri.

Saini, G. R. 1969. "Farm Size, Productivity and Returns to Scale." *Economic and Political Weekly* (June 28).

Sen, A. K. 1962. "An Aspect of Indian Agriculture." *Economic Weekly* (Annual Number).

_____. 1966. "Peasants and Dualism with or without Surplus Labor." *Journal of Political Economy* (October).

_____. 1966. "Size of Holding and Productivity." *Economic Weekly* (Annual Number).

Sen, B. 1970. "Opportunities in the Green Revolution." *Economic and Political Weekly* (March 28):A-33-40.

_____. 1974. *The Green Revolution in India—A Perspective.* New York.

Siddhu, Surjit S. 1974. "Relative Efficiency in Wheat Production in the Indian Punjab." *American Economic Review* (September).

Srivastava, V. K., Nagadevara, V., and Heady, E. O. 1973. "Resource Productivity, Returns to Scale and Farm Size in Indian Agriculture: Some Recent Evidence." *Australian Journal of Agricultural Economics* (April).

Yotopoulos, P. A., Lau, L. J., and Somel, K. 1970. "Labor Intensity and Relative Efficiency in Indian Agriculture." *Food Research Institute Studies* 9(1):43-55.

Annex A.1

SELECTION OF FARM HOUSEHOLDS FOR ANALYSIS

The NCAER panel survey of rural Indian households, 1968–69 to 1970–71, has data for 4,118 households. The survey included cultivators and noncultivators; the selection of farm households from this sample was made on the following basis:

a) Only households that did not change status in any of the three years were selected, i.e., those that were cultivators for each of the three years. This reduced the sample to 2,459 farm households. (783 were noncultivators for all three years and the rest changed their status at least once).

b) In order to estimate properly the effects of land ownership on production, households that had invested in land in any of the three years were not selected for final analysis.

c) Any cultivating household that had a gross cultivated area of less than 0.05 acres for any of the three years was omitted. (Households with a "small" plot of land were classified by NCAER as cultivating 0.01 acres.) Any calculation of production will show these households to have an "unreasonably" high value of income per acre.

d) Any household that had land leased out during the third year of the survey was omitted. This was unfortunate, but necessary due to the lack of data on the amount of land leased out.

e) If any of the variables had "missing values," the entire observation was omitted. This was necessary to obtain a consistent series for the variables involved in the analysis.

f) If income per acre was less than or equal to zero or greater than Rs. 3,000 for any of the three years, the household was eliminated from analysis. The lower bound was chosen for obvious reasons. The upper bound of Rs. 3,000 was chosen because this was the maximum observed for the third year of the survey (1970–71 has the most "reliable" data of the three years of the survey). This was done to eliminate any "outliers" from the analysis.

It should be mentioned that the landownership figures for the first year (1968–69) are suspect. This information was made available in a private communication from NCAER. Rather than eliminate any households with inconsistent land ownership data, the ownership figure for the third year of the survey, 1970–71, was imposed for the other two years. This procedure was based on NCAER's assertion that the figures for land ownership are most accurate for 1970–71. Since only households that had zero investment in land for each of the three years were selected for analysis, they must have had the same amount of land for all the years. Consequently, the imputation of land ownership figures of the third year for 1968–69 and 1969–70 is justified. [26]

g) The "final" sample of cultivators selected for analysis was 1,772. Out of these, 1,444 households used positive amounts of both intermediate and capital inputs as reported in the survey.

Annex A.2
FAMILY LABOR INPUT IN FARM PRODUCTION

The NCAER survey did not collect any information on the family labor input in farm production. This is a serious omission, since family labor is a major input on most farms and often accounts for 100 percent of the labor input on small farms (under 5 acres). In the literature, dualism in the labor market has been emphasized as a major causal factor explaining the inverse relationship between farm size and land productivity. Thus, it would have been desirable to have a direct measure of labor input to test whether small farms did indeed apply more labor per acre. Lacking this direct data, a synthetic measure of labor input, L', was constructed and used for analysis.

There are two components of labor input on farms: (a) $L1$—hired labor and (b) $L2$—family labor. If the two are assumed to be of equal quality, then direct addition will provide an estimate of total labor input: that is, $L' = L1 + L2$.

(a) $L1$—*Hired Labor.* An estimate of total wage payments made (if any) for hired labor, H_L, is available for each farm. In order to convert these payments into man-days, an estimate of the wage rate is needed. Though wage rates at individual farm level would be desirable, one has to settle for a certain amount of aggregation—village, block, district, or state. Village data are generally not available; selected district-wage data are collected by Directorate of Statistics, Ministry of Agriculture, Government of India, and published in "Agricultural Wages in India." The last such published data are available only through 1964. Unpublished data for 1969-70 was obtained from Mark Rosenzweig of Yale University.

The wage rate for "male field labor" was chosen as the basic unit for analysis, and the procedure of imputation of this wage was to select an estimate for it at the *lowest* level of aggregation; thus, when block data were not available, district data were used, failing which an estimate for the average rate for the state was used. The district estimate was the most common, and state estimates for the years 1966-67 to 1971-72 are published in Jose (1974). Since the unpublished disaggregated data were only available for 1969-70, and the analysis was done for 1970-71, growth rates in wages as reported in Jose were used for final imputation of money wage rates for each household. The wage rate figure for the state of Rajasthan was taken from Bardhan (1973b), who used National Sample Survey data to arrive at his average figures for the individual states.

This procedure assigns to each farm (household) a wage rate, w, estimate. If hired labor had been used by the farm, or outside employment secured by a household member, the estimate of the wage rate can be used to compute the man-days involved. Thus, $L1 = H_L/w$.

(b) *Computation of Family Labor Input* - L2.   The NCAER survey allows one to identify the earners E, nonearners NE and family workers *FW* for each household. The distinguishing feature between earners and family workers is that the former have at least some outside employment. This distinction does not apply to the head of the household, who is always classified as an earner. A nonearner can safely be assumed to be one who does no work—on- or off-farm. Thus, total family labor input in farm production, *L2*, is composed of *M1*—earners input in farm production, and *M2*—family workers labor input in farm production.

Earners Input in Farm Production-M1. If *e* represents the sum of all outside earnings, and if the total number of working days per earner *M* are known, then

$$M1 = (M - e/w) \cdot E.$$

A straightforward assumption would be to impute "full employment" equal to 300 days for each earner. Studies on Indian agriculture, however, have consistently shown an increasing trend in total employment with farm size; that is, a large-farm earner is likely to be employed for a greater number of days during the year than a small-farm earner. Thus, imputation of a constant number of working days for all farmers might overestimate the on-farm employment for small farmers. To guard against this bias, an attempt was made to compute estimates of varying employment by farm size. Unfortunately, few such published estimates exist, and none on a national basis for the late sixties. Chaudhri (1974) has, on the basis of Farm Management data, some estimates for farm-worker employment (Table A.A–1). Though these figures are for the Punjab, they nevertheless were taken to be indicative of national patterns. Combining the Ferozepur and Punjab figures, a regression of employment with farm size yielded the following result. The result of the equation allows one to impute greater employment to large-farm family members—an approximation that is consistent with reality.[27]

An estimate of *M1*, on-farm labor input by earners, is
$$M1 = (M - e/w) \cdot E = (288.3 + .596(\text{farm size}) - e/w) \cdot E.$$

If *M1* < 0, a zero value was assumed. This procedure may underestimate the family labor input for farm members who earn a higher than average wage. Though this bias is present, it should be mentioned that most of the farms with "negative" on-farm work by earners were medium-sized farms. (Average farm size = 9.8, *m* = 185 farms.) This implies that the estimate of *M* for medium-sized farms may be an underestimate, since it is expected that earners on these farms do put in some work on the farm.

Table A.A-1. Annual Labor Input of a Family Farm Worker

Size group (acres)	Average size of farm	8-hour days per year
Ferozepur, Punjab 1968-70		
Less than 14.82	10.72	288
14.82-22.24	18.58	307
22.24-34.59	27.75	309
34.59-59.30	43.24	328
Over 59.30	83.72	325
Average	30.74	298
Punjab, all regions 1967-70		
Less than 10	6.73	273
10 -17.5	13.4	292
17.5-25	20.8	309
Over 25	35.11	319
Average	20.87	300

Source: Chaudhri (1974).

M2—Family Worker Input in Farm Production.   Family workers with no outside earnings also provide labor for farm production. If this component of family labor was small on all farms, then it could be safely ignored. However, large farms are likely to have more of their own labor force recorded as family workers rather than earners, because there is a greater amount of on-farm work available. An extreme case would be a family worker who is fully occupied on a large farm; this worker would appear in the NCAER classification as a family worker. On the other hand, even a few days (rather than full employment) of on-farm labor classifies a person as a family worker.[28] This extreme variation in family worker input makes it hazardous to ignore it, especially given the fact that such a procedure would seriously underestimate the labor input on large farms. (Variation can also be expected to be present due to factors such as cropping intensity, HYV cultivation, sex composition of family, etc.).

An alternative method is to construct work profiles for family workers. What is known is that the nature of this employment is approximately proportional to farm size—it rises from a low figure to 300 days (full employment) for large farms. But what size farms keep their family members fully employed? An approximation is to assume that the average large farm (> 15 acres) is of such a size. The average size of a large farm was 28.8 acres and the cultivated acreage 30.6 acres. The latter figure is more appropriate, since work input can be expected to vary with cropping intensity.

If 300 days is taken to be full employment, then a family worker works

$M2/FW = 300/30.6$, or approximately 10 days/acre/family worker.

It is a reasonable assumption that family workers work at the same rate, regardless of farm size. Thus, an estimate of $M2$, family worker input into farm production is:

$M2 = FW \cdot$ area cultivated $\cdot 10$ days per acre.

This construction of $M2$ automatically imputes less total work to family workers on small farms than on large farms.

Computation of L2—Family Labor Input in Farm Production.

The constructed figure of $L2$, is:
$L2 = M1 + M2$ days of labor, where $L2$, $M1$, $M2$ are defined above.

For very small farmers (N $= 62$, average farm size $= 1.3$ acres), the average estimate of $L2$ was equal to 555 days. In keeping with the "worst case" procedure, these farms (and one farm that had an estimate of zero labor input) were eliminated from computation of labor estimates. Thus, only 1,709 (1,772 $-$ 62 $-$ 1) observations were used for analysis.

The average estimate of L' ($= L1 + L2$) for these 1,709 farms was 82 days/acre. Table A-11 of the main text shows this estimate to be fairly close to other direct estimates of labor input/acre. This favorable comparison partially vindicates the use of L' (rather than a direct estimate) for hypothesis testing.

A Selective Survey of Evidence on Farm Size and Factor Productivity in Other Countries

Scattered evidence on the relationship between farm size and productivity exists for many countries, though in few besides India has it been the subject of intensive analysis. This survey is designed to broaden the scope of our investigation of this issue and to note types of evidence not showing up on the countries considered in detail in Chapter 4 and which may enrich our body of hypotheses to explain the differences between small and large farms.

TAIWAN

The data from Taiwan is of special interest because of the very small absolute size of nearly all farms. Despite this, the land productivity advantage of smaller farms over large ones is marked; farms of less than half a hectare produce twice as much per hectare as those of over two hectares. This suggests the possibility of considerable potential output increases from a more equal farm-size distribution even in this very land-scarce context.

JAPAN

In contrast to virtually all the developing countries, land productivity in postwar Japan does not differ significantly by size (Table

194

Table B-1. Earnings[a] by Farm Size (of Cultivated Land), Taiwan 1965

Farm size (hectares)	Persons per family	Farm income[b]			Farm family earnings		Distribution of nonfarm receipts				Nonfarm receipts as a share of family income
		Per family	Per person	Per hectare	Per family	Per person	Rent on estate	Labor earnings	"Sideline" activities	Other	
<0.5	6.76	15.7	2.32	40.1	24.2	3.58	7.11	36.21	42.17	14.51	.351
0.5–1.0	7.20	25.6	3.55	32.8	34.0	4.72	6.66	28.38	44.45	20.51	.247
1.0–1.5	7.51	36.7	4.89	28.5	44.7	5.95	12.88	19.26	38.64	29.22	.179
1.5–2.0	9.75	43.6	4.47	24.1	51.4	5.27	9.90	27.32	29.26	33.52	.151
≥2.0	11.62	66.9	5.76	21.5	75.9	6.53	18.37	15.06	29.47	37.10	.119
All farms	8.23	34.7	4.22	26.5	43.1	5.24	10.33	26.06	38.37	25.24	.195

[a]Thousands of NT$.

[b]Farm receipts minus farm expenses.

Source: Joint Commission on Rural Reconstruction in China (U.S. and China), Taiwan Agricultural Statistics, 1901–1965. Economic Digest Series #8, Taipei, Taiwan, 1966, pp. 219–29.

B-2). Possibly the small range over which farm size varies prevents the phenomenon observed in other countries from appearing, although, as just noted, this is not the case in Taiwan. Alternatively, the prevalence of off-farm employment opportunities may be a key factor.

Another interesting hypothesis bearing on the unusual farm size/factor productivity relation in Japan is that many of the small farmers tend to be absentee (at least before the postwar agrarian reforms) or part-time farmers. It has been hypothesized in the prewar period that of the 700,000 landowners with less than three *cho* of land, most were absentee owners who had moved to the cities. They were small merchants, white-collar workers, government officials, and so on.[1] Since World War II and the land reform, part-time farming has become much more prevalent and appears to have greatly reduced the differences in family income as a function of farm size. When power tillers were finally purchased in sizable quantities in the 1960s, their function was primarily to reduce labor inputs, especially on the larger farms, but also on the small ones.[2] The fact that an operator was only part-time in agriculture was mentioned with some frequency as a reason for machinery purchase.[3] This suggests that the opportunity cost of labor was not notably lower on the small farms.

"Data from the Farm Household Survey in 1960 show that individual crop yields are somewhat higher on the larger farms. But the multiple-cropping ratio is larger for small farms, indicating that cropland is used more intensively on smaller units. Total receipts per unit of cultivated area are slightly smaller on farms with more than 2 *cho* (about 5 acres) than on smaller farms. Small farms use much more labor per unit of cultivated area than do larger farms. While total output per acre is larger on the small farms, there is some evidence that with economic development and the greater use of capital the larger farms are becoming more intensive. A recent study shows that while rice yields are now higher on the larger farms, the reverse was true during the 1930s (Ogura 1963: 76, 376). This apparently reflects the influence on yields of fertilizers, pesticides, and other purchased inputs that are used in somewhat larger amounts on the larger farms. During the 1930s the higher rice yield on small farms was associated with larger labor and manure inputs."[4]

MEXICO

Mexican information is of interest because the agricultural censuses permit rough estimates of factor productivities by very broad size

Table B-2. Land Productivity, Labor Productivity, and the Labor/Land Ratio by Farm Size, Japan

Farm size (tan)[a]	Value-added/tan		Labor hours/tan		Value-added/labor (yen per hour)		Percent of resources		Number of farm households (in thousands) (1960)
	1952–54 (1)	1959–61 (2)	1952–54 (3)	1959–61 (4)	1952–54 (5)	1959–61 (6)	Labor hours (1960) (7)	Land (1960) (8)	(9)
<5	13.0	15.6	428.6	339.0	303	460	15.70	14.54	1,266
5–10	14.8	16.7	433.7	356.4	341	468	33.92	29.87	991
10–15	13.9	16.6	344.8	316.4	403	525	27.10	26.88	907
15–20	13.6	16.8	305.3	274.3	445	612	13.43	15.37	1,001
>20	13.7	16.3	268.7	232.2	509	701	9.85	13.42	404

[a]One tan equals 0.1 hectare or 0.245 acres.

Sources: Columns (1) through (4) are from Hiromitsu Kaneda, "Sources and Rates of Productivity Gains in Japanese agriculture, as Compared with the U.S. Experience," *Journal of Farm Economics* 49 (5) (1967): 1448. Columns (5) and (6) are calculated on the basis of the previous ones. The estimate in column (8) is based on Ministry of Agriculture and Forestry, *Agricultural Statistics,* as reproduced in Taheo Misawa, "An Analysis of Part-Time Farming in the Postwar Period," in Kazushi Ohkawa, Bruce F. Johnston, and Hiromitsu Kaneda. *Agriculture and Economic Growth: Japan's Experience* (Tokyo: University of Tokyo Press, 1969), p. 251. Hokkaido and Okinawa are excluded from these figures. Column (7) estimates the distribution of labor hours, using the data from columns (8) and (4).

categories, and with *ejido* farms treated separately as far back as 1940. Land productivity, with land measured by value, was seven times higher on small private farms than on large ones in 1940 and 3.5 times higher in 1960 (Table B-3). Capital productivity, on the other hand, was higher on large farms in both years, as a result of the greater relative production of livestock on small private farms, where it constituted 62 percent of total output in 1960, as contrasted with 29 percent on large private farms and 21 percent on *ejidos*.[5] (The output/capital ratio was slightly higher on small than on large farms in each of crop production and livestock production.) Value of output per peso of land and capital was lower on the large farms in 1940, but higher in 1960, having increased dramatically over the two decades, due in part to a shift from livestock to crops. *Ejidos* tended to have similar productivity of land and capital taken together as did small private farms, land productivity however being much lower and capital productivity substantially higher.

The dramatic increase in the value of output per peso of land and capital on large farms probably reflects the governmental support for this type of agriculture, via public infrastructural expenditures, credit, etc. Relative productivities are, clearly, sensitive to government policy.

LAND-ABUNDANT AFRICAN COUNTRIES

Agriculture, like other sectors, has received less study in most African countries than elsewhere in the world. This is particularly unfortunate from the perspective of our study, since almost the only developing countries commonly believed not to be land scarce are found in Africa.

Table B-3. Productivity Measures by Major Size and Tenure Groups, Mexico, 1940, 1960

	1940			1960		
	Large	Small	*Ejidos*	Large	Small	*Ejidos*
Average products						
Per value of land	0.24	1.55	0.45	0.33	1.17	0.36
Per value of capital[a]	0.73	0.36	0.89	0.86	0.46	0.83
Per value of land & capital	0.17	0.29	0.30	0.42	0.33	0.25
Per worker	8,700	1,500	2,040	35,600	2,900	5,150

[a]On farm capital.

Source: Shlomo Eckstein et al, *Land Reform in Latin America: Bolivia, Chile, Mexico, Peru and Venezuela*, World Bank Staff Working Paper No. 275, April 1978, Appendix C, p. 9.

Much of African agriculture has been characterized by communal land ownership and some of it by shifting cultivation. While neither characteristic renders irrelevant the general question of size-productivity associations, it complicates them considerably and makes empirical work more difficult.

The low technological level of much of African agriculture helps to explain the apparent lack of a land scarcity in many regions. With little public infrastructure (transportation systems, communications, etc.) and an insufficient combination of capital and technology to make high land-labor ratios feasible, little pressure had developed to change the relatively informal communal patterns of land-holding. With the increasing incursion of new technologies, many borrowed from the developed countries, this situation is changing and pressure on the land is being felt. Rapid population growth naturally contributes to it.

In the past, many of the large farms were foreign plantations, and much of the inequality in the agricultural income distribution was thus associated with the foreign-local population division. Given the much greater colonial government attention to and assistance of expatriate agriculture, it may have achieved relatively high land productivity in a number of countries. Some of the present-day biases against heavy labor use were less marked in the colonial period.

It seems a fair appraisal that current trends in most African countries will soon bring the serious land problems that have in the past been more characteristic of Asia and Latin America. It can no longer be assumed that income distribution (foreigners aside) is relatively equitable in land-abundant African countries.

The evidence on the farm size-productivity relationship in Kenya is consistent with that of most other countries. A recent ILO report[6] says:

A number of large farmers lack adequate capital and managerial ability to use all their available land effectively. This is one of the reasons why large farms tend to have a lower proportion of land under crops, lower output and lower employment per usable acre. These tendencies are well illustrated by a recent survey of large farms under African ownership in Trans-Nzoia district, the results of which are summarised in table 39[B-4]. There are some exceptions to these tendencies, especially among farms between 1,000 and 1,250 acres in area. But in all these three respects farms of less than 250 acres do best on the average.

Small holdings are in these respects a viable alternative to large farms. This is well illustrated by comparing table 39[B-4] with table 40[B-5], which summarises similar information drawn from surveys of the settlement schemes. Even on the settlement schemes, there is a large decline in land utilisation on holdings over 20 acres (8 hectares) in size. And as with the sample of large farms, the general

Table B-4. Output, Gross Profit, Land Use and Employment by Farm Size on Large Farms in the Trans-Nzoia District, Kenya, 1970–71

Farm-size group (acres)	Average farm size in group (usable acres)	Gross output (sh. per usable acre)	Gross profit before interest (sh. per usable acre)	Land use		Stocking rate (grazing acres per unit of stock)	Employment[1] (man-year equivalents per 1,000 usable acres)
				Land under crops (percent)			
Less than 250	183	248	48	46		3.2	93
250–499	326	161	49	21		3.1	62
500–749	546	133	27	24		3.8	43
750–999	816	113	16	19		6.2	44
1,000–1,249	1,012	89	24	13		4.4	34
1,250–1,499	1,194	149	42	18		4.2	46
1,500–2,000	1,502	128	45	10		4.3	28
2,000 or more	2,979	65	9	9		7.1	14
All large farms	890	117	29	16		4.8	36

[1]This refers to hired labor only, and neglects family labor, partners, and cooperative members.

Source: Kenya, Ministry of Finance and Planning, Statistics Division: *An economic survey of African-owned farms in Trans-Nzoia, 1970–71.* Farm Economic Survey Report No. 28 (1972).

Table B-5. Output, Net Profit, Land Use and Labor Input by Farm Size on Settlement Schemes, Kenya, 1967-68

Farm-size group (acres)	Average farm size in group (acres)	Gross output (sh. per acre)	Net profit (sh. per acre)	Land use		Labor inputs[1] (man-year equivalents per 1,000 acres)
				Land under crops (percent)	Stocking rate (grazing acres per unit of stock)	
Less than 10	7.3	635	424	45	0.9	808
10–19.9	13.8	250	139	30	2.6	399
20–29.9	23.5	156	86	24	3.0	234
30–39.9	34.7	161	66	16	3.8	159
40–49.9	44.4	113	51	14	4.1	124
50–59.9	52.3	98	49	13	5.1	111
60–69.9	64.5	98	42	19	5.3	109
70 or more	124.8	111	61	14	3.6	70
All settlement farms	30.5	156	81	19	3.5	190

[1]This includes family labor and is therefore not comparable with the labor inputs in table 39[B-4].

Source: Kenya, Ministry of Finance and Planning, Statistics Division: An economic appraisal of the settlement schemes, 1964–65—1967–68. Farm Economic Survey Report No. 27 (1971).

tendency is that the smaller the holding, the larger the gross output and employment per usable acre. For several reasons, the data from the two surveys are not entirely comparable. Nevertheless, taken together, they establish a strong presumption for thinking that both employment and output tend to be higher on smaller farms.

MALAWI

Not all African countries, even sub-Saharan ones, have abundant land. Malawi exemplifies the cases with high population/land ratios. Differences among farms of different sizes are very similar to those observed in Asia and Latin America. Although the agricultural survey of 1968-69 reveals higher cash income (whether gross or net) per acre on large farms than on small ones (Table B-6), when the considerable home consumption is taken into account, it appears that total output per acre is a decreasing function of size of holding. Table B-6 presents low and high estimates of home consumption, with necessarily arbitrary guesses as to its relative importance by size of holding.[7] One factor that would seem to be involved in the markedly inverse relation between size and value-added per acre that results is a higher share of land producing two or more products simultaneously on the smaller farms, an interesting form of intensive land use. It is noteworthy also in Malawi that, for the most part, the families on farms of less than 6 acres earn much of their incomes off the farms.

Both uninformed colonial thought and the pro-large farm biases discussed elsewhere in this study have contributed to the idea that African small farmers are noneconomic, inefficient, and so on. The weight of evidence now quite contradicts such positions and a new (not yet quite) conventional wisdom has emerged on the price responsiveness and general economic responsiveness of this farmer. There can be little doubt that he must continue to play a crucial role in African development. In defending his potential against the usual arguments in favor of land concentration, it will be important to have more quantified evidence as to the relative productivity of small farms.

OTHER COUNTRIES

Analyses or statistics on the farm-size factor-productivity relationship exist for a number of other developing countries. The usual in-

Table B-6. Cash Income and Other Characteristics of Farms by Size, Malawi, 1968–69

Size of holding (acres)	Current cash receipts per acre (1)	Current farm expenditure per acre (2)	Current net farm income per acre (3)	Current net farm income per farm (4)	Other current income per farm (5)	Total current income per farm (6)
<1.9	35.8	13.5	22.6	26.7	258.8	285.5
2.0–3.9	26.9	8.0	18.9	54.7	224.0	278.8
4.0–5.9	28.6	6.3	22.3	106.9	215.3	322.1
6.0–11.9	38.7	9.1	29.6	230.3	275.5	505.8
>12.0	37.6	9.0	28.6	425.9	319.2	745.1
All farms	33.2	8.7	24.5	93.4	243.0	336.4

Estimates of value-added per acre where share of home consumption is assumed to be: Low (7)	High (8)	Estimates of home consumption per holding Low (9)	High (10)	Share of home consumption in total income Low (11)	High (12)	Share of income from off-farm Low home consumption (13)	High home consumption (14)	Share of income from non-agriculture Low home consumption (15)	High home consumption (16)
83.2	231.5	71.6	246.8	21.7	48.8	72.4	48.6	72.4	49.6
56.0	147.0	107.5	370.7	32.4	62.3	58.0	34.5	58.0	34.5
52.4	126.1	144.3	497.5	40.1	70.1	46.2	26.3	46.2	26.3
52.0	109.0	179.1	617.5	39.4	69.1	40.2	24.5	40.2	24.5
43.0	78.4	215.0	741.3	40.2	69.9	33.2	21.5	33.2	21.5
59.7	146.0	134.3	463.0	35.6	65.6	51.6	30.4	51.6	30.4

Source: National Statistical Office, Malawi Government, *National Sample Survey of Agriculture 1968–69*. Zomba, 1970, p. 42.

verse relation with land productivity has been noted for many countries of Latin America, including Argentina, Chile, and Guatemala.[8] A detailed study by Buck showed its presence in pre-revolutionary China,[9] and Korean data paint a similar picture.[10]

In short, it is clearly the normal relationship. In most countries, the big question is not its presence, but whether it is due primarily to factors that render it irrelevant from a policy point of view (e.g., differences in land quality) or to factors that imply a high level of relative efficiency for small farms.

Relative Land-Utilization Intensity across Farm-Size Groups in Relationship to Country Factor Endowment

William R. Cline

Consider two countries, 1 and 2, with equal population sizes and equal agricultural labor forces, but with λ times the endowment of land per capita in country 2 as in country 1. Suppose the agrarian structure is identical in the two countries, in proportional terms: the large-farm sector controls the fraction ϕ of the land and the small-farm sector controls the fraction $(1 - \phi)$; the large-farm sector has the fraction ψ of the total labor force at its disposal, while the small-farm sector has the fraction $1 - \psi$. In keeping with the tendency of smaller farms to use higher inputs of labor relative to land, $\phi > \psi$. Define indicator Z as a measure of relative land utilization intensity for large farms, equal to the average product of land on large farms divided by the average product of land on small farms. Then it will be shown below that if the elasticity of substitution between land and labor in the production function is less than unity, relative large-farm land utilization Z will be lower in the country with a more abundant land endowment (country 2); if the elasticity of substitution is unity, the relative land-use intensity by large farms will be constant across countries, regardless of land endowment; and if the elasticity of substitution is greater than unity, the relative land-use intensity by large farms will rise across countries as relative land endowment rises. It will also be shown that in all cases, so long as the small-farm sector's share of labor force exceeds its share of available land, the relative land-use intensity measure Z will be less than unity.

Case A. *Unitary Elasticity of Substitution.* Consider the case of unitary elasticity of substitution, with a Cobb–Douglas production function. Assume constant returns to scale (the situation usually found empirically in developing country agriculture). Then all farms in the small-farm sector may be collapsed into a single production unit, as may those in the large-farm sector. With the production function:

(1) $Q = A^\alpha N^\beta,$ where Q = output

A = land area input (assume equal to total land available on the farm)

N = labor input (assume equal to total labor force available to the farm)

we may write

(2) $Q_1{}^L = (\phi A_1)^\alpha (\psi N_1)^\beta$

(3) $Q_1{}^s = \{(1 - \phi)A_1\}^\alpha \{(1 - \psi)N_1\}^\beta$

where superscript s = small-farm sector L = large-farm sector; subscript = country 1, 2.

The measure of relative large-farm land utilization Z for country 1 will then be:

(4) $Z_1 = \dfrac{Q_1{}^L/A_1{}^L}{Q_1{}^s/A_1{}^s} = \dfrac{\{(\phi A_1)^\alpha (\psi N_1)^\beta\}/(\phi A_1)}{[\{(1 - \phi)A_1\}^\alpha \{(1 - \psi)N_1\}^\beta]/\{(1 - \phi)A_1\}}$

For country 2, all variables are identical except that the land available is λ times as great: $A_2 = \lambda A_1$; $N_2 = N_1$.

(5) $Z_2 = \dfrac{\{(\phi\lambda A_1)^\alpha(\psi N_1)^\beta\}/(\phi\lambda A_1)}{[\{(1 - \phi)\lambda A_1\}^\alpha \{(1 - \psi)N_1\}^\beta]/\{(1 - \phi)\lambda A_1\}}$

Since all terms λ in Equation (5) cancel, $Z_2 = Z_1$. Thus, it is demonstrated that relative large-farm land utilization should remain constant across countries regardless of land endowment per capita, if the elasticity of substitution between land and labor is unitary. This conclusion means that whatever production gains were obtainable through structural reform of agriculture in a land-abundant country could also be expected to be achieved (in proportional terms) in a land-scarce country, so long as land and labor have unitary substitution elasticity.

Case B. *Constant Elasticity of Substitution Production Function.* Suppose that the elasticity of substitution between land and labor is different from unity and, in the normal case, below unity. This case may be analyzed using the CES production function:

(6) $Q = \{\delta A^{-\rho} + (1 - \delta)N^{-\rho}\}^{-1/\rho},$

where $\dfrac{1}{1 + \rho} = |\sigma|$, the elasticity of substitution and $\rho \geq -1$.

If $\rho = -1$, the elasticity of substitution is infinity; if $\rho = 0$, elasticity of substitution is unitary; if $\rho > 0$, the elasticity of substitution is less than unity, presumably the normal case.

The proposition to be proved is that if the elasticity of substitution is less than unity, relative large-farm land utilization Z falls as relative land abundance rises across countries.

Specifying the production function in terms of output per land area,

(7) $Q/A = \{\delta A^{-\rho} + (1 - \delta)N^{-\rho}\}^{-1/\rho} A^{-1}$

$$= \left\{\delta + (1 - \delta)\left(\frac{N}{A}\right)^{-\rho}\right\}^{-1/\rho}.$$

Recalling that large farms have shares ϕ and ψ of land and labor respectively, and small farms have the corresponding shares $(1 - \phi)$ and $(1 - \psi)$: recalling that country 2 has the same labor (N_1) as country 1, but λ times as much land; and using Equation (7), we may write the ratio of relative large-farm land utilization Z in country 1 to that in country 2 as:

(8) $Z_1/Z_2 = \dfrac{\dfrac{\left(\delta + (1 - \delta)\left\{\dfrac{(1 - \psi)N_1}{(1 - \phi)A_1}\right\}^{-\rho}\right)^{1/\rho}}{\left(\delta + (1 - \delta)\left\{\dfrac{\psi N_1}{\phi A_1}\right\}^{-\rho}\right)^{1/\rho}}}{\dfrac{\left(\delta + (1 - \delta)\left\{\dfrac{(1 - \psi)N_1}{(1 - \phi)\lambda A_1}\right\}^{-\rho}\right)^{1/\rho}}{\left(\delta + (1 - \delta)\left\{\dfrac{\psi N_1}{\phi\lambda A_1}\right\}^{-\rho}\right)^{1/\rho}}} \overset{?}{>} 1.$

(Note that the denominators and numerators of both Z_1 and Z_2 are switched to permit the exponent $1/\rho$ to be positive.)

To simplify Equation (8), let:

$$x = \frac{1 - \psi}{1 - \phi}\frac{N_1}{A_1} \quad \text{and} \quad y = \frac{\psi}{\phi}\frac{N_1}{A_1}.$$

Substituting x and y for their corresponding terms; taking the power ρ of both sides of Equation (8) (which does not change the direction of inequality since $\rho > 0$ in the "normal" case of less than unitary elasticity of substitution); and consolidating the terms of the fraction, then shifting the denominator to the right-hand side, we obtain:

(9) $\qquad \{\delta + (1 - \delta)x^{-\rho}\}\{\delta + (1 - \delta)\lambda^{\rho}y^{-\rho}\}$

$\qquad \overset{?}{>} \{\delta + (1 - \delta)y^{-\rho}\}\{\delta + (1 - \delta)x^{-\rho}\lambda^{\rho}\}.$

After multiplying the terms in Equation (9) and eliminating identical terms appearing on both sides, we obtain:

(10) $\quad \delta(1 - \delta)\lambda^{\rho}y^{-\rho} + \delta(1 - \delta)x^{-\rho} \overset{?}{>} \delta(1 - \delta)x^{-\rho}\lambda^{\rho} + \delta(1 - \delta)y^{-\rho}$

Dividing both sides by $\delta(1 - \delta)$, we obtain:

(11) $\qquad (\lambda^{\rho} - 1)y^{-\rho} \overset{?}{>} (\lambda^{\rho} - 1)x^{-\rho}.$

Since $\lambda > 1$, $\lambda^{\rho} - 1 > 0$, and division of both sides by the term in parentheses leaves the direction of inequality unchanged. Then, taking the power $-1/\rho$ of both sides and reversing the inequality (since $\rho > 0$ in the "normal" case of less than unitary elasticity of substitution), we obtain

(12) $\qquad y \overset{?}{<} x.$

Recalling the definitions of x and y, it is clear that the condition of inequality (12) is met. That is, by construction, the large-farm share of labor force is less than large-farm share of land available, ϕ, so that x/y must be greater than unity (that is, $x/y = \{(1 - \psi)/(1 - \phi)\}/\{\psi/\phi\}$, where the numerator in brackets must be greater than unity and the denominator in brackets must be less than unity) and therefore $y < x$; QED.

To recapitulate, Equations (7) through (12) demonstrate that when the elasticity of substitution is less than unity, the degree of land utilization on large farms relative to that on small will fall, across countries, as relative land-abundance rises—for any given "agrarian structure," defined as the share of total land and total labor in the large-farm sector.

The second proposition to be proved is that when elasticity of substitution is greater than unity, the relative large-farm land utilization Z rises as relative land abundance rises across countries. Thus, considering Equation (8), it is to be shown that the left-hand side is less than unity (rather than greater than unity as in the "normal" case.)

Let *LHS* be the left-hand side of (8). Then it is to be shown that:

(13) $\qquad LHS \overset{?}{<} 1 \quad$ when $\rho < 0$

Taking the power ρ of both sides now reverses the inequality. Pursuing the same other steps as before in going from (8) to (9), therefore, yields precisely the same resulting expression as before (9). Since the steps from (9) to (10) do not involve special manipulation of ρ, the proof in this second case also obtains an expression identical to (11). However, since $\lambda^\rho < 1$, when $\rho < 0$, division by $(\lambda^\rho - 1)$ now yields a reversal in the inequality, so that:

(14) $y^{-\rho} \overset{?}{<} x^{-\rho}$

(that is, Equation (11) divided by $\lambda^\rho - 1$).
This time, however, taking the power $-1/\rho$ of both sides does not reverse the inequality, so that we obtain the same final expression as before (12):

(15) $y \overset{?}{<} x.$

Since (15) does not involve the parameter ρ, and since the condition was found true before, then this second proof is complete. That is, if the elasticity of substitution were greater than unity, relative large-farm land utilization would rise rather than fall across countries as relative land abundance rose.

Finally, it is to be shown that Z, relative large-farm land utilization, is always less than unity (output per farm area is less on large farms than on small). This fact is more apparent intuitively than the previous two propositions, since it results directly from the phenomenon of diminishing returns to one factor applied in larger proportions to another factor. That is, with the agrarian structure such that more land is always combined with relatively less labor on large farms, the average product of land on large farms will be less than that on small farms. In terms of the equations above, returning to (7) the relative large-farm land utilization for country 1 will be:

(16) $$Z_1 = \frac{\left(\delta + (1 - \delta)\left\{\dfrac{\psi N_1}{\phi A_1}\right\}^{-\rho}\right)^{-1/\rho}}{\left(\delta + (1 - \delta)\left\{\dfrac{(1 - \psi)N_1}{(1 - \phi)A_I}\right\}^{-\rho}\right)^{-1/\rho}} \overset{?}{<} 1.$$

Taking the power $-\rho$ of both sides and reversing the inequality (for the normal case of less than unitary elasticity of substitution, $\rho > 0$), we obtain:

(17) $\delta + (1 - \delta)\left(\dfrac{\psi N_1}{\phi A_1}\right)^{-\rho} \overset{?}{>} \delta + (1 - \delta)\left(\dfrac{(1 - \psi)N_1}{(1 - \phi)A_1}\right)^{-\rho}.$

Eliminating terms δ and $1 - \delta$, and taking power $-1/\rho$ of both sides (once again reversing the inequality);

(18) $\quad \dfrac{\psi N_1}{\phi A_1} \overset{?}{<} \dfrac{(1 - \psi)N_1}{(1 - \phi)A_1} \quad$ or $\quad \dfrac{\psi}{\phi} \overset{?}{<} \dfrac{1 - \psi}{1 - \phi}.$

By construction $\psi < \phi$, so that $1 - \psi > 1 - \phi$. Therefore, in (18) the left-hand side is less than unity and the right-hand side is greater than unity, so that the inequality condition is met. It is therefore demonstrated that Z, the ratio of average productivity of land on large farms to that on small farms, is less than unity.

Note that this last conclusion holds even if the elasticity of substitution is greater than unity ($\rho < 0$). In economic terms, this fact means that diminishing returns to the land factor still hold true, even if the elasticity of substitution between factors is greater than unity (but less than infinite). In algebraic terms, this fact may be observed by noting that in the proof here (Equations 16 through 18) there were exactly two reversals of the inequality sign, stemming from the fact that $\rho > 0$ in the normal case. At these two steps there would be no reversal of inequality in the case with $\rho < 0$, but since there were an even number of inequality reversals in the former case, there is no difference in the final outcome between the two cases. In short, in an agrarian structure in which the large-farm sector disposes of a larger share of total land than its share of total labor, the relative degree of land utilization by large farms will be less than that by small farms, regardless of the elasticity of substitution between the two factors.

APPENDIX D.

Statistical Appendix

Table D-1. Cropland as a Percentage of Farm Area by Farm-Size Group, Selected Countries (Approx. 1960)

Size group (ha.)	Brazil	Chile	Colombia	Peru	Uruguay
A. Crop area as % of farm area					
0–1	86	87	74	87	—
1–2	88	83	76	83	52
2–5	75	77	68	74	52
5–10	58	68	56	60	58
10–20	44	55	44	48	52
20–50	29	43	31	34	41
50–100	19	36	21	24	32
100–200	14	35	16	20	27
200–500	10	34	11	15	18
500–1,000	7	27	9	11	11
Over 1,000	2	6	3	5	7
All farms	11	14	18	15	13
B. Percentage of country total cropland in group					
0–1	0.3	0.4	1.9	4.3	—
1–2	1.2	0.9	4.2	7.8	0.2
2–5	5.4	2.4	11.3	18.7	0.6
5–10	6.9	3.5	12.9	11.1	2.3
10–20	11.9	5.2	13.8	7.5	4.5
20–50	21.4	8.9	16.3	6.7	9.1
50–100	12.8	8.3	11.1	4.0	9.7
100–200	10.7	10.1	9.3	4.1	12.3
200–500	12.9	16.4	9.0	5.8	17.6
500–1,000	7.2	13.2	4.6	4.2	12.8
Over 1,000	9.3	30.7	5.7	25.8	30.9

210

Table D-1. (Continued)

Size group (ha.)	Brazil	Chile	Colombia	Peru	Uruguay
	C. Percentage of country total farm area in group				
0–1	a	a	a	a	a
1–2	0.2	0.2	1.0	1.4	—
2–5	0.8	0.5	3.1	3.8	0.2
5–10	1.4	0.8	4.3	2.7	0.5
10–20	3.1	1.4	5.8	2.3	1.2
20–50	8.3	3.0	9.7	3.0	2.9
50–100	7.6	3.3	9.9	2.5	4.0
100–200	8.7	4.1	11.0	3.1	6.1
200–500	14.4	7.1	14.7	5.7	12.8
500–1,000	11.4	7.0	10.0	5.8	15.4
Over 1,000	44.1	72.6	30.5	69.7	56.9

[a]Less than 1%. Percentages for total area in farms over 1 hectare.

Table D-1. (Continued)

Size group (ha.)	Venezuela	Costa Rica	Nicaragua	Panama	Ceylon
	A. Crop area as a % of farm area				
0–1	90	82	76	88	86
1–2	90	95	78	89	90
2–5	84	67	68	84	88
5–10	77	67	53	69	90
10–20	68	44	43	54	89
20–50	55	31	35	37	88
50–100	48	26	30	25	87
100–200	40	19	27	16	84
200–500	35	17	21	11	73
500–1,000	29	17	15	6	..
Over 1,000	10	17	6	10	..
All farms	20	23	23	31	85
	B. Percentage of country total cropland in group				
0–1	0.2	0.4	0.2	0.5	15.6
1–2	0.9	1.4	1.2	2.6	17.3
2–5	4.8	4.4	5.7	11.5	21.7
5–10	5.9	7.3	5.9	14.7	9.1
10–20	6.6	9.8	8.1	18.6	5.9
20–50	8.7	18.8	17.1	23.6	5.6
50–100	6.6	15.9	17.4	12.9	4.0
100–200	7.3	9.8	16.2	6.0	4.7
200–500	11.8	11.6	14.9	3.7	16.1
500–1,000	10.3	7.2	6.1	0.9	—
Over 1,000	36.9	13.4	7.2	5.0	—

Table D-1. (Continued)

Size group (ha.)	Venezuela	Costa Rica	Nicaragua	Panama	Ceylon
C. Percentage of country total farm area in group					
0–1	a	a	a	a	15.4
1–2	0.2	0.3	0.4	0.9	16.4
2–5	1.1	1.5	1.9	4.2	20.9
5–10	1.5	2.5	2.6	6.5	8.6
10–20	2.0	5.1	4.4	10.7	5.6
20–50	3.1	14.1	11.3	19.7	5.5
50–100	2.8	13.9	13.5	15.8	4.0
100–200	3.6	11.8	13.9	11.1	4.8
200–500	6.8	15.2	16.4	10.5	18.8
500–1,000	7.1	9.5	9.5	4.8	—
Over 1,000	71.8	26.1	26.1	15.8	—

Table D-1. (Continued)

Size group (ha.)	Taiwan	India	Japan	Korea	Pakistan
A. Crop area as a % of farm area					
0–1	71	94	91	33	85
1–2	81	94	91	47	89
2–5	80	93	83	45	89
5–10	77	91	72	..	86
10–20	16	88	61	..	78
20–50	20	85	33	..	61
50–100	63	..	..	..	45
100–200	84	..	..	..	29
200–500	89	..	..	..	..
500–1,000	74	..	..	..	..
Over 1,000	..	..	..	..	..
All farms	77	91	85	39	80
B. Percentage of country total cropland in group					
0–1	31.1	6.9	32.9	44.6	7.8
1–2	32.7	12.6	36.5	39.8	13.6
2–5	25.2	28.3	19.1	15.6	30.3
5–10	4.3	22.7	6.0	—	23.8
10–20	—	18.1	4.3	—	14.3
20–50	0.1	11.4	1.2	—	6.4
50–100	0.4	—	—	—	2.2
100–200	1.5	—	—	—	1.6
200–500	3.9	—	—	—	—
500–1,000	0.8	—	—	—	—
Over 1,000	—	—	—	—	—

Table D-1. (Continued)

Size group (ha.)	Taiwan	India	Japan	Korea	Pakistan
C. Percentage of country total farm area in group					
0-1	33.6	6.7	30.6	53.1	7.4
1-2	31.2	12.1	33.8	33.4	12.2
2-5	24.2	27.8	19.6	13.5	27.3
5-10	4.4	22.7	7.1	—	22.1
10-20	0.3	18.5	6.0	—	14.5
20-50	0.6	9.4	3.0	—	8.4
50-100	0.4	2.8	—	—	3.9
100-200	1.4	—	—	—	4.3
200-500	3.4	—	—	—	—
500-1,000	0.8	—	—	—	—
Over 1,000	—	—	—	—	—

Table D-1. (Continued)

Size group (ha.)	Philippines	Thailand	Turkey	Kenya	UAR
A. Crop area as % of farm area					
0-1	96	90	98	69	100
1-2	97	91	97	61	99
2-5	96	90	97	49	98
5-10	89	87	95	34	97
10-20	81	85	90	26	94
20-50	78	82	91	32	84
50-100	76	..	52	40	..
100-200	73	..	32	37	..
200-500	44	..	40	32	..
500-1,000	..	..	40	27	..
Over 1,000	..	11	49	13	..
All farms	86	88	92	21	96
B. Percentage of country total cropland in group					
0-1	1.8	2.8	2.7	3.9	16.1
1-2	11.6	8.8	4.6	9.5	21.6
2-5	34.8	33.9	17.9	18.6	22.7
5-10	24.5	34.6	24.2	11.6	11.1
10-20	14.5	15.4	23.4	11.2	8.3
20-50	5.1	4.5	16.4	0.2	8.8
50-100	1.8	—	4.2	0.6	14.4
100-200	1.7	—	2.1	1.6	—
200-500	4.2	—	1.7	9.8	—
500-1,000	—	—	2.8	10.5	—
Over 1,000	—	—	—	22.5	—

Table D-1. (Continued)

Size group (ha.)	Philippines	Thailand	Turkey	Kenya	UAR
	C. Percentage of country total farm area in group				
0-1	1.6	2.8	2.5	1.5	15.5
1-2	10.2	8.5	4.3	4.1	21.0
2-5	31.2	33.1	16.9	10.0	22.2
5-10	23.7	34.9	23.3	8.9	11.1
10-20	15.3	15.9	23.2	11.2	8.3
20-50	5.6	4.5	16.6	0.2	9.0
50-100	2.1	0.4	4.4	0.4	13.1
100-200	2.0	—	2.0	1.2	—
200-500	8.2	—	2.0	8.0	—
500-1,000	—	—	2.4	10.2	—
Over 1,000	—	—	2.4	44.3	—

Note: Cropland is defined as arable land plus land under permanent crops. Arable land includes land in temporary crops, temporary meadows, and temporarily fallow land.
.. not applicable
— negligible

Sources: Food and Agriculture Organization, *Report on the 1960 World Census of Agriculture*, vol. 5, Tables 2.7, 2.8, 2.3, 2.4, 2.10, 3.3.

Table D-2. Land Endowment per Agricultural Population, Selected Countries

Country	A Agricultural population '70 (1,000)	B Total area (1,000 ha.)	C Agricultural area (1,000 ha.)	(year)	E = B/A (ha/person)	F = C/A (ha/person)
Argentina	3,697	277,689	170,975	(68)	75.11	46.25
Bolivia	2,714	109,858	28,365[a]	(63)	40.48	10.45
Brazil	40,635	851,197	141,356[b]	(70)	20.95	3.48
Chile	2,484	75,695	15,814[a]	(65)	30.47	6.37
Colombia	9,652	113,891	22,138	(70)	11.80	2.29
Costa Rica	802	5,070	2,362	(72)	6.32	2.95
Ecuador	3,264	28,356	6,015	(68)	8.69	1.84
Guatemala	3,203	10,889	2,499[c]	(64)	3.40	0.78
Honduras	1,803	11,209	4,236	(63)	6.22	2.35
Mexico	23,636	202,206	97,258[c]	(70)	8.56	4.11
Nicaragua	1,129	13,000	1,793	(63)	11.51	1.59
Panama	632	7,565	1,683	(70)	11.97	2.66
Peru	6,189	128,522	30,380	(71)	20.77	4.91
Uruguay	482	17,751	15,480[c]	(70)	36.83	32.12
Venezuela	2,823	91,205	19,061[c]	(61)	32.31	6.75
Greece	4,134	13,194	8,870	(66)	3.19	2.15
Turkey	24,560	78,058	53,749	(71)	3.18	2.19
U.A.R.	18,545	100,145	2,852	(72)	5.40	0.15
Ceylon (Sri Lanka)	6,591	6,561	2,418	(71)	1.00	0.37
India	364,823	328,048[d]	178,680[d,e]	(71)	0.90	0.49
Pakistan	43,810	80,394[f]	24,235[f]	(69)	1.84	0.55
Japan	21,564	37,227	6,246	(72)	1.73	0.29
Korea, Rep.	17,132	9,848	2,329[c]	(69)	0.57	0.14
Philippines	26,489	30,000	11,631	(71)	1.13	0.44
Taiwan	5,300[i]	3,475	n.a.	(61)	0.66	0.18[j]

Table D-2 (Continued)

Country	A Agricultural population '70	B Total area	C Agricultural area	(year)	$E = B/A$	$F = C/A$ (ha/person)
Thailand	27,663	51,400	15,939	(71)	1.86	0.58
Ghana	4,946	23,854	13,811[a,g]	(68)	4.82	2.79
Kenya	8,761	58,264	5,614[c]	(60)	6.65	0.64
Nigeria	36,900	92,398	46,795	(61)	2.50	1.27
Malawi	3,887	11,848	3,236[h]	(59)	3.05	0.83
Tanzania	11,370	94,509	56,453	(70)	8.31	4.97

Source: Food and Agriculture Organization Production Yearbook 1973, Tables 1, 5 (pp. 3–7, 17–20).

Agricultural area = arable land, land under permanent crops, permanent meadows and pasture. Excludes "forests and woodlands" and "other land" (the latter including urban areas, water bodies, and unused but potentially usable land).

[a] Arable land used in calculation refers to land under temporary crops.
[b] Arable land used in calculation refers to arable land on agricultural holdings.
[c] Pastures and meadows refer to those on agricultural holdings.
[d] Including Kashmir—Jammu.
[e] Data refers to reporting area of 305,510 tho. hectares.
[f] Excluding Kashmir—Jammu.
[g] Permanent meadows, pastures refer to savanna.
[h] 1972.

[i] *Source:* U. S. Department of Agriculture, *Changes in Agriculture in 26 Developing Nations, 1948 to 1963*, pp. 62, 63, 66.
[j] Assumes same ratio col. F/col. E as for average among Japan, the Philippines, and Korea.

Table D–3. Colombia: Farm Income and Expenses by Size Group, INCORA Borrowers' Sample, 1969[a] (Pesos)

Farm size (hectares)	Gross farm cash income 1	Other farm income 2	Consumption of farm produce 3	Total farm income (1 + 2 + 3) 4	Operating expenses 5	Net farm income (4 − 5) 6	Off-farm income 7	Total family income (6 + 7) 8	Net farm income as % of family income 9
0–1	18,723	991	790	20,504	16,916	3,588	8,711	12,299	29.18
1–4.99	20,608	1,176	1,134	22,918	11,899	11,019	2,349	13,369	82.43
5–9.99	24,448	1,431	1,512	27,390	13,683	13,707	1,719	15,426	88.86
10–14.99	29,153	1,629	1,436	32,218	18,461	13,757	1,709	15,466	88.95
15–19.99	29,734	1,559	1,995	33,289	16,338	16,950	2,011	18,961	89.40
20–49.99	23,937	2,092	1,827	27,857	13,088	14,768	2,042	16,811	87.85
50–99.99	19,996	2,141	2,445	24,581	10,214	14,368	1,764	16,132	89.06
100 and over	25,918	2,197	3,604	31,719	13,337	18,382	1,888	20,270	90.69
Average	23,963	1,714	1,860	27,538	13,466	14,071	2,031	16,103	87.39

[a] 2,897 total observations.

Source: Agency for International Development, General Working Document 17. Small Farm Analysis. Preliminary Results: Income Distribution, by James R. Horst and Thomas Walker, December 1972, p. 2.

Table D-4. Colombia: Characteristics of 474 Farm Subsample of the INCORA Borrowers Sample, 1969

Farm size (ha.)[a]	Value of production per ha. (pesos)		Value of land-based production per ha. (pesos)		Value of crop output per cultivated ha. (pesos)	Value of output of land-based livestk activ. per ha. of pasture (pesos)	Value of production per farm, gross (pesos)	Value of prod. net of operat. expense /gross value of prod. (%)	Share of val. of prod. consum. on farm (%)	Net cash farm income per farm (pesos)	Off-farm income per farm (pesos)	Income per farm (pesos)	Share from off-farm (%)
	Est. 1 1a	Est. 2 1b	Est. 1 2a	Est. 2 2b	3	4	5	6	7	8	9	10	11
0–0.99	18,012	…	14,154	…	10,776	16,599	7,908	59.95	14.03	4,894	10,958	15,852	69.13
1–4.99	6,305	…	4,892	…	7,989	2,429	18,873	54.62	6.17	9,517	3,544	13,061	27.13
5–9.99	4,068	…	3,641	…	5,909	1,021	26,510	58.46	6.50	15,943	1,368	17,311	7.90
10–14.99	2,245	…	2,052	…	4,745	696	25,680	58.22	7.45	13,651	1,520	15,171	10.10
15–19.99	2,603	…	2,569	…	7,458	872	33,632	51.52	8.26	15,704	2,493	18,197	13.20
20–49.99	1,455	…	1,442	…	5,297	509	31,306	65.71	6.41	18,968	3,867	22,835	16.93
50–99.99	1,742	…	1,472	…	8,333	961	49,404	51.11	8.96	20,282	11,517	31,799	36.22
100 & over	671	…	671	…	2,043	414	19,135	81.61	15.36	14,020	0	14,020	0
All farms	3,002	2,158	2,652	1,906	6,057	910	24,011	57.59	6.91	13,256	3,010	16,266	18.50

[a]Number of observations, respectively: 21, 159, 132, 73, 26, 46, 6, 2: 467 total.

Notes: Col. 1. Value of production from p. 15 (all page references in this note refer to the table source); area for estimate 1 comes from p. 11, "total computed area." Sample size is that shown on p. 11. Est. 2 total is from p. 18. There seems to be no corresponding data by size category. The apparent source of the discrepancy (though in reference to a smaller 152 farm subsample) was noted by A.I.D. (AWD #2, p. 40). The unclassified share was 40.3% for that sample (a rapidly increasing function of size) and 30% in this larger 474 farm sample. For the 2,783 farms reported in GWD #17U, it i: 45.3% (ibid., p. 4) and is again an increasing function of size.

Col. 5 is based on the value of production figures of p. 15 and the number of farms of p. 11 (that is, 474), on the assumption that the lower value of production figure on p. 15 (than on p. 18) is due to the exclusion of 7 farms.

Col. 6 is based on a smaller sample than col. 5, specifically 401 farms: see p. 16.

Col. 7 is from p. 15; size of sample used is not indicated.

Cols. 8–11 are based on the data of pages 4–10, which include 467 farms. It is not clear whether income in kind is in fact excluded or not; the same is true for investment in kind.

Source: Agency for International Development, *General Working Document # 17C. Small Farm Economics: Preliminary Results of a 474 Farm Subsample of INCORA Borrowers,* by Dana Dalrymple, Samuel Davis, Cathy Gleason, and Beverly Lowenstein. August 1972.

Table D-5. Mean Palay Yields by Crop Semester, Presence or Absence of Irrigation, Variety of Palay Planted, and Tenure Group, in Nueva Ecija Province and in the Central Luzon Region As a Whole (in 44 kg. Sacks)

Crop semester	Owners	Lessees	Share tenants
Central Luzon[a]			
1968/69	49.8	51.6	51.1
1967/68	53.3	51.0	49.0
1964/65	41.3	45.7	47.7
Nueva Ecija[b]			
Irrigated			
High-yielding variety			
January-June 1971	62.49	69.38	64.97
January-June 1970	50.46	66.05	62.64
January-June 1969	45.29	56.65	64.98
July-December 1971	27.16	35.45	37.54
July-December 1970	53.13	61.33	62.30
July-December 1969	51.23	64.19	63.18
July-December 1968	57.12	53.15	55.96
Traditional variety			
January-June 1971	33.33	67.68	52.20
January-June 1970	54.32	51.70	48.48
January-June 1969	36.94	46.23	51.10
July-December 1971	28.71	38.05	47.72
July-December 1970	45.44	55.34	52.64
July-December 1969	53.79	55.18	56.86
July-December 1968	53.62	50.46	52.39
Rain-fed			
High-yielding variety			
July-December 1971	24.65	23.62	26.23
July-December 1970	57.39	39.13	40.20
July-December 1969	46.52	55.78	51.76
July-December 1968	46.82	63.85	48.02
Traditional variety			
July-December 1971	24.71	26.01	25.82
July-December 1970	40.38	41.74	42.40
Traditional variety (cont.)			
July-December 1969	44.46	47.04	44.62
July-December 1968	38.39	40.59	42.94

[a]From a study by Sandoval and Gaon, as reported in the source for this table (listed below).

[b]From R. P. de los Reyes, M. Mangahas, and F. J. Murray, *Land Reform and Agricultural Improvement in Nueva Ecija-Phase One*, 1973, as reported in the source for this table (listed below).

Source: International Labour Office *Sharing in Development: A Program of Employment, Equity and Growth for the Philippines* (Geneva: International Labour Office, 1974), p. 485.

Table D-6. Source of Income of Operators in Ceylon, 1962

Size of holding	Full-time operators	Part-time operators		Total operators
		Main income from agriculture	Main income from nonagriculture	
0[a]	380	280	2,830	3,490
0 ≤ 1	132,750	62,210	218,441	413,401
1–2	137,979	52,640	64,030	254,649
2–5	224,610	54,601	40,020	319,231
5–50	139,771	22,301	15,371	177,443
Subtotal Nonestate	635,490	192,032	340,692	
Estate (>50)	5,451	252	185	5,888
Total	640,941	192,284	340,877	1,174,102

[a]Produce, livestock, etc.

Source: Ceylon, Department of Census and Statistics, *1972 Census of Agriculture,* vol. 1, *Agricultural Land, Agricultural Operators and Tenure,* The Government Press, Ceylon, pp. 58, 90–91. The definition of income is unfortunately not precisely specified (ibid., p. 33); in principle it should include income in kind as well as cash income.

Table D-7. Comparison of 'Ownerships' and 'Landholdings' Distribution Patterns in Egypt, 1961

Size-class (feddans)	No. of ownerships (000's)	No. of holdings (000's)	No. of holdings as a percentage of number of ownerships	Total area of ownerships (000 feddans)	Total area of holdings (000 feddans)	Area of holdings as % of area of ownerships
<5	2,919	1,381	47.3	3,172	2,354	74
5-<10	80	170	212	526	1,101	209
10-<20	65	57	88	638	743	117
20-<50	26	24	92	818	689	84
50-<100	6	6	100	430	430	100
≥100	5	4	80	500	906	181
Total	3,101	1,642	53	6,084	6,223[a]	100

[a]The total area of holdings exceeds the total area of ownerships by 2%. A possible source of the discrepancy between the two figures—apart from any statistical and definitional differences—may be that the figure for the total area of ownerships is exclusive of *government properties*.

Source: Mahmoud Abdel-Fadil, *Development, Income Distribution and Social Change in Rural Egypt 1952–1970* (Cambridge: Cambridge University Press, 1976), p. 16.

Notes

CHAPTER 1

1. B. F. Johnston and J. B. Cownie, "The Seed-Fertilizer Revolution and Labor Force Absorption," *American Economic Review* (September 1969).
2. R. Albert Berry, "Land Distribution, Income Distribution, and the Productive Efficiency of Colombian Agriculture," *Food Research Institute Studies* 12(3) (1973).
3. William R. Cline, *Economic Consequences of a Land Reform in Brazil* (Amsterdam: North-Holland Publishing Co., 1970).

CHAPTER 2

1. Among empirical studies that have focused on this distinction is that of L. Lau and P. Yotopoulos, "A Test for Relative Efficiency and Application to Indian Agriculture," *American Economic Review* (March 1971).
2. An excellent recent review of the issues surrounding mechanization is William C. Merrill, *Agricultural Mechanization.* Occasional Paper No. 1, Economics and Sector Planning Division, Office of Agriculture, U.S. Agency for International Development, Washington, 1975. See also H. Kaneda, "Economic Implications of the 'Green Revolution' and the Strategy of Agricultural Development in West Pakistan," *Pakistan Development Review* (Summer 1969); S. Bose and E. Clark, "Some Basic Considerations on Agricultural Mechanization in West Pakistan," *Pakistan Development Review* (August 1969); M. Yudelman, G. Butler, and R. Banerji, *Technological Change in Agriculture and Employment in Developing Countries* (Paris: Organization for Economic Cooperation and Development, 1971); K. Abercrombie, "Agricultural Mechanization and Employment in Latin America," *International Labour Review,* 106(1) (July 1972); and I. Ahmed, "The Green Revolution, Mechanization and Employment" (Geneva: International Labour Office, 1975, processed).

Opponents of this view contend that, despite abundant labor, mechanization is socially profitable in some developing countries because it permits double-cropping and/or the release of land otherwise needed for fodder for bullocks. Under some circumstances this argument is doubtless correct, although the contribution of a given type of machine may depend very much on the precise alternative state. For example, introducing a tractor on a given middle- or large-size farm can raise total output, especially if the farm has a shortage of power. Splitting the farm up into a number of small units might lead to a still higher output level. Thus, the optimal agrarian structure might involve few machines, a second best could involve many, and a third best, few. In general, there is little evidence that a high level of mechanization would be a feature of an optimal agricultural strategy in many LDC's. See, for example, A. Singh and M. Billings, "The Effect of Technology on Farm Employment in Two Indian States," in R. Ridker and N. Lubell (eds.), *Employment and Unemployment Problems of the Near East and South Asia,* vol. 2, pp. 502-34 (Delhi: Vikas Publications, 1971).

3. J. M. Brewster, "The Machine Process in Agriculture and Industry," *Journal of Farm Economics* 32 (February 1950): 69-81.

4. E. O. Heady and John L. Dillon, *Agricultural Production Functions* (Ames, Iowa: Iowa State University Press, 1961), p. 630.

5. Cline, *Economic Consequences*..., pp. 58-72.

6. Surjit S. Sidhu, "Relative Efficiency in Wheat Production in the Indian Punjab," *American Economic Review* (September 1974); P. K. Bardhan, "Size, Productivity and Returns to Scale: An Analysis of Farm Level Data in Indian Agriculture," *Journal of Political Economy* (November/December 1973); Lau and Yotopoulos, "A Test ... ."

7. Different farm sizes could be the result of different optimal sizes of operation associated with different products or combinations of products. With homogenous factors and perfect markets (for output and input) and unique optimal sizes for each product, farms of different sizes could not be found producing the same product. Sometimes a finding of constant returns reflects, as much as anything else, the inability of productive units to exist if their relative efficiency is not reasonably close to that of the most efficient size. If this were a basic reason for the constant-returns finding in agriculture, despite substantial returns in the production functions of individual products, one would expect to find farms producing a given item clustered around the optimal size range. The fact that, even among farms producing a given item, there is often a wide range of sizes suggests that the constant-returns findings cannot be explained in this way.

8. For a model examining "capitalist land reform" with compensation see W. R. Cline, "Policy Instruments for Rural Income Redistribution," in Charles R. Frank, Jr., and Richard C. Webb (eds.), *Income Distribution and Growth in the Less-Developed Countries* (Washington, D.C.: Brookings Institution, 1977), pp. 281-336.

9. A. V. Chayanov, *The Theory of Peasant Economy,* D. Thorner, B. Kerblay, R. E. F. Smith (eds.), (Homewood, Ill.: Richard D. Irwin, 1966); A. K. Sen, "Peasants and Dualism with or without Surplus Labor," *Journal of Political Economy* 74 (October 1966): 425-50; D. Kanel, "Size of Farm and Economic Development," *Indian Journal of Agricultural Economics* 22 (2) (April-June 1967);26-44; Cline, *Economic Consequences* ...; Berry, "Land Distribution ..."; K. Griffin, *The Political Economy of Agrarian Change; an Essay on the Green Revolution* (Cambridge, Mass.: Harvard University Press, 1974).

10. The marginal product of a factor is the increase in production contributed by one additional unit of that factor, while all other inputs are held constant. The average product of the factor is merely the ratio of total production to the total number of units of the factor used.

11. W. Arthur Lewis, "Economic Development with Unlimited Supplies of Labor," *The Manchester School* 22 (May 1954): 139-91; J. C. H. Fei and G. Ranis, *Development of the Surplus Labor Economy: Theory and Policy* (Homewood, Ill.: Richard D. Irwin, 1964).

12. Some empirical studies have come up with this result, others have not. One of the earlier studies was that of Mellor and Stevens in a Thai village. (John W. Mellor and Robert D. Stevens, "The Average and Marginal Product of Farm Labor in Underdeveloped Economies," *Journal of Farm Economics* 38 [August 1956]: 780-91.) They concluded that the marginal product of labor (MPL) was not significantly different from zero at the 5 percent confidence level. Mellor later noted that the data was rough; the definition of labor included

persons "available for farm work" whether actually working or not. All farms were assumed to have the same production function. A number of more recent studies have compared the MPL on small and large farms; most such studies have indeed found it to be lower on small farms. Saini's recent study for the Punjab and Uttar Pradesh states of India (for the years 1955-56 and 1956-57) found an MPL averaging about 20 percent higher on farms hiring 50 percent or more of the total labor used on the farm than on farms hiring less than 25 percent of the labor, measured at the geometric mean level of inputs. (G. R. Saini, "Resource Use Efficiency in Agriculture," *Indian Journal of Agricultural Economics* 24 (April-June 1969.)

In selected regions of Colombia, Thirsk estimated the marginal value product of labor, finding it low and well below recorded wage rates in two fairly heavily populated departments. The samples were small however. (Wayne Thirsk, *The Economics of Farm Mechanization in Colombia,* Ph.D. dissertation, Yale University, 1972, p. 123.)

A recent analysis of the Muda River area in Malaysia, with a data set substantially superior to most, estimates the MPL (at the geometric means) to be very close to the wage rate on both small and large farms, a little below the wage on the former and above it on the latter. This region has a particularly active labor market (Howard Barnum and Lyn Squire, "Technology and Relative Economic Efficiency," World Bank, Development Economics Department, Studies in Employment and Rural Development, No. 34, December 1976, p. 21).

In several empirical calculations, where labor applied on small farms was costed at going wage rates, the net profits of the farm came out negative. See, for example, A. K. Sen, "An Aspect of Indian Agriculture," *Economic Weekly*, Annual Number, vol. 14 (1962). Unless such a study has been able to take account of possible differences in productivity of labor by farm size, the conclusions cannot be relied on.

Overall, the build-up of information has suggested that labor surplus is less than the higher estimates made by some observers in the 1940s and 1950s. (Charles Kao, Kurt Anschel, and Carl Eicher, "Disguised Unemployment in Agriculture: A Survey," in Carl Eicher and Lawrence Witt, *Agriculture in Economic Development* [New York: McGraw-Hill, 1964].) At the same time, the systematic evidence of lower average labor productivity on small farms and the evidence of lower marginal productivity in some countries suggests that the marginal product on the farm is often below the wage rate. It would be amazing if this result did not emerge in cases where transport and communications are difficult. Note that this finding does not contradict the proposition that farms may be allocatively efficient when the true opportunity cost of the resources they command is taken into account. (One of the early arguments of this proposition was in W. David Hopper, "Allocation Efficiency in Traditional Indian Agriculture," *Journal of Farm Economics* 47 [1965].)

In short, both measurement and conceptual difficulties make empirical studies of the labor surplus issue difficult to carry out and difficult to assess. It is plausible to expect differences among countries and regions; possibly in some cases there is little gap between the wage and the marginal product of labor on small farms. But the persuasive theoretical arguments and a good share of the empirical results point to a significant gap, so the presumption must be that such gaps are frequent.

13. Parallel considerations apply in the context of renters, who buy the services of land temporarily (e.g., a crop season, a year, or whatever) rather than indefinitely; the price of the land's use is the rent they pay.

14. There is little empirical evidence on land price differentials by farm size because of the difficulties in comparing qualities. So our proposition is based on impressions and on the theoretical arguments cited.

15. For evidence relating to Brazil, see W. R. Cline, "Interrelationships Between Agricultural Strategy and Rural Income Distribution," *Food Research Institute Studies* 12(2) (1973): 150. The issue has been widely debated in the Asian and African contexts as

well. In an excellent recent survey of the effects of farm mechanization in developing countries, Merrill notes:

> During the early stages of mechanization most new machines have little effect on yields. Although some studies report a high correlation between horsepower per hectare and yields or find that farms using tractors have higher yields, a closer look usually reveals that the higher yields are the result of using improved varieties, more fertilizer, better water control, or improved cultivation practices rather than machines per se. It appears that yield increases accounted for by mechanization alone are seldom greater than 10 percent. Many researchers assign almost all yield increases to other technological changes which frequently occur simultaneously with, but independent of, mechanization.

William C. Merrill, Agricultural Mechanization, Economics and Sector Planning Division, Office of Agriculture, Technical Assistance Bureau, U.S. Agency for International Development, Occasional Paper, No. 1, September 1975, p. 8.

16. For evidence of a relatively high degree of substitutability between labor and farm machinery, see Wayne R. Thirsk, "Factor Substitution in Colombian Agriculture," *American Journal of Agricultural Economics* 56 (February 1974):73-84.

17. The sort of land productivity comparisons usually made involve valuing output of a given item at the same price for all farms.

18. In Colombia, for example, many of the very large farms (1,000 hectares and up) are in remote areas. And, on average, farm size appears to be smaller near cities. In the *municipio* of Cali (Colombia's third largest city) average farm size in 1960 was 20.6 hectares, compared to 23 for the whole department. In the special district of Bogotá, however, it was 14.3 hectares, compared with 10.5 hectares for the whole department, possibly reflecting the preference just cited.

19. An additional circularity relating land use and land price has sometimes been suggested. The fact that relatively high cultivation rates and output per total area take place on a given parcel may become capitalized in the price assigned to the parcel's land. As a result, higher land prices for smaller farms may be due to superior soil quality or to superior demonstrated production of the land attributable in fact to the greater application of nonland inputs (especially labor). We have seen no studies throwing light directly on this issue.

Furthermore, in cases where smaller farms are, on average, closer to towns or cities than large ones, their prices for land will in some cases tend to be inflated due to that proximity and will overestimate (relatively speaking) the economic potential of the land.

20. In many of the specific discussions that follow, however, we are constrained by data limitations to measure land in terms of area. While this fact diminishes our understanding as to why input ratios and factor productivities differ between small and large farms, it does not weaken the overall conclusions, since the sector-wide calculations are designed to take account of varying economic potential of land across farm sizes.

21. This description appears to fit Colombia quite accurately (section 4.2). For Northeastern Brazil, yields per hectare cultivated appear instead to be constant across farm sizes. See M. D. Sund, *Land Tenure and Economic Performance of Agricultural Establishments in Northeastern Brazil*, University of Wisconsin, Ph.D. thesis, 1965. In China, as of the 1930s this was true as well. In the Philippines, as of the 1960s, no systematic differences emerge from the data; different crops present different stories. In Pakistan, there is evidence of higher yields on larger farms for some crops and not for others. Few studies have attempted to dissaggregate in such a way as to allow for land quality differences, so the data do not permit strong conclusions at this point.

22. We do not, however, deny the existence of possible output benefits from such transfers. It has long been argued that nonownership discourages a farmer from making profitable long-run investments on the farm, weakens potentially productive community

cooperation, and so on. These arguments, some of them involving mechanisms that would be hard to identify empirically, may well be important, but the available statistics do not demonstrate their validity and make it natural to conclude, tentatively at least, that size of operational unit is a much more important determinant of efficiency than is tenure.

23. Note that the previous caveat that the very smallest farms may apply too much labor would thus become irrelevant, because all farms would be of the same size in constant quality land area and would possess the same labor force, the available family labor. An equal distribution of available land among the entire rural labor force on a family farm basis will generally result in parcels significantly larger than the smallest prereform farms. Furthermore, even if a single-farm size were identified as having the highest social efficiency under current conditions (i.e., the size at which total social factor productivity stopped rising from the levels of the very smallest farms and began declining over the large range of remaining farm sizes), that size could not be interpreted to be a unique optimal size for the establishment of postreform parcels.

24. For a discussion of incentive problems on the large cooperative farms created by land reform in Chile under Allende, particularly with respect to the diversion of cooperative resources into small private plots within the cooperative farms, see S. Barraclough and J. Fernandez, *Diagnostico de la Reforma Agraria Chilena* (Mexico: Siglo Veintiuno Editores, 1974).

25. See, for example, the negative position taken by Dandekar and Rath with respect to creating large numbers of very small farms capable of absorbing the rural labor force in India. V. M. Dandekar and N. Rath, "Poverty in India—II: Policies and Programmes," *Economic and Political Weekly* 6(2) (January 9, 1971): 106–46.

26. Srivasta and Heady (p. 512) estimated elasticities of −0.28 and −0.49 for the Indian Punjab and Uttar Pradesh in 1967–69. Yotopoulos, Lau, and Somel estimated substitution elasticities of approximately −0.3 on all farms, but as high as −0.94 on small farms for India, and reported that the overall estimate appeared implausibly low (pp. 47–48). Bardhan found for seven out of eight regional estimates for India that the unitary elasticity Cobb-Douglas form could not be statistically rejected in favor of the nonunitary constant elasticity of substitution (CES) form (p. 1376). U. K. Srivasta and E. O. Heady, "Technological Change and Relative Factor Shares in Indian Agriculture: An Empirical Analysis," *American Journal of Agricultural Economics* 55(3) (August 1973): 509–14; P. Yotopoulos, L. Lau, K. Somel, "Labor Intensity and Relative Efficiency in Indian Agriculture," *Food Research Institute Studies* 9(1) (1970): 43–55; P. K. Bardhan, "Size, Productivity and Returns to Scale: An Analysis of Farm Level Data in Indian Agriculture," *Journal of Political Economy* (November/December 1973): 1370–86.

However, since the CES production function estimate typically requires statistical tests based on the relationship of the output/labor ratio (or the ratio of capital and land to labor) to the wage/rental ratio, and because—as discussed above—the appropriate concept for labor's cost on family farms is not the wage rate, one must view CES estimates with caution because of the high likelihood of errors in variables. Moreover, with errors in variables one might expect a downward bias in the estimated elasticity of substitution.

27. This last case is mainly a curiosity, since it is unlikely that the elasticity of substitution is above unity, let alone infinite. The intuitive interpretation of this case is as follows. With infinitely elastic substitution, the output from a single factor is wholly independent of how much of the other factor is available. Therefore, if the land resource is doubled moving from country 1 to country 2, the output produced by land alone doubles, while that produced by labor alone holds constant. But the large farm, with much land and little labor, obtains most of its output from land, while the small farm obtains little of its output from land. Therefore, a doubling of only the output due to land gives a much larger percentage rise for total output for the large farm than for the small.

28. For an earlier review of this literature, see Cline, "Policy instruments . . . ."

29. S. Cheung, "Private Property Rights and Sharecropping," *Journal of Political Economy* 76(6) (November/December 1968): 1107-22.

30. P. K. Bardhan and T. N. Srinivasan, "Cropsharing Tenancy in Agriculture: A Theoretical and Empirical Analysis," *American Economic Review* 51(1) (March 1971): 48-64.

31. A flaw commented upon by D. Newberry, "Cropsharing Tenancy in Agriculture: Comment," *American Economic Review* 64(6) (December 1974): 1060-66.

32. C. Bell and P. Zusman, "A Bargaining Theoretic Approach to Cropsharing Contracts" (Washington, D.C.: 1975, mimeo.).

33. J. Stiglitz, "Incentives and Risk Sharing in Sharecropping," *Review of Economic Studies* 41(2) (1974), pp. 219-55.

34. Some discussion of empirical findings and a review of theoretical issues is presented by J. C. Hsiao, "The Theory of Share Tenancy Revisited," *Journal of Political Economy* 83(5) (October 1975): 1023-32.

35. Distribution of landownership is a determinant of the amount of tenanted land, of course, where owners of large areas do not wish to or cannot cultivate it all. When they rent it out in small plots, either on a cash or a share basis, there may be little output loss from the concentrated ownership of land. When they operate it themselves, output loss does typically occur.

36. Among useful studies of certain aspects of these dynamic relationships are Michael Schluter, "Differential Rates of Adoption of the New Seed Varieties in India; the Problem of the Small Farm," Cornell University, Department of Agricultural Economics, Occasional Paper No. 47, August 1971; M. Schluter, "The Interaction of Credit and Uncertainty in Determining Resource Allocation and Incomes on Small Farms, Surat District, India," Cornell University, Department of Agricultural Economics, Occasional Paper No. 68, February 1974.

37. For evidence on the high productivity of additional credit-financed modern inputs on small farms in Colombia, see W. Thirsk, "Rural Credit and Income Distribution in Colombia," Rice University Program of Development Studies Paper No. 51 (Houston: 1974, mimeo.). For a report on similar evidence for Brazil, see Cline, "Policy instruments . . . ." The view that small-farm credit often is unproductive emerges in U.S. Agency for International Development, *A.I.D. Spring Review of Small Farmer Credit: Small Farmer Credit Summary Papers XX* (Washington, D.C.: Agency for International Development, 1973). Central to this issue, of course, is how well the credit institutions are structured and managed. In a number of countries, the record is bad on these accounts and major restructuring is called for.

38. Dalrymple and Jones suggest a provocative parallel between this already completed cycle of adoption of high-yielding varieties in Mexico and its recent early phases in the Green Revolution in Asia. D. Dalrymple and W. Jones, "Evaluating the 'Green Revolution,'" paper prepared for joint meeting of American Association for the Advancement of Science and Consejo Nacional de Ciencia y Tecnologia, Mexico City, June 20, 1973, mimeo.

39. Among these theories are the life cycle and the permanent income hypotheses. See W. R. Cline, *Potential Effects of Income Redistribution on Economic Growth: Latin American Cases* (New York: Praeger Publishers, 1972).

40. Cline, "Interrelationships . . . ."

41. Surjit Bhalla, "An Analysis of Savings in Rural India," (Washington, D.C.: 1975, mimeo.).

42. This point may be seen by referring to the familiar Harrod–Domar growth model, in which the growth rate equals the savings rate divided by the capital/output ratio.

CHAPTER 3

1. Food and Agriculture Organization, *Report on the 1960 Census of Agriculture,* vol. 5, *Analysis and International Comparison of Census Results* (Rome: Food and Agriculture Organization, 1971).

2. The remainder of this study relies heavily on the use of regression analysis, a statistical procedure that selects coefficients for independent variables to provide the best possible fit between the observed values of the dependent variable and those implied by the equation estimated. The criterion for the best fit is the "least squares" condition: the coefficients are selected so that the sum of squared residuals (that is, the sum over all observations of the square of the difference between the actual and the predicted value of the dependent variable for each) is minimized.

Two statistics in such tests are especially important: the multiple correlation coefficient of determination, R^2, which indicates the percentage of total variation explained by the regression (with the barred term $\bar{R}^2$ referring to this statistic after adjustment to take into account the number of observations less the number of independent variables used for the test, or the "degrees of freedom"); and the t-statistic, which is the ratio of the coefficient estimated to the standard error of the estimate for that coefficient. As the R^2 approaches unity complete explanation is approached; as the t-statistic rises to values of 2.0 or higher, generally (or, as the standard error falls below one-half of the magnitude of the coefficient estimated), the estimated coefficient is significantly different from zero in statistical terms (at the 5 percent level of confidence; that is, on grounds that would lead one to conclude erroneously that a relation existed, when one in fact did not, only 5 percent of the time).

3. The Gini coefficient varies from 0 for perfectly equal distribution to 1 for completely unequal distribution. On a "Lorenz curve" diagram of the cumulative percent of number of farms (horizontally) against the cumulative percent of land in the farms (vertically), it equals the area between the curve and the diagonal of the diagram, divided by the entire area under that diagonal.

4. The World Bank study refers to concentration of land ownership, but the data probably refer to size distribution of farm operations rather than ownership units. Note that for those countries in which World Bank estimates of the Gini coefficient of land concentration are available (Table 3–5), the estimates are generally close to our estimates (Table 3–3).

5. Of course, in a comparison of output per hectare with average farm size, it is necessary to remove the influence of population pressure on the land before drawing policy implications. More densely populated countries tend to have both smaller farm sizes and higher output per hectare than sparsely populated countries. For this reason, the contrasts among countries within Asia (mentioned in the text) are much more meaningful than contrasts between land-scarce Asia and land-abundant Latin America.

CHAPTER 4

1. W. R. Cline, *Economic Consequences of a Land Reform in Brazil.*

2. In a recent production function study for Northeastern Brazil, Scandizzo and Barbosa also have found returns to scale to be constant for general agriculture. They do find some evidence of increasing returns to scale when the data are organized by specific-crop sectors, but these results appear to be significantly different from constant returns (in the statistical sense) for only two out of five sectors (cotton and cocoa, with results for rice, sugar cane, and mixed crops showing t-ratios below critical levels for the test on increasing returns to scale). Pasquale L. Scandizzo and Tulio Barbosa, "Substituição e Produtividade de Fatores na

Agricultura Nordestina," *Pesquisa e Planejamento Econômico* 7 (2) (August 1977): 382, 394.

3. Each farm is classified as belonging to the livestock sector if it receives half or more of its output value from livestock. If the farm receives half or more of its output from crops, then it is classified into a specific-crop sector if either (a) more than half of its crop output value comes from the product in question; or (b) more than 30 percent of total farm output value comes from the product.

4. Cline, *Economic Consequences* . . . , pp. 91–94.

5. Pasquale L. Scandizzo e Tulio Barbosa, "Substituicao e Produtividade . . . .

6. In a set of grouped average data, much of the variation caused by miscellaneous exogenous factors will be cancelled, or averaged, out; by contrast, the attempt to explain all variation of individual farm observations in large numbers with a limited number of variables is bound to leave a major portion of variance unexplained, even though strongly confirming the specific hypothesis test in terms of a highly significant ratio of the coefficient estimate to its standard error. (This observation should also be kept in mind in assessing the statistical results reported in the following sections of this study.)

7. In the form $VA/X = a + b \log X$, the ratio b/a tells the steepness with which value-added per hectare declines as farm size rises. This ratio was approximately -0.1 and -0.15 for sugar in Pernambuco and cattle in Ceara in 1962–63, respectively. (Cline, *Economic Consequences* . . . p. 92.) In the estimates of Table 4-3 here, the corresponding ratios are approximately -0.14 for sugar and -0.24 for livestock. Thus, the steepness of the inverse relationship between farm size and productivity has remained practically unchanged or, if anything, worsened.

8. Unweighted averages of the factor-use elasticities for the four Northeastern product sectors in the Getulio Vargas Foundation data were: labor, 0.43; capital, 0.57; seed-fertilizer, 0.64 (ibid., pp. 112–13). The corresponding elasticities reported here in Table 4-5 are: labor, 0.38; capital, 0.63; seed-fertilizer, 0.69.

9. A 15 percent social cost of capital for Brazil is estimated in Edmar L. Bacha, Aloisio B. de Araujo, Milton da Mata, and Rui Modenesi, *Analise Governamental de Projetos de Investimentos no Brasil: Procedimentos e Recomendacoes* (Rio de Janeiro: IPEA, 1971). Sensitivity analysis applying a social cost of capital of 10 percent yields results almost identical to those in Table 4-7 in terms of relative total factor productivity by farm size.

10. The January 1973 minimum wage level for the Northeast, 182.4 cruzeiros per month (or US $342 per man-year), is taken from Instituto Nacional de Colonizacao e Reforma Agraria, *Sistema Nacional de Cadastro Rural: Informativo Tecnico 1: Indices Basicos* (Rio de Janeiro: Instituto Nacional de Colonizacao e Reforma Agraria, 1974).

11. Cline, *Economic Consequences* . . . , pp. 128–30.

12. Although the yield differentials were taken from 1966 data.

13. Farms and land operated by their owners rose by 7.1 and 16.9 percent, respectively, while rented farms and land (excluding sharecropping) fell by 50.2 and 21.3 percent, respectively, sharecropped farms and land fell by 32.4 and 16.2 percent, respectively, and farms and land farmed without title (*colonato*) changed by 2.0 and -11.5 percent, respectively. (This last change implies that a number of large farms previously held without title became titled during the intercensal period.) The number of farms operated by an administrator rose by 100 percent and the land in them by 30 percent, to reach approximately 40 percent of all land reported in the 1970-71 census.

14. Real-value-added in agriculture rose by 43.1 percent over the decade, according to national accounts estimates, and land in farms by 13.4 percent. Land listed as in use for crops or as pasture rose by 27.8 percent, however, so that if all output were assumed to be produced on this land, productivity on it would have risen by only 12 percent, or a little over 1 percent per year. As between the two agricultural censuses, area listed as currently under

crops rose faster than the volume of production, but this difference may be due to different timing of the two censuses. The share of land in fallow in the latter year was much higher; that under crops was just 8.1 percent higher in 1970-71 than in 1960. On this matter, independent estimates of areas under cultivation are probably more indicative than the censuses. According to Kalmanovitz's figures, for 17 major crops the area rose by 11.3 percent over this period, implying an annual increase in value of output per hectare of approximately 2.4 percent. (Salomon Kalmanovitz, "La Agricultura en Colombia, 1950-72," in DANE, *Boletin Mensual de Estadistica,* 276 (July 1974): 145.)

15. For a more detailed discussion, see A. Berry, "Some Recent Trends in Colombian Agriculture," mimeo., 1976. Note that the share of land under temporary crops rose only for farms above 60 hectares, although it did so from a very low base and remained very low at the end of the decade.

16. The fact that the sample is not representative is also suggested by the result that total output per farm does not increase monotonically with farm size, nor does average size of farm area increase with increasing size of farm—defined as total investment in durable goods plus total sales value of production plus total operating expenses (variable costs). Agency for International Development Sector Analysis Division, Bureau for Latin America, *General Working Document No. 17 U, Small Farm Analysis Preliminary Results: Employment, Availability and Utilization,* by James R. Horst and Thomas Walker, January 1973, p. 6.

17. On many of the Instituto Nacional de Colonizacion y Reforma Agraria questionnaires, reported cultivated land plus pasture land exceeded farm area. It is not clear whether this contradiction resulted from data errors or from some form of double counting.

18. The high rice yields on the smallest farms (under 0.2 hectare) cannot be considered of much significance, both because the amount of land is so small and because errors of observation (e.g., rounding to the nearest tenth of a hectare) may lead to substantial errors in the yield figures.

19. Vernon W. Ruttan, "Tenure and Productivity of Philippine Rice Producing Farms," *Philippine Economic Journal* 5(1) (1966): 42-63.

20. J. P. Estanislao, "A Note on Differential Farm Productivity, by Tenure," *Philippine Economic Journal* 4(1) (1965): 120. The study cited by Estanislao is Horst and Judith Von Oppenfeld, J. C. Sta. Iglesia, and P. R. Sandoval, *Farm Management, Land Use and Tenancy in the Philippines* (University of the Philippines, August 1957), p. 114.

21. Generoso F. Rivera and Robert T. McMillan, *An Economic and Social Survey of Rural Households in Central Luzon* (Philcusa—U.S. Operations Mission to the Philippines, 1954), pp. 68, 71.

22. Vernon W. Ruttan, "Land Reform and National Economic Development," G. P. Sicat (ed.), *The Philippine Economy in the 1960's* (Institute of Economic Development and Research, University of the Philippines, 1964), pp. 104-5.

23. Lack of a systematic differential between these two forms is confirmed by more recent data from Central Luzon and Nueva Ecija (Table D-5, Appendix D). That table also shows a continuing tendency for yields to be lowest on owner-operated farms in most crop years.

24. A more recent survey (1969 and 1970) in Nueva Ecija, however, shows no overall tendency for leaseholders to spend more per hectare on fertilizers than share tenants; farms are not classified by size. (Ateneo de Manila University, Institute of Philippine Culture, *Land Reform and Agricultural Improvement in Nueva Ecija: Phase One,* by R. P. de los Reyes, M. Mangahas and F. J. Murray, 1973, typescript, Tables 6 and 7, as quoted in International Labor Office, *Sharing in Development: A Program of Employment, Equity and Growth for the Philippines* [Geneva: International Labor Organization, 1974], p. 488.)

25. De los Reyes et al., *Land Reform* ..., Tables 9-11.

26. Based on figures presented in Horst and Judith Von Oppenfeld, *et al., Farm Management ....*

27. The figures presented by Estanislao, "Differential Farm Productivity . . .," imply averages of 1,014 for owners, 1,640 for part owners, and 2,266 for tenants.

28. Bureau of Agricultural Economics, *Agricultural Economics, Statistics, and Market News Digest* 6(46) (November 15, 1972), p. 3. In this set of farms, yields were highest for owners. It is therefore doubtful whether they are representative.

29. Quoting the recent International Labour Office report: "These results are not entirely unexpected. Evidence has been emerging that it is common for landowners to make certain important decisions (especially regarding variety to be planted) jointly with the tenant farmer. The quantity of fertilizer to be applied is often controlled by the amount of credit the landowner provides, and there are indeed many cases in which the landowner provides the fertilizer directly. This tends to counteract the disincentive for share tenants to apply variable inputs if they worked the land of a totally absentee landowner. The recent finding that almost nine-tenths of the landowners have small estates, tends to lend further support to the landowner-participation hypothesis." (ILO, *Sharing in Development*, p. 486).

30. See Mahar Mangahas, "An Economic Theory of Tenant and Landlord Based on a Philippine Case," in Lloyd G. Reynolds (ed.), *Agriculture in Development Theory* (New Haven: Yale University Press, 1975), pp. 138–61; and Mahar Mangahas, Virginia A. Miralas, and Romana P. de los Reyes, *Tenants, Lessees, Owners: Welfare Implications of Tenure Change* (Quezon City: Institute of Philippine Culture, Ateneo de Manila University, 1975).

31. Discussion and figures in this section refer to the present Pakistan, even for years when Bangladesh was part of Pakistan.

32. Presented mainly in Mahmood Hasan Khan, *The Economics of the Green Revolution in Pakistan* (New York: Praeger Publishers, 1975).

33. A very substantial portion of total farm area is rented in Pakistan. At the time of the 1959-60 agricultural census this share was about 49 percent; it tended to increase with size to well over 50 percent in the range 7.5 to 25 acres and fall sharply for the farms over 50 acres, although it was still 39 percent for those of 50 to 150 acres. By 1971, the share of land rented by the operator was 45 percent. At all sizes it is predominantly sharecropping.

Fragmentation is also notable in Pakistan, especially in certain regions. In the North West Frontier Province there are, on the average, almost four separate plots per farm.

34. Note that the figure for total value of product is in fact not quite production value as such, because for livestock it corresponds to value-added. Value of fodder output is not included in the total. Note also that we exclude the smallest size category and the largest from most of the comparisons, on the grounds that their output is relatively small. Also the very high figure for the smallest farms reflects the much greater importance of livestock (especially poultry) there than on larger farms. Presumably, a considerable share of the inputs for that livestock does not come from the small farms themselves, but from grazing on open land.

35. Herring and Chaudhry note that the farms in the Farm Accounts and Family Budget Surveys (FAFBS) in the Punjab were carefully selected to represent conditions there; further, the likelihood that they may be reasonably representative is increased by the fact that the average gross income per cultivated acre between 1966-67 and 1968-69 in the sample closely approximated the average for West Pakistan in the same period. (Ronald Herring and M. Ghaffar Chaudhry, "The 1972 Land Reforms in Pakistan and Their Economic Implications: A Preliminary Analysis," *Pakistan Development Review* 13[3] [Autumn 1974]: 262.)

36. Note that in the last two equations the elasticity of gross income per acre with respect to farm size at the point of means is -0.28 and -0.20 respectively.

37. The coefficient is -146 instead of -187, and the t-statistic is -2.39 instead of -4.84. As measures of productivity net farm income (gross income minus purchased inputs and hired labor costs) and value-added (gross income minus purchased inputs) are more

relevant than is gross farm income. The impact of size, whether measured in total acres or in cultivated acres, remains systematically negative, regardless of which dependent variable is used.

38. Since the equation constrained the size-productivity relationship to be the same in each region, the calculation (from the fitted equation) of yield differentials by size for a given region would not be expected to be precise.

39. From Hiromitsu Kaneda and Mohammed Ghaffar, "Output Effect of Tubewells on the Agriculture of the Punjab: Some Empirical Results," *Pakistan Development Review* 10(1) (Spring 1970): 68–87.

40. This would appear to be due in part (perhaps mostly) to lower fodder land quality on the larger farms, in part to greater foraging on public lands by animals on the smaller farms, and in part to the greater labor that can be applied to care of the animals on the smaller farms.

41. M. Naseem, *Field Survey of Small Farms in Sahiwal District, Pakistan,* Agency for International Development Spring Review of Small Farmer Credit, vol. 14, February 1973, no. SR 114.

42. K. M. Azam, "The Future of the Green Revolution in West Pakistan: A Choice of Strategy," *International Journal of Agrarian Affairs* 5(6) (March 1973): 417, 418.

43. Ibid., p. 418.

44. The fact that most categories appear to have surpluses of income over expenditures suggests that income may have been better reported than in most other surveys, plausible given the much more precise design, whereby field workers stationed in the sample villages maintained year-round records.

45. The "big landowners" are distinguished from the peasant proprietors by the fact that their holdings are larger, but the dividing line between the two groups is not uniform across the sample villages and varies with local conditions. The figures suggest quite high savings rates for the big landowners. In 1968–69, for example, it averaged 50.3 percent, according to these figures. For all farmers, over 1965–70 it averaged 26 percent. These figures are probably overestimates; though they are not totally implausible in light of the rapid income increases characterizing parts of the Punjab during precisely this period, they had also been high in most earlier years. Possibly, expenditures have been underreported or income overreported. For the lowest income occupational groups (agricultural laborers, artisans, etc.) the reported savings rate tends to be low over a period of years, lending greater credence to the data.

46. Two measures of savings per cultivated acre were constructed; in both cases the family's overall S/Y ratio was applied to that share of its income earned on the farm. This basic calculation (used strictly for "big landowners" and "peasants") was as follows:

$$\left(\frac{\text{Total family savings}}{\text{Total net family income}} \times \text{Net farm income} \right) \div \text{Cultivated acres.}$$

For the first variable, $(S/CA)_1$, it was assumed for tenant cultivators that the share of the rent they paid that would be saved (by the recipient) was equal to the "tenants" savings rate; for the second, $(S/CA)_2$, it was assumed that the share of the rental income saved was equal to the average savings rate of the big landowners in that region.

47. E.g., Azam, "Green Revolution in West Pakistan . . . ."

48. This figure may be suspect; the comparable one in 1972 is much lower, and there is no obvious reason for a decline between the two years.

49. Thousands of nutrient tons consumed were reported as 19.4 in 1959–60 and 381.9 in 1971–72. (Government of Pakistan, Ministry of Food, Agriculture, Underdeveloped Areas and Land Reforms, *Agricultural Statistics of Pakistan 1975* [Islamabad, 1975], p. 186.)

50. Note that a comparison of the percent of farms adopting often provides data more favorable to the large farms than a comparison of percent of land under the new variety.

51. Refugio I. Rochen, "Dwarf Wheat Adoption by Barani Small Holders of Hazara District: Technological Change in Action," Islamabad, Ford Foundation Preliminary Report, 1970.

52. Azam, "Green Revolution in West Pakistan . . . ,"

53. How the difference between price weights and caloric weights affects the calculations is not clear.

54. Khan, *Green Revolution in Pakistan* . . . , pp. 119-20.

55. Although for 1960 the datum—column (3) of Table 4-37—refers to all crops, except fodder, rather than just the five used in Khan's analysis.

56. This estimate appears to be consistent with the results reported by Khan in a recent paper. M. H. Khan, "Land Productivity, Farm Size and Returns to Scale in Pakistan Agriculture," mimeo., November 1976. He uses regression analysis on the farm sample to test the relationship of farm size with output per net sown area; with only net sown area as the independent variable, he finds a negative coefficient for the sample as a whole, for the Punjab farms, and, more strongly, for Sind farms; it appears also for six of the eight districts. The relation for new wheat, new rice, and cotton taken individually tends to be positive, suggesting that the negative overall relationship is a result of differences in crop composition. When labor and capital inputs are also included in the regressions the coefficient of net sown area is more frequently positive. These more recent results must be reconciled with the earlier ones. In 1960, the inverse relation between output per unit of land and farm size was more marked when the land unit was cultivated area than when it was net sown area (Table 4-31).

57. Note also that although villages to be sampled in a given district were chosen on a random basis, farms within the village were not. (Kahn, "Land Productivity . . . ," pp. 4-6). There is no obvious reason that this should have created a bias vis-à-vis the farm-size/productivity question, however.

58. Khan, "Land Productivity . . . ," p. 9.

59. A point emphasized by McInerney and Donaldson in World Bank, "The Consequences of Farm Tractors . . . ."

60. This phenomenon is well known; see, e.g., McInerney and Donaldson. What remains to be seen is whether or not it is the major factor behind the decline in tenanted land, and whether or not it will have an important negative impact on income distribution.

61. On this, see the discussion by H. Barnum and L. Squire "Technology and Relative Economic Efficiency," World Bank, Development Economics Department, Employment and Rural Development Division, December 1976.

62. In this case, size of area used for paddy and area not normally used for paddy, this latter apparently excluding the house lot. Note also that since there were few single-croppers, nearly all of our analysis focuses on the double-croppers, where cell sizes are large enough to allow good levels of confidence.

63. One relong equals approximately 0.7 acre.

64. In an analysis based on the same Muda River Survey, but using a smaller sample (386 farmers instead of the 762 used here) Barnum and Squire ("Technology and Relative Economic Efficiency") found a statistically insignificant difference of only about 5 percent in rice output per relong. One source of the different results is the inclusion of other crops than rice in our analysis, since our yield/relong data shows the farms of less than 5 relongs with an advantage of only 10 percent over farms of more than 5 relongs (based on Table 4-50). A higher share of farm output on the smallest farms is of nonpadi items. Also, the differential in value-added per relong is greater than that in value of output per relong, since the ratio of purchased inputs to value of farm output increases with farm size (Table 4-48). A third pos-

sible factor is our use of land area at the beginning of the year rather than average over the year, a factor that leads to a relative overestimation of land productivity on farms of less than 5 relongs of 8.5 percent (vis-à-vis farms of greater than 5 relongs). The remaining (small) inconsistency between our figures and those of Barnum and Squire may be due to their exclusion of a small number of farms with acid soils and other farms that had not reported certain information on labor utilization.

65. The index includes hired labor measured by wages paid plus female family hours assumed to be worth 0.828 Malaysian dollars and male family hours 1.656. An alternative index, where it was assumed that an hour of hired labor is worth the same on all farms sizes, i.e., 0.9 for females and 1.8 for males, produced similar results.

66. Barnum and Squire ("Technology and Relative Economic Efficiency," p. 8) found labor productivity in rice about 10 percent higher on farms above 5 relongs than on those below 5 relongs. Possibly this difference is due to their consideration of rice alone, or to their use of total labor hours as the measure of labor input rather than labor hours weighted by whether hired or family, female or male. In either case, the differential is small.

67. Some of the positive association between farm size and labor productivity in country-wide analyses may be due to aggregation across nonhomogeneous regions. Often regions with larger average farm size will have higher incomes and, if labor markets are better within regions than between them, higher labor productivity on all farm sizes than will regions with low average farm size. Since the data on labor inputs for Muda are in terms of time actually worked rather than time available (as in most such calculations) it may be that the low labor productivity usually found on small farms is due in part to a lower ratio of time worked to time available for work.

68. Y. Huang, "Tenancy Patterns, Productivity, and Rentals in Malaysia," *Economic Development and Cultural Change* 23 (4) (July 1975): 703–18.

69. Note, however, that in the smaller subsample of 386 farms Barnum and Squire ("Technology and Relative Economic Efficiency," p. 8) found the opposite result (though not statistically significant) for rice. Land was measured by area, capital by flow of services, and labor by hours of input. Several of the methodological differences discussed above may contribute to this discrepancy in results.

70. Income is gross of depreciation on capital equipment, but such depreciation would not lower it by more than a few percentage points at most. Capital stock has been rising quickly in the region, so depreciation would be a fairly small share of current purchases of capital goods. Such purchases range from less than 1 percent of family income for the smallest farm size to about 6 percent for the largest. If depreciation were one-half of new purchases, the savings rate of the largest farms would fall from 20 percent to 17 percent.

71. Although the Muda survey data is, relatively speaking, of very high quality, the savings data are naturally less accurate than most of the other figures.

72. The families in size categories (2), (3), and (4) have heads of below average age, though not dramatically so.

73. Except in the unlikely circumstance that other families were willing to subsidize them permanently.

CHAPTER 5

1. A qualification of this procedure involves the implicit assumption about labor input. Suppose the farm size resulting from dividing total land by the total number of rural families is x^*. The production associated with farms of size x^* at present may involve the use of more labor or less labor than that available from precisely one family of average size. As a result the computation of expected output on the land reform parcel may be over- or

underestimated. With some knowledge of the marginal product of labor, adjustments to the first calculation could be made to allow for this error. In practice, however, the labor input on currently existing farms of the size that would result from complete land redistribution into family farms is usually quite close to the labor available from a single family. Furthermore, in conditions of low marginal product of labor, the change in output per parcel that would be implied by a correction for any divergences between current and postreform labor input on farms of parcel size would be limited.

2. By contrast, a land reform creating a privileged sector of relatively large parcels for a small elite of the rural work force would fail to do so, although it seems unlikely that even this type of reform would actually reduce total employment. New, prosperous parcel recipients in this type of reform might replace hired labor formerly used on the farms of large owners with their own family labor, but this negative effect would probably be swamped by the positive effect of an increase in total agricultural labor requirements associated with increased utilization of land formerly in large farms.

3. W. R. Cline, *Economic Consequences* . . . .

4. It should be noted that although the table reports prospective increase in output from land redistribution based on current patterns of output per physical area by farm size, similar results are obtained when the analysis is based on output per land value. Regions in which average land quality (price per hectare) is higher on larger farms approximately equal in importance regions in which average land quality is lower on larger farms.

5. Ibid., pp. 146-48.

6. Calculated from ibid., pp. 146-48, 152.

7. There is an abundant literature on land reform experience. See, for example, Doreen Warriner, "Results of Land Reform in Asian and Latin American Countries," *Food Research Institute Studies* 12 (2) (1973); and Schlomo Eckstein, Gordon Donald, Douglas Horton, and Thomas Carroll, *Land Reform in Latin America: Bolivia, Chile, Mexico, Peru and Venezuela* (Washington, D.C.: World Bank, 1978, Staff Working Paper No. 275). The recent cases of Chilean and Peruvian land reform are described in William R. Cline, "Policy Instruments . . . ".

8. Schlomo Eckstein, et al., *Land Reform in Latin America* . . . .

9. Doreen Warriner, "Results of Land Reform . . . ."

10. World Bank, *Land Reform: Sector PolicyPaper* (Washington, D.C., 1975), p. 68.

11. Keith Griffin, *Land Concentration and Rural Poverty* (New York: Holmes & Meier, 1976).

12. Even apart from the fact that land reform advocates will be able to cite successful historical precedents and land reform opponents unsuccessful ones.

13. It is possible that in some circumstances the response of owners to such restriction would be minimal and that in fact the desired result of transferring windfall or monopoly income shares from owners to tenants could be achieved at little risk of eviction. There is a need for further theoretical and empirical work examining the conditions under which this situation would hold true. More generally, however, policy-makers must expect tenant evictions as the result of restrictions on rental and sharecropping.

14. What seems to emerge from the data now available is that there are good reasons for families combining farm and off-farm activities; there are no good reasons to assume that government intervention would lead to greater efficiency. In countries where considerable off-farm employment opportunities exist, small-farm families earn substantial shares of their income from off-farm employment. Thus, in Ceylon in 1962, about 30 percent of operators earned most of their income from nonagricultural activities (Appendix Table D-6), as did over half of those with less than one acre. In Malawi (1968-69), the share of family income from off-farm activities was high—30-50 percent for all households surveyed and 50-70 percent for those with less than two acres (Table B-6). One-quarter to one-half of all farm families earned more off the farm than on. In the Muda River area of Malaya, farms of less

than one acre got about half their income from off-farm activities and those of one to two acres about 30 percent (Table 4-49). Although less quantitative, evidence is widespread that in most countries farmers with small plots complement their farm income from such activities. In some countries, the reason they have the plots in the first place is part of an arrangement whereby they provide labor to larger farmers.

Cross-country comparisons suggest that when there are diseconomies from operation of very small plots, their owners tend to rent them out to other farmers (and find full-time off-farm jobs themselves). In Egypt, after the major land reform of 1952 left the country with a predominance of very small farms, the agricultural census of 1961 showed many more small ownership plots than operational holdings (Table D-7) and only about half as many production units as owned units. In parts of India, land redistribution into very small units has also been followed by such a consolidation via market forces. The evidence that such consolidation does on occasion occur on its own (i.e., without government intervention) strengthens the presumption that where it does not occur, there are good reasons for its absence in terms of efficiency.

This is not, of course, to argue that land markets operate with near perfect efficiency. It is often argued that farm fragmentation lowers efficiency (though the evidence does not, on balance, suggest that this effect is a dramatic one) and it is wondered why the land market does not lead via purchase and sale to a more efficient allocation of land among farmers. But to expect that when one farmer wants to expand, his neighbor will want to contract operations, or that the market will be able to solve a complex maximization problem of this sort, is probably unrealistic. It might also be unrealistic to expect government intervention to improve on the market, unless a high level of expertise was available.

15. As reported in World Bank Staff Working Paper #210, "The Consequences of Farm Tractors in Pakistan," prepared by John P. McInerney and Graham F. Donaldson, February 1975, p. ii.

16. Don Kanel, "The Role of Land Tenure in the Modernization of Agriculture," mimeo. Paper presented at the Purdue University Workshop on Small Farm Agriculture in Developing Nations, November 1972, pp. 2-4.

APPENDIX A

1. The general expectation would be in the affirmative; better education, easier access to inputs and lesser risk are all factors that place the large farmer in a better position to adopt the new technology than his smaller and poorer neighbors. Even if the extent of adoption is controlled, the large farmer may still have an advantage because of the crucial dependence of HYV performance on the proper use of water, pesticides, and fertilizers.

2. Variations in adoption behavior, for example, may not show up in a local study if most of the farmers have adopted the new technology (cf., wheat in Punjab). Extension and credit agencies perform differently in different areas and are most likely to have performed well in the successful areas. If access to these agencies is dependent on farm size, then a study of successful areas may not highlight the inequities involved.

3. The motivation for this debate is not hard to discern. If small farmers were economically more productive, then policies like land reform would have both an equity and an efficiency basis.

4. Ideally, R should include in it any revenue from livestock operation. Though such data were available for the third year, for the preceding two years the only available figure was for *net* livestock income. Requirements of consistency dictated that livestock receipts be excluded from the analysis. Note, however, that the definition of R made little difference to the results of the third year.

5. It is interesting to note that Cline's study (1970) for Brazil (a land-*abundant* country) shows that farms primarily differ across sizes in their land-use intensity and that these differences account for the variations in output/acre, i.e., large farms bring less of their cultivable land into operation and therefore achieve lower output per total area. By contrast, differences in land use by farm size in India (a land-*scarce* country) take the form of differences in cropping intensity.

6. The question asked in the village schedule was "What were the prices for the different types of land that were ruling in the village during the reference period." Thus, it is expected that these prices reflect the average price prevailing in the village and therefore incorporate farms of all sizes.

7. This result can be construed to partially support Sen's (1964) contention that on an interregional basis, one would expect a negative relationship between farm size and soil fertility. "If two pieces of land are of the same size, but holding A is more fertile than holding B, the former will provide a greater opportunity for earning income, so that family size may expand faster in the former case. This will lead to a quicker subdivision of A than of B, and soon a correlation may be established between the smallness of the size of holdings and the fertility of the soil. This argument is easy to see in the context of interregional variation, because often it has been observed that in fertile areas population expands faster both because of natural increase as well as migration." Note that the "distress sales" hypothesis of differing soil quality is not totally applicable on an interregional basis, it being much more relevant on an intraregional basis. In any case, there is no way to differentiate between the hypotheses on the basis of the observed correlation.

8. It should be reiterated that the quality index, P, does not control for within-region differences in soil quality. Since the regional prices are based on relatively small samples (20-50 farms) and reflect in some sense the average price prevailing in the village, it is doubtful that the error of omission is large.

9. This can easily be shown by differentiating equation 5' with respect to P. The maximum point of y, for a given land size, occurs when $\log P = (a'/b') - (1 + \log A)$. According to the estimates presented for this equation in Table A-2, the maximum point of y is reached for $P = 12,000$, $5,950$ and $3,570$ for farms of sizes 7.5 acres (mean), 15 acres (medium) and 25 acres (large), respectively. These values of P are well within the observed range—Rs. 200 to 13,500. The mean value of $P = $ Rs. 2476.

10. Note that if coefficient b was not significantly different from zero, this would not prove that there are no differences in farm productivity between large and small farms. This is because irrigation differences, which may be endogenous to farm decisions, have been assumed to be exogenous by the model.

11. This finding means that the statistical results establish a strong central tendency for output per farm area to fall as farm size rises. The policy implications of this trend hold, regardless of the existence in some of the sectors of a fairly wide band of variation around it (low R^2) due to extraneous factors.

12. The results for model 3, though not presented, also confirm the presence of a negative relationship at the level of individual crops. Indeed, the coefficient for the scale term, b', was invariably more significant than the coefficient for b reported in Table A-3. The coefficient for maize and sugar cane are now significant at the 1 percent level, and for jowar at the 10 percent level.

13. When all farms are considered together, then ones of different size may specialize in different products (some of which have economies of scale up to a certain level of output, say) leading to different factor proportions on farms of different sizes. All farms would still have the same ratio of output to inputs, in the absence of one of the two differences noted below.

14. A homogenous production function is assumed. If a nonhomothetic production function is postulated, then differences in factor ratios will result, even with perfect factor markets.

15. This can be shown as follows. Assume that "land" is fixed for each farm. Let $R =$ profits, $pQ =$ price times quantity of output, $M =$ factors other than land, and $H =$ land. If all peasants are profit maximizers, then

$$R = pQ - P_m M.$$

where $Q = M^a H^b$, $a + b = 1$, and $Pm =$ price of other inputs.
First order conditions:

$$\frac{\delta R}{\delta M} = Pa\frac{Q}{M} - P_m = 0$$

M is the only choice variable, since land is fixed. Therefore, $Q/M = P_m/pa$. So long as P_m is constant across all farms, and considering that p is also constant, then all farm sizes will have identical ratios of output to nonland inputs, namely,

$$\frac{Q_i}{M_i} = \frac{Q_j}{M_j} = \frac{P_m}{P_a}, \text{ where } i \text{ and } j \text{ are different farm sizes.}$$

Now, $\dfrac{Q_i}{Q_j} = \dfrac{M_i}{M_j} = \dfrac{M_i{}^a H_i{}^b}{M_j{}^a H_j{}^b}$.

Or $\dfrac{Q_i}{Q_j} = \left(\dfrac{M_i}{M_j}\right)^a \left(\dfrac{H_i}{H_j}\right)^b$,

dividing both sides by $\left(\dfrac{M_i}{M_j}\right)^a$ and its equivalent $\left(\dfrac{Q_i}{Q_j}\right)^a$ we obtain

$$\left(\frac{Q_i}{Q_j}\right)^{1-a} = \left(\frac{H_i}{H_j}\right)^b,$$

if constant returns to scale are assumed, then $1 - a = b$, and $Q_i/H_j = Q_i/H_j$, or land productivity, does not change with farm size. If constant returns to scale are not assumed, then output per area does vary but only because of scale considerations and not because land is fixed.

16. Considerable interest attaches to the question of the effect of tenancy on output. Section 3.6 examines the available evidence in the National Council of Applied Economic Research (NCAER) data; the general conclusion that emerges is that tenancy has no effect on output.

17. That the structure of the cost curve is different for the different sized farms is suggested by the fact that the large farmers obtained *more* funds at a lower rate of interest. Differences in interest rates reported in the Table A-7 are therefore not reflecting a common upward sloping supply curve of funds.

18. The number of observations is 1,443 rather than 1,772 because of two considerations: (a) no input could be zero for estimation in log forms, and (b) construction of L' eliminated some observations (see annex A.2).

19. The capital/labor ratio of the largest size group (over 25 acres), however, does not follow the rising trend of the first three size groups (and, indeed, is lower than that for each of the other three groups). This anomaly may be due to the synthetic nature of the labor variable, which tends to underestimate family labor (if there is any bias) and therefore small-farm labor.

20. In both the equations, an explicit term for HYV cultivation, percentage of area under HYV, was added. Though the new variable was significant, it did not affect the nature of the results and, in particular, the magnitude of the land coefficient, A. Given the necessity of irrigation for successful cultivation of the new varieties, the two variables, irrigation and HYV cultivation, are highly correlated. Thus, since irrigation differences are already included in model 4, addition of an HYV term does not make much difference in the results.

21. Of course, there is no reason necessarily to expect this relationship to change. If the underlying structure of the markets remains constant, and if adoption of the profitable technology is equal across farms, then the structure of interfarm behavior should remain the same. The validity of these assumptions is examined in the next few pages.

22. This inference would, of course, depend on the reasons for nonadoption by small farmers. Only if cause could be attributed to noneconomic factors, such as "backwardness," would this negative conclusion about land reform be relevant, because economic sources of differences in adoption of improved techniques could be addressed through the implementation of proper credit and extension policies in a reform.

23. This is for the model that includes land price and percent of area under irrigation as independent variables. For the basic model, including only logarithm of farm area, the decline in the absolute value of the coefficient on farm size is only 23 percent over the period.

24. The literature on adoption has usually ignored the limitation of irrigation on adoption differences. These studies indicate differences in adoption behavior by the percentage of adopter farms. A more relevant index of adoption patterns, in the short run, is the percentage of irrigated farms that have adopted the new technology. In the long run, irrigation differences can be considered endogenous, and then the index of adoption rates (adopters/total farms) becomes meaningful. Both indices are presented in Table A-17. The small farmer, with better irrigation, has only an *initial* advantage. Once the profitability of the new technology is proven, irrigation patterns and adoption rates can be expected to change. And if access to irrigation capital is "biased," the advantage of the new technology should shift in favor of the large farmer. This is apparently what happened in India in 1968-69 to 1970-71 (see discussion below, and Table A-17).

25. Further support for the contention that small farmers have not lagged behind in adoption is given by Sen (1974). Summarizing the evidence on adoption patterns in India, he states: "the average small farmer happens to be at least as progressive as any other farmer in respect of attitude toward innovation, risk bearing and application of recommended package of inputs," and "there is evidence that while in some locations the operators of large farms have led the adoption of high yielding varieties, small and medium size farmers have quickly followed; in others, it is the operators of small and medium size farms who have been in the lead with respect to adoption" (p. 53).

26. The net area irrigated for the first and second years had also to be accordingly adjusted. The procedure used was as follows: (i) the proportion of land reported to be irrigated in the first (and second) year was imputed to the land owned in the third year; and (ii) if this procedure resulted in a greater acreage being irrigated in the first two years, then the irrigated acreage of the third year was assumed.

27. A "worst-case" approach has deliberately been employed in the construction of a figure for family labor input. This synthetic figure is used in the text to show that small farmers use more labor/acres than large farmers. Unless a worst-case methodology is employed, one might be "biasing" the results in the expected direction.

28. The NCAER data show an average of 1.5 earners and 1.2 family workers per farm. On large farms (> 25 acres), there are 1.2 earners and 2.5 family workers—the difference from the average reflects the tendency for large farms to have workers classified as family workers rather than earners. (Female family workers are considered to be equal to 0.75 male family workers, in terms of work units.)

APPENDIX B

1. The great importance of the nonoperating owners is shown in the figures of the thirties and forties. See, for example, Takekazu Ogura (ed.), *Agricultural Development in Modern Japan* (Tokyo: Fuji Publishing Co., Ltd., 1966), p. 61.

2. Ohkawa, Kazushi, Bruce Johnston, and Hiromitsu Kaneda, *Agriculture and Economic Growth: Japan's Experience* (Princeton: Princeton University Press, 1970), p. 156.

3. Ibid., p. 160.

4. Kenneth L. Backman and Raymond P. Christensen, "The Economics of Farm Size," in Herman Southworth and Bruce Johnston, *Agriculture and Economic Growth* (Ithica: Cornell University Press, 1970), p. 247. The study of Ogura cited is from Takekazu Ogura, *Agricultural Development in Modern Japan* (Tokyo: Fuji Publishing Co., Ltd., 1963).

5. Eckstein, et al., *Land Reform in Latin America* . . . , Appendix C, p. 9.

6. International Labor Organization, *Employment, Incomes, and Equality: A Strategy for increasing Productive Employment in Kenya,* International Labor Organization, 1972, pp. 166–67.

7. Consumption data from the same survey revealed that food accounted for 31.5 percent of total cash consumption expenditure; food, beverages, and tobacco accounted for 38.8 percent. For farm households at the income level of Malawi, it would be expected that food would take up 50–70 percent of total consumption, so that home consumption would be 27–56 percent of total consumption. In fact, there is presumably considerable home consumption of other items too, so home consumption of food might more likely be 20–40 percent of total consumption, but still 1.2–4.0 times purchased food. This latter was 114.4 shillings per holding; total current farm receipts per holding were 126.3 shillings. If home-consumed food thus averaged 134.3–463.0 shillings it would constitute a large share of total output. If home consumption were assumed to be three times as large on the top farms as on the smallest ones (and specifically for the five sizes in the relative magnitude of 1.0, 1.5, 2.0, 2.5, and 3.0) then the low and high assumptions about its overall importance produce the results in Table B-6.

8. Comite Interamericano de Desarrollo Agricola, *Monografías Sobre Algunos Aspectos de la Tenencia de la Tierra y el Desarrollo Rural en America Latina,* Organizacion de los Estados Americanos, Washington, 1970, p. 34.

9. John Lossing Buck, *Land Utilization in China* (New York: Paragon Book Reprint Corp., 1968), and by the same author, *Chinese Farm Economics* (Chicago: University of Chicago Press, 1930).

10. See Bank of Korea, Research Department, *Economic Statistics Year Book,* 1960, p. 278.

Index

(Page numbers in italics designate tables.)

Africa, productivity/farm size in, 198–202
Agricultural policies. *See also* Land reform
  for developing countries, 29–30
  implications concerning, 228 n.5
  for India, 144
  land redistribution, output and, 7
  output and, 237 n.11
  small farm productivity/land reform
    and, 128–40
  small farms/high production and, 1–4
"Agricultural Wages in India" (government
    publication), 190
AID. *See* U.S. Agency for International
    Development (AID)
Algeria, 136
Animals. *See* Livestock; *names of specific
    animals*
Argentina, 203
Azam, K. M., 89–90, 95, 96

Bangladesh, 231 n.31
Barbosa, Tulio, 51
Bardhan, P. K., 25, 26, 148, 157, 175,
    190
Bell, C., 26
Bennett, R. L., 157
Berry, R. Albert, 58, 65, 67
Bhagwati, J. N., 148
Bhalla, Surjit, 108
Bharadwaj, K., 150, 156
"Biomodal" strategy on agriculture, 1
Bolivia, 135, 136
Borrowing. *See* Credit
Brazil
  cropland in, *210–11*

factor combinations and testing in,
    52–54
factor use/farm size in, *53, 55*
farm level testing by product group in,
    48–52
intensive hypothesis tests for, 44–58
land productivity by farm size in, 44–48,
    49, 50, 52, 127
land redistribution in, 131
production per unit available land in, *46*
returns (production) to scale (of farm)
    and, 6
saving rates in, 28
social factor productivity in, 54, *56–57,*
    58
yields in, 225 n.21
Buck, John Woosing, 203
Bureau of Agricultural Economics
    (BAECON/Philippines), 75, 77

Capital
  costs, India, 159–61, 184
  HYV adoption and, 178
  land redistribution and, 131
  land value and, Malaysia, 116–20
  owned farms and, 74
  shift toward, farm size and, 52–54, *55,*
    58, 111, 114
  social factor productivity and, 54, 57
  tenant farms and, 75
Capital/labor ratio (India), 170–72
Capital-market imperfections, 10–11, 27,
    29, 60
Cattle. *See also* Livestock
  as crop replacement, 15

241

Library of Congress Cataloging in Publication Data

Berry, R   Albert, 1937–
    Agrarian structure and productivity in
developing countries.

    Includes bibliographical references and index.
    1. Underdeveloped areas—Agriculture.
2. Farms, Size of.   I. Cline, William R., joint
author. II. Title.
HD1417.B387   338.1'09172'4   78-20524
ISBN 0-8018-2190-8